HOW THE CITY REALLY WORKS

THE TIMES

HOW THE CITY REALLY WORKS

2nd edition

The definitive guide to money and investing in London's square mile

Alexander Davidson

KOGAN PAGE

London and Philadelphia

Publisher's note

Every possible effort has been made to ensure that the information contained in this book is accurate at the time of going to press, and the publishers and author cannot accept responsibility for any errors or omissions, however caused. No responsibility for loss or damage occasioned to any person acting, or refraining from action, as a result of the material in this publication can be accepted by the editor, the publisher or the author.

First published in Great Britain and the United States in 2006 by Kogan Page Limited
Second edition 2008

120 Pentonville Road
London N1 9JN
United Kingdom
www.kogan-page.co.uk

525 South 4th Street, #241
Philadelphia PA 19147
USA

The views expressed in this book are those of the author, and are not necessarily the same as those of Times Newspapers Ltd.

ISBN 978 0 7494 5084 7

British Library Cataloguing-in-Publication Data

A CIP record for this book is available from the British Library.

Library of Congress Cataloging-in-Publication Data

Davidson, Alexander, 1957–
How the city really works : the definitive guide to money and investing in London's square mile / Alex Davidson.
p. cm.
ISBN 978-0-7494-5084-7
1. Finance--England--London. 2. Financial institutions--England--London. 3. Stock exchanges--England--London. I. Title.
HG186.G72L6653 2008
332.109421--dc22

2007047300

Typeset by JS Typesetting Ltd, Porthcawl, Mid Glamorgan
Printed and bound in Great Britain by Bell & Bain Ltd, Glasgow

For Acelia, Michael and Victoria, still at school,
and for Philip and Eleanor, who, since the first edition
of this book was out, have spread their wings and
gone to University.

This book is for still for you,

To celebrate a wonderful childhood and
to look forward to what is to come,

With love

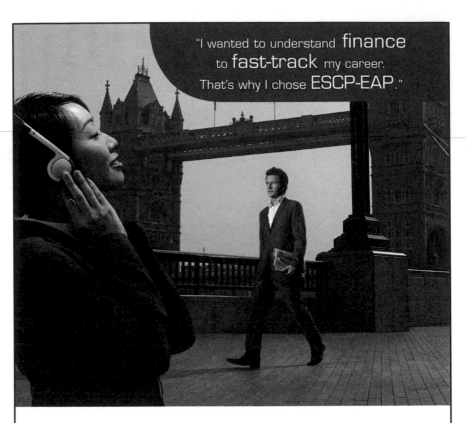

Contents

CITYJET
FOR AIR FRANCE
Take off from the heart of Londor
The largest European networ
direct from London Ci
Belfast City – Dublin – Dundee – Edinburgh – Geneva – Nice – Paris – Strasbourg – Zuri
airfrance.co.u

Aberdeen – The Independent Asset Manager

Aberdeen Asset Management PLC is an international investment management group, managing assets for both institutions and private individuals from offices around the world. Our mission is to deliver superior fund performance across diverse asset classes in which we believe we have a sustainable competitive edge.

We manage currency, fixed income and equities (quoted and private) in segregated, closed and open-ended pooled structures. We also run a sizeable European property business.

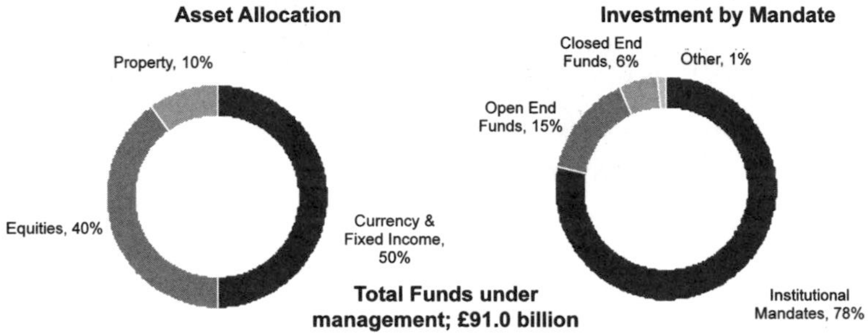

At Aberdeen we pride ourselves on original thinking and research. We also believe strongly in portfolio transparency. Implicit in our style is a rejection of commoditised products and closet indexing; our business therefore stands or falls on whether we can genuinely add value to client wealth.

We operate as an independent company, free of the conflicts of interest that can affect integrated financial groups. Although we are publicly quoted, management and staff are significant owners of the business. Asset management is all that we do.

Our equity process dates from the early 1990s. The process is continuously evolving but its central tenets are an emphasis on original research, the identification of businesses that we can understand and the elimination of downside risks through price disciplines. While it originated in Asia, our approach works equally in developed markets, since fundamentals drive returns over the long term.

Our aim is to add value by identifying good quality securities, defined chiefly in terms of management and business model, which are attractively priced.

Stock selection is the key source of equity alpha. We downplay benchmarks in portfolio construction since these provide little clue to future performance, we always visit companies before investing, making thousands of visits annually to existing and prospective holdings. Every contact is documented in detail. If a security fails our screens, we will not own it, irrespective of its index weight.

Our mainstream strategies are simple: we buy-and-hold, add on the dips, and take profits on price run-ups. This reduces transaction costs and keeps portfolios focused. We rarely pursue short-term returns for mainstream strategies, albeit for specialist portfolios, activity may be more dynamic.

We employ over 75 equity investment professionals globally. Portfolio decisions are made collectively, and we avoid cultivating 'star' managers. Cross-coverage of securities also increases objectivity and lessens reliance on individuals.

We're delighted to be able to offer you a selection of 16 investment companies that give you the opportunity to tap into some of the most dynamic investment markets around the world – with Aberdeen's team professional fund managers to support you.

Our expertise focuses on six areas: the UK, UK high income, Asia, globally invested funds, specialist funds focused on a particular market sector and tracker funds. In this way, the range allows you to pinpoint investment markets very precisely so you can meet particular needs within your portfolio.

Investing in our range of investment trusts couldn't be easier or more cost effective. We offer four ways to invest – and two are tax efficient. Just choose whether you want to invest in our Share Plan, Investment Plan for Children, tax-efficient ISA or make a PEP transfer. Our low cost investment plans mean that there is no initial costA to you. Our Share Plan and Investment Plan for Children have no annual charge, and our PEP transfer and ISA have a low annual charge of £24 (plus VAT).

Whichever investment trust you are interested in, please ensure that it is suitable for your appetite and tolerance for risk. Higher risk investments may compensate for their higher volatility and uncertainty by offering potentially higher returns than lower investments. But this is not guaranteed.

The source for all figures: Aberdeen Asset Manager, as at 31 August 2007

* There is 0.5% government stamp duty

company's finance department. There have been instances however, of lawyers and financial journalists who wish to develop their financial expertise.

Nevertheless, relevant experience is required, and the typical participant profile since the programme began, has six to seven years' experience. Hand picked from an ever-growing pool of applicants, Masters in Finance participants are of widely varying nationalities. However, what they all share is a high level of intellectual ability, the capacity for hard work and the motivation to take on a demanding and challenging commitment. This ensures that a wealth of experience is brought to the programme, enabling learning from fellow world-class participants as well as world-class faculty.

Participants soon learn the value of being surrounded by fellow high-achieving professionals, as every effort is made to teach material in an involving manner. Lectures are accompanied by case studies, group work and guest speakers. "An advantage of being in the world's financial centre," Ms Vinck enthuses, "is the ability to bring case studies to life by bringing in key players who were actually involved, such as the CFO."

Completion of the Masters in Finance programme gives many graduates the required in-roads for a successful finance career in London: 56% of the 2006 class have named the UK as their primary work location, whereas only 13% of the class were working in the UK before they started the degree. There are of course success stories in abundance further afield too, testament to the consolidation of London Business School as an internationally recognised leader of finance education.

A recent review of graduate salaries reveals similar patterns of success – the median salary of 2006 Masters in Finance graduates working in the UK is £107,605 (including bonuses). As Glyn Jones, 2005 graduate and Executive Director of Finance at UBS puts it, "the benefit you derive isn't just the first job, or your next pay rise, though certainly for me, it paid for itself extremely quickly. The payback period is much longer, emotionally as well as in career terms."

To keep up with changes in the marketplace, and in response to direct feedback requested from participants, the School continually reviews and updates programme content. Ms Vinck recently oversaw the launch of electives such as Private Equity, Credit Risk and Hedge Funds to ensure the programme remains "aligned with what's happening in the industry."

Graduates of the Masters in Finance programme continually refer to London Business School as "a fabulous brand that opens doors and gets them places." And with 27,000 alumni leading global organisations, running governments, transforming communities and starting new businesses in over 100 countries around the world, the facts speak for themselves.

It doesn't take a finance expert to see that with a Masters in Finance from London Business School, the numbers are stacked in your favour.

For more information about Masters in Finance at London Business School, please visit www.london.edu/mif/tt0208/ or email finance@london.edu or call +44 (0)20 7000 7599

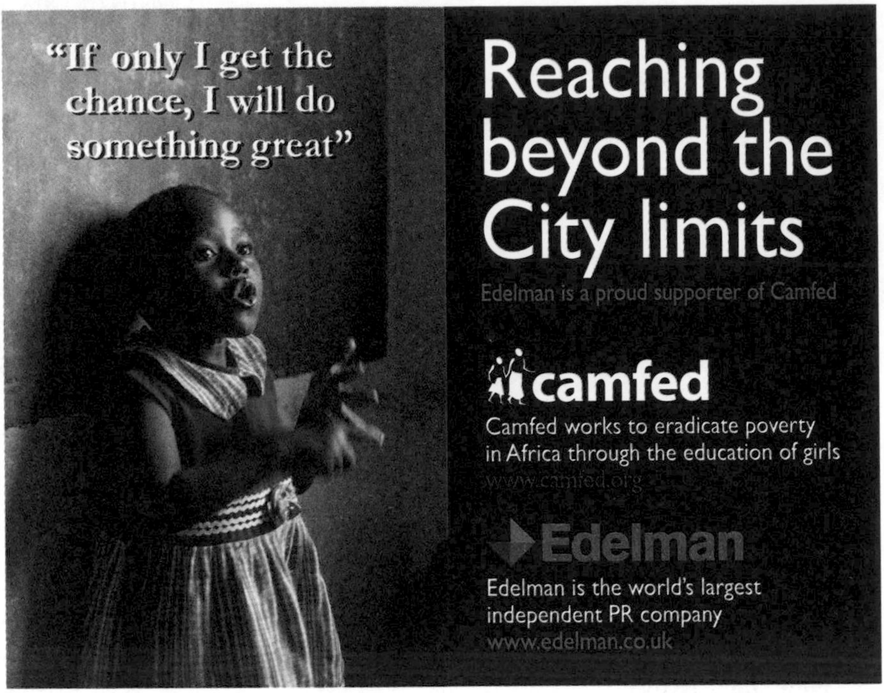
"If only I get the chance, I will do something great"
Reaching beyond the City limits
Edelman is a proud supporter of Camfed
camfed
Camfed works to eradicate poverty in Africa through the education of girls
www.camfed.org
Edelman
Edelman is the world's largest independent PR company
www.edelman.co.uk

It's also about the benefits for pension funds from what private equity has "left for the next man", in the form of returns on IPOs of companies previously taken private. Contrary to the industry's asset stripping stereotype, private equity firms tend not to trash the businesses they back – if they did, why would the investment community buy them back when they come to be relisted?

US studies have found that private equity-backed companies refloated on American stock markets have outperformed other IPOs and wider market benchmarks, and it has become conventional wisdom that this better performance reflects the improved financial discipline and efficiency private equity has brought to these businesses. Admittedly studies in the UK and other non-US markets have shown a more mixed performance: my research (*Private Equity Backed IPOs in UK, date?*) among IPOs that came to market in the UK between 1992 and 2003 found that while ex-private equity businesses have performed better than other IPOs, they haven't necessarily beaten the wider stock market.

However this research also identified another potentially important benefit for investors: private equity-backed floatations have tended to deliver more consistent, homogeneous long-term performance than other listings. Measured over successive six-monthly intervals, private equity-backed floats have repeatedly outperformed other UK IPOs. Their average aftermarket performance has been less likely to be driven by a few exceptionally good issues and they have had a better probability of delivering a positive return.

These more reliable returns have made this category of IPOs an attractive, less risky bet for conservative institutional investors such as pension funds. With pension fund mandates generally carrying performance and risk targets, screening IPOs according to whether they are private equity-backed can therefore be a useful tool for limiting the downside of buying into new listings.

As well as reflecting how businesses have been improved, the explanation for this more predictable IPO performance could lie in the way private equity houses remain incentivised in the ongoing success of former investments. Often private equity firms won't completely divest of a holding in an IPO, and many will retain significant stakes for a year or so after the listing. They will therefore continue to have a direct interest in the company being managed properly and delivering value. They may provide valuable monitoring of the company, and – through contacts with analysts – help its profile through facilitating the exchange of information between the business and other investors.

Crucially too, private equity firms have reputations at stake; being associated with failures may well create difficulties for future listings of investments. This feeds into IPO pricing: canny private equity houses won't be over-greedy when they come to sell for fear of killing the golden goose for future IPOs.

The tendency of private equity firms to concentrate on particular industries – where the value-adding potential is greatest – may also help the overall performance of their IPOs.

The private equity industry argues that the necessary pain involved in its restructuring of companies results in healthier, fitter, more stable and productive enterprises – with more sustainable futures.

This transformational pain, however uncomfortable for those directly affected, also makes such businesses attractive investments for pension funds. And that means helping produce wider economic and social benefits for the much larger number of people who are pension fund beneficiaries.

To talk to any of our finance, management or actuarial academics please don't hestiate to get in touch with Gemma Lines, Director of Marketing and Communications at Cass on +44 (0)20 7040 8600. To find out about our MBA, specialist masters or undergraduate programmes, please visit our website: www.cass.city.ac.uk

The City Office is an important new venture and its establishment follows wide ranging consultation with practitioners, trade associations and other stakeholders. The Office, guided by an Advisory Group of senior City practitioners, helps shape new thinking about the future direction of the financial services market in the enlarged EU, and enables the City to develop further its approach to strategic, pan-EU issues.

The Lord Mayor of the City of London, a respected ambassador for financial services, also plays a key role in promoting the Square Mile, within the EU and beyond. Over the past year, the Lord Mayor has visited 20 countries across the globe.

The City is rightly proud of its prestigious status at a domestic, European and international level, and the City Corporation works hard to help maintain this position. We are very aware however, that we must never become complacent and that success cannot be left to chance.

If the City is to continue to thrive, the infrastructure and public services of London as a whole must be modern and efficient, to accommodate population growth and to sustain economic development. Transport projects are particularly important, in order to maintain London's credibility as a place to do international business, and we are delighted with the Government's decision to give the go-ahead to Crossrail.

The world of finance is fast-moving, yet London stays ahead of the pace. It is sensitive to the pulse of the international market place, because it is at the heart of it – it is in all our interests to make sure that it remains there.

Michael Snyder is Chairman of the Policy and Resources Committee at the City of London Corporation

The City of London Corporation – In Partnership with the City

www.cityoflondon.gov.uk

Questions and Answers – *Gareth Syms, TD Waterhouse*

Gareth Syms is the Manager of the TD Waterhouse Investor Centre based in Holborn. Day to day Gareth and his team offer support and help for customers looking to take control of their investments using TD Waterhouse's share dealing service.

So what are the services that TD Waterhouse offer?
We offer a variety of trading and investment tools to the UK retail investor. These include everything from a Self Invested Personal Pension (SIPP) account to more high risk derivative trading accounts such as CFDs and Financial Spread Betting.

Who in particular do you cater for?
Really it's a broad range of people across the UK. In general our customers have a reasonable understanding of aspects of the UK market, however we have many customers who now trade International markets too. We also offer a number of educational tools to assist customers with their investment decisions.

Trading can seem pretty daunting, how easy is it to get started?
It's relatively easy to get started but we suggest that a basic understanding of what your trading or investment strategy is, is desirable. It's all about deciding what your objectives are and what your appetite for risk is.

In terms of how to trade we have a dedicated Customer Service line and a wide range of information available online, but if the customer wants to speak to someone face to face, we have our Investor Centre based in London. Here customers can learn everything from the basics of how to trade all the way through to more advanced technical analysis and fundamental analysis.

What support do you give to traders – beginners and advanced?
It is important to note that our service is Execution Only. We do not offer investment advice. As a result our customers will be self directed in the way they trade, but when they have a need for assistance or require additional services, our Customer Services and Investor Centre teams are on hand to help. There are also helpful seminars run regularly at the Investor Centre on getting started, and there are good articles on the tdwaterhouse.co.uk site to help you understand the basics.

For more advanced traders we offer the TD Waterhouse ProTrader® product which gives access to Level 2 and live streaming prices, plus more advanced charting options. We offer seminars on how to use them, and on more sophisticated financial products.

What changes have you seen over the last few years?
The biggest change has been the amount of business we do online. We have a very comprehensive website that most of our customers use to trade. Only a few years ago the majority of our business was done over the telephone. Those days though are long gone.

In the Investor Centre we've also seen a significant increase in the level of knowledge our customers display. They tend to be moving towards not only diversifying their portfolios but also expanding the accounts they use for trading and investment purposes. For example one customer not only has a trading account but also has begun to manage their own pension through the TD Waterhouse SIPP, and to assist with their trading strategy they are also opting to use Financial Spread Betting and CFDs. However, these accounts carry a varying degree of risk so our customers need to be aware of these prior to making their investment decisions.

We've also seen customers develop a greater understanding of the mechanics of the market and this is largely down to their attendance at the regular seminars that we run.

What is the main question you get asked in the Investor Centre?
People tend to ask if we give advice. We don't – it's important to note that we offer an Execution Only service. Customers place orders either through our website or over the telephone and the cost is very competitive when compared to a traditional advisory broker. It also means that customers are responsible for their own financial decisions.

Does trading have to be a high risk occupation?
That all depends on your investment or trading strategy. One thing to remember is, at TD Waterhouse you can diversify your portfolio and spread the risk by investing in our high interest rate savings account; investing in managed funds through our Fund Supermarket; or trade ETFs. If you feel the UK market presents more risk than an overseas market, you are able to invest on 16 overseas exchanges including North American and European markets.

We also find that customers often choose to invest using their ISA allowance and this provides them with a tax efficient wrapper, so they get to keep their profits without worrying about Capital Gains Tax. A particular benefit of this is that we charge zero administration fee if your account valuation is £3,600 or more. It is important to note however that any equity based investment strategy carries a level of risk as the performance of equities can result in a loss to the capital invested.

Contact Details
Address
Investor Centre
TD Waterhouse
Mid City Place
71 High Holborn
London
WC1V 6TD

Telephone
0845 601 6205

Web
tdwaterhouse.co.uk

Opening hours
Monday-Friday
8.00am-5.00pm

Royal Opening for Docklands Business School

Earlier this year, Her Majesty The Queen and His Royal Highness The Duke of Edinburgh visited Docklands to open the University of East London's magnificent new Business School and Knowledge Dock Centre, part of a £130 million investment programme at the university.

Located on the waterfront of the Royal Albert Dock, the Business School provides innovative programmes in all aspects of business and management. With its vast, curved roof forming a magnificent wing-shaped canopy, it provides a bright, spacious and vibrant learning environment with state-of-the-art facilities including a library open 24 hours a day.

The University of East London Business School is a leading provider of business and management education in the London Thames Gateway. In a global economy that is increasingly knowledge-based, we are continually innovating to develop new, more efficient and business-oriented programmes that meet the needs of students and employers alike.

Innovation and partnership

Innovation and flexibility in programme content and delivery are key to success. We offer evening and weekend modular programmes and are a leader in the field of distance learning, enabling students to gain valuable career-enhancing qualifications from their own homes and workplaces.

Our new postgraduate prospectus includes innovative MBA and Masters programmes in areas such as international business and public services. We have particularly strong subject fields in finance, economics and accounting; entrepreneurship, project and risk management; strategy operations management and marketing; and human resources and organisational behaviour.

The School has a long tradition of delivering high-quality management training to major organisations as diverse as Ford Europe, Logica and the NHS. It has close partnerships with institutions in key markets such as China and South East Asia

I found the lecturers and professors very helpful and they genuinely wanted us to do well. They were very flexible in their approach to student development.

Towards the end of my MSc, I was looking for an opportunity to move into economic modelling. I would not have secured my current job at HM Treasury without my Masters. I also regularly bump into past lecturers running refresher courses at the Treasury."

Zebedee Nii-Naate, Graduate Diploma in Economics and MSc Economics

"The course's multi-disciplinary approach provides a firm grounding and well-balanced foundation for those interested in pursuing a career in quantitative finance, risk management or furthering their interest in research work.

The calibre of the teaching staff is very high and they are always willing to work with students even outside normal hours. The modules are scheduled and designed to cater for the needs of working professionals. Additional revision classes are often offered, where answers to questions and further direction on taught materials, project work and research interests are provided."

Ruben Garcia Moral, MSc Financial Engineering

Email: **courses@ems.bbk.ac.uk**

Web: **www.ems.bbk.ac.uk/welcome**

Tel: **020 7631 6406**

How does the City really work?

The concept of how the City really works is an interesting angle for BPP Professional Education. As a leading provider of financial services training, most of the top business professionals from the leading organisations in the City currently train with us. So we effectively give them the skills that they need to make the City work – a key overall role. From investment administration staff to top level analysts and directors, we offer training courses that will see them right through their career. From the ones they need to get on the ladder and meet the standards required by the regulatory bodies, to the top professional qualifications that stand them out from the crowd and get them to the very top of the career ladder.

What courses could BPP offer you?

BPP is a leading provider of financial services training, offering you more choice than many other training providers. Our training is split up into two key areas:

- **Threshold competency training** – the skills that you need to do your job
    - **Investment Administration Qualification (IAQ™)** – mainly for back office and administration staff
    - **SII Certificates** – mainly for front office staff in client facing roles
    - **Investment Management Certificate** – for those working in the fund management industry
    - **Islamic Finance Qualification** – for specialists in this area, specifically Sharia'a compliant finance
- **Professional level training** – professional level skills that will set you apart
    - **CFA® Program** – the globally recognised 'gold-standard' in investment banking
    - **CF qualification** – for corporate finance specialists
    - **SII Diploma** – for UK based finance professionals working in specialist areas
    - **SII Diploma in Investment Compliance** – for regulation and compliance professionals
    - **SII Diploma in Investment Operations** – for investment operations professionals
    - **SIIM (Wealth Management)** – for private client and wealth management professionals

Why should you train with BPP?

As well as training with a company that's got one of the strongest reputations for

Acknowledgements

This book owes everything to the City professionals who gave freely of their valuable time in providing interviews, source material and other help. At the same time, the text is independent, and is neither endorsed nor approved by any institutions or individuals named in the acknowledgements or elsewhere. The selection of facts and themes, and the opinions expressed, are the author's alone.

Among those who helped, in no particular order, are the Bank of England, the British Bankers' Association, the Building Societies Association, the Council of Mortgage Lenders, the Baltic Exchange, the London Metal Exchange, the FDA (Factors and Discounters Association), FTSE International Limited, the Association of Investment Companies, the Alternative Investment Management Association, and the UK Debt Management Office. Chris Hodge, head of corporate governance, at the Financial Reporting Council, helped enormously on corporate governance.

Denis Peters, corporate communications director at Euroclear, gave both editions of this book a full reading, far outside the call of duty. He has made valuable comments and criticisms and picked up many useful points, and has significantly improved the text.

At the London Stock Exchange, Hugh Brown, manager of product management and development, was helpful in explaining developments in trading systems. At Equiduct, Bob Fuller, chief executive officer, took a lot of trouble in answering questions. Peter Randall, director at Chi-X, gave me some useful input. At PLUS Markets Group, Nemone Wynn-Evans, director of business development, gave me much useful insight into how her business works. Ian Marsh, professor of finance at Cass Business School, was willing to discuss at length his interesting study into the cost of trade execution of UK equities.

The Financial Services Authority and the Association of British Insurers have invited me to conferences and taken trouble to answer questions in my

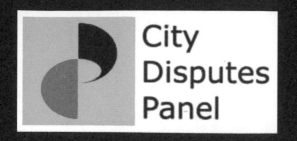

Whilst providing all of the services offered by the CDP since 1994, the new portfolio includes cost controlled models for mediation, arbitration and neutral evaluation. This demonstrates how CDP is responding to the evolving needs of the City. CDP will continue to offer innovative solutions suitable for use in the dynamic City environment of the 21st century.

CDP does not impose routine processes on users. It works with them to develop the most appropriate solutions to match their circumstances. This may include the use of bespoke contract clauses providing for the appointment of CDP in the event of a dispute, conflict or other difference between the contracting parties. Often the facilitative approach can result in a structured process tailor made for the parties.

As CDP looks to the future, it is worth recalling the words of Alderman David Lewis interviewed in *The Times* on his election as Lord Mayor in November 2007. Referring to the conduct of business in the City, he said "Integrity. Trust. Fairness. Honesty. Hard work. Charity. Helping others. These are the ageless values that my father taught me and my school taught me. I think a little bit of that is being diluted". At CDP, the core values of independence, integrity and impartiality will always be available to our users. We are in the City, for the City and supported by the City.

For further information, please visit the CDP website at **www.citydisputespanel.org.uk** to view the type of approaches available and specimen contract clauses, or call Catherine Hammond on **020 7520 3824**. If you are not in need of a specialist provider of conflict management and dispute resolution services just now, then bookmark this page, add the CDP website to your favourites or add the details to your contacts list.

If you do have a problem, remember; with the City Disputes Panel involved, creating effective solutions is easier than you think.

work as a journalist, and I have incorporated some of their insights in the book. The Serious Fraud Office has been helpful in updating me on progress. The Insurance Fraud Bureau has brought me up to date with what it is achieving. My thanks are due to the International Association of Insurance Fraud Agencies for kindly inviting me to its 2007 annual meeting. Detective Superintendent David Clarke filled me in with developments at the City of London Police related to combating fraud. Alan McQuillan, interim director of the Assets Recovery Agency, was exceptionally helpful in answering questions.

Both Lloyd's and the International Underwriting Association of London were helpful in providing me with source material for the insurance sections of this book. Equitas checked and amended copy.

The Department of Work and Pensions and the Pension Regulator helpfully clarified some issues about pension legislation. I am grateful to the Bourse Consult for its report *The Competitive Impact of London's Financial Market Infrastructure*, April 2007. It changed some of my ideas.

Ken Wild, global IFRS leader at Deloitte & Touche, kindly checked some material on accounting. Thayne Forbes, joint managing director at Intangible Business, usefully commented on my coverage of the findings of a survey by his firm on acquisitions and related goodwill in the accounts.

I thank Jim Rogers for some valuable comments on my new chapter on commodities. Buchanan Communications was extremely helpful in giving me a broad perspective of how investor relations work. Hill & Knowlton gave background insights into how PR practitioners operate.

Other parties who helped include the Bank of International Settlements, the Finance & Leasing Association, Egg and First Direct, as well as the Association of Private Client Investment Managers and Stockbrokers. Compeer kindly made research available, and Charles Newsome, investment manager at Christows, commented helpfully on the text.

Deutsche Börse helped me on exchanges and LCH.Clearnet provided perspectives on clearing. Euronext.liffe, EDX London, the Baltic Exchange and GFI Group helped on derivatives. ICAP helped on derivatives, and, through its website resources, on foreign exchange for the second edition. Jill Leyland, Economic Adviser to World Gold Council, explained gold markets. Peter Sceats, expert witness and consultant director of business development at TFS London, gave some perspectives.

The Financial Ombudsman Service explained its services. Anna Bowes at Chase de Vere Financial Solutions, Justin Modray, Kevin Carr of Lifesearch and Tom McPhail, Head of Pensions Research at Hargreaves Lansdown, helped with the original personal finance chapter.

The International Capital Market Association commented on the bonds coverage. Chris Furness, senior currency strategist at 4CAST, gave me insight

into foreign exchange. David Styles, assistant director, corporate law and governance directorate, the Department of Trade and Industry helped on corporate governance. Peter Staddon, head of technical services at the British Insurance Brokers' Association, read and helpfully commented on drafts for the first edition.

Many others helped with this project, including some at the highest level in City firms and trade associations, but preferred to stay anonymous. I would like to thank you all, as well as anybody whose name I have inadvertently omitted. The help that I received was great. The errors are all mine.

Important note

This book aims to explain the City understandably, using simple language and generic examples. The wording does not have the status of legal definitions, and this guide is for educational purposes. It should not be used as a definitive source or, in particular, as a substitute for investment advice. The book is necessarily selective and seeks to cover only the main City activities. It may reflect some of the author's preferences. The City changes quickly and the details in this book may become out of date, but the overview will stay true.

Abbreviations

When I use the name of an organisation for the first time in a chapter, I spell it out in full. Subsequently, I usually abbreviate it. For example, you will find the Financial Services Authority referred to subsequently as the FSA, and the London Stock Exchange as the LSE.

Introduction

The City of London is vast and complex. It is developing not just every month but every day and every minute. It has progressed even since this book went to press. Technology struggles to keep up. New exotic products – particularly in derivatives – grab market share in an increasingly international marketplace.

The demand for the first edition of this book was far greater than I had envisaged and this second edition is not before time. As in the first edition, I have enhanced and livened up the text with material taken from the City itself.

This book aims to explain the City in language you can understand. If you do not know what the City is, or have a hazy knowledge but want to find out more, this book will give you the necessary overview.

You will find out here how the Bank of England sets interest rates, and I include some coverage of its role in money markets, taking into account recent reforms. We will take a look at how the Bank reacts, in cooperation with the Treasury and the regulator, when liquidity on money markets seizes up. We will take a brief look at the liquidity problems that hit mortgage bank Northern Rock in September 2007. We will cover the foreign exchange market, and why the strong pound has had an overall beneficial effect on the economy.

There is a new chapter, my own sneaking favourite, reflecting the growing importance in the City of addressing financial fraud, and there is another on money laundering. Research for these chapters has taken input from government officials, lawyers and fraud-busting bodies such as the City of London police and the Serious Fraud Office.

As before, we give the stock market early prominence in the book. You will find here enough to help you get started as an equities investor and to understand market news. The London Stock Exchange has entered a new era as a result of EU legislation. This book explores the Exchange's latest trading technologies, and the competition. We cover related developments in clearing and settlement.

You will read about how capital markets work. A new chapter on new issues looks at the choice of markets in London. In another chapter, we focus on how investment banks bring companies to the market. Analysts are a link in the chain, but regulatory developments have placed restrictions on them, and we will see where they stand in a new chapter. We will cover valuation techniques such as discounted cash flow analysis and EBITDA, and I will explain the City's dependence on earnings per share. The book provides an overview of technical analysis.

We explore how the big institutional investors as well as private investors work. We cover hedge funds and how they move markets. We delve into some of the more esoteric areas of the City such as shipping and metals.

In the City today, derivatives are becoming increasingly sophisticated, and are used for both speculating and hedging. This book provides clear basic explanations of how they work, both on exchange and over the counter. I have included a separate chapter explaining how commodity futures work, and some current thinking about investment prospects in this area.

You will find money markets with government bonds in one chapter, and corporate bonds with credit derivatives in another. We focus on concerns about credit risk, triggered by defaults in US sub-prime mortgages, which are packaged in the bond market as collateralised debt obligations and are hedged by derivatives.

The commercial insurance market now claims that it is underwriting more cautiously than in the past. In this book, we will try to see whether it lives up to its claim, and how well it will stand a market downturn. I will explain how the London insurance market, including Lloyd's, works. There is a new chapter on reinsurance, which covers the impact of catastrophes such as Hurricane Katrina in 2005, and how insurers have started to tap capital markets for extra reinsurance capacity.

In personal finance, we will take a critical look at pension reform, and controversies related to sales of payment protection insurance. We look at current thinking on mortgages. Elsewhere, we compare types of pooled investment.

Since the first edition was published, regulation and corporate governance have evolved, and this book covers how they work today. We focus on the role of the Financial Services Authority and the development of its principles-based regulatory regime, which is not always helped by the onset of EU financial services legislation.

The City relies on the communication professionals to convey its message to the public and to itself. In a new chapter, we focus on the complex interlinks between public relations, investor relations and the press, including tip sheets and the internet as well as newspapers, magazines and news agencies. We consider the role of primary and secondary information providers. You will find out how to read between the lines of press coverage.

If you want to work in the City, or have started doing so and need a broad overview, let this book be your guide. The approach here is practical as well as theoretical. It covers the City as it works today. The text is so designed that you may read it consecutively, or may dip into chapters – because not everybody will want to understand every area of the City all at once.

If you have had little or no exposure to the City, I hope this book will be a treat for you. I have tapped the expertise of the professionals and offer a flavour of their world. I have drawn on my own experience of working as a share dealer, as well as in financial journalism.

If you are an investor, this book will fill in the gaps missing from your broker's explanations or the financial press. This text will help with some professional examinations but is no substitute for your course texts. Feedback from the first edition suggests this book is of considerable help as background reading for students of economics and business, both at sixth form level and in more advanced studies.

It is in the throb of real experience that textbooks fall short – which, to be fair, is in keeping with their aim. This book gives you an experience that is perhaps closer to the knuckle. It was fun to prepare this second edition for you, and I hope you will enjoy reading it.

1

The City of London

Introduction

In this chapter we will define the City of London in geographical and product terms, and see how it has developed from the cosy club that it was until the mid-1980s to the competitive international marketplace it is today.

The City defined

To define the City, we need to consider its range of activities and its geographical positioning. There is some overlap. The City covers wholesale financial services, which are money and/or financial instrument exchanges between professionals, or between professionals and companies or governments, but also some retail activity.

Broadly speaking, the City operates in or around the geographical *square mile* in the centre of London. A stockbroker dealing with retail clients is considered part of the City provided that it operates within or near the square mile. But the retail stockbroker operating from the provinces is not a City firm unless it has a head office based there.

Somebody who works at a City head office of a clearing bank can claim to work in the City, but a colleague working for a provincial branch cannot. If a firm only sells insurance, pensions and unit trusts, this is not in itself City activity, even if it operates in the square mile. But stockbrokers considered part of the City also offer these general financial services. Commercial insurance professionals who work in the London market are part of the City.

The firm's base is usually where senior management is located, and this is fundamental even in an era where electronic links cross geographical boundaries with ease. The City relies still on face-to-face contact.

Over the years, even the physical boundaries have extended beyond the traditional square mile. One of the most important City locations is Canary Wharf, part of the Docklands, where some leading investment banks, including Morgan Stanley and Credit Suisse, are based, as well as the Financial Services Authority (FSA), which regulates all financial services in the UK. Schroder Salomon Smith Barney has an office in Victoria.

Sometimes, the London operation has foreign ownership, which is not seen as detrimental. For example, London exchange ICE Futures is owned by Atlanta-based Intercontinental Exchange, and the London International Financial Futures Exchange (LIFFE) is owned by NYSE Euronext.

Financial markets

Financial markets give borrowers an opportunity to raise capital, making contact with lenders through banks and other intermediaries. Commercial banks take deposits and lend them to borrowers. Investment banks sell the securities of corporate or government issuers to investors. Securities may be debt instruments, such as syndicated loans or bonds, or may be shares. Following issue, securities may be traded on relevant markets.

From the investor's perspective, cash deposits and bonds are at the low end of the risk spectrum, and equities and derivatives are at the high end. Institutional investors allocate assets across their portfolios to spread the risk. They may hedge their positions with derivatives so, if they lose a substantial sum on their main portfolio, they will gain on the derivatives, and the reverse.

Traders also speculate on derivatives, as well as on underlying equities or other financial instruments. They have a more short-term approach than investors, which means that they look more at mergers and acquisitions rumours, pending earnings announcements and news flow than at a company's fundamentals.

The City as a world leader

London is behind only New York as a global financial market and, in some areas, it is ahead. It is the clear leader in Europe.

In cross-border bank lending, the UK has a 20 per cent global market share (March 2006), unchanged over a three-year period, and the United States has 9 per cent, according to the May 2007 issue of *International Financial Markets in the UK*, published by International Financial Services London (IFSL). In foreign exchange turnover (April 2006), the UK has a 32 per cent share, unchanged from the previous year, against the 18 per cent share of the United States, its nearest rival. The UK has a 42 per cent turnover in foreign equities, down from 43 per cent in 2005, and compared with 33 per cent in the United States. The UK is the market leader in international bonds (2006), with 70 per cent of the secondary market, unchanged since 1992.

In over-the-counter (OTC) derivatives, the UK has a 43 per cent market share (April 2004), of which about three-quarters are interest rate swaps and similar products, which makes it the global leader, according to IFSL statistics. The United States has 24 per cent. In marine insurance net premium income, the UK has a 20 per cent market share (2005), while the United States has 11 per cent. London's share of world hedge fund assets reached 21 per cent in June 2006, which represents a steady gain since 2003, when it was 14 per cent, but it has a long way to catch up with the United States at 66 per cent.

No gain without pain

London has concentrated expertise, is well placed in the time zones between New York and Japan, and its regulatory regime sets international standards. To reach this position, the City has historically taken risks. The United States has invented such products as exchange-traded funds, financial derivatives and credit derivatives, and the City of London has adopted and exploited them.

The City has reached its current status through trial and error over the decades. In the 19th century the UK merchant banks, now more usually known by the US term *investment banks*, developed rapidly but, with the advent of the First World War in 1914, some failed to retrieve moneys owed to them and almost collapsed. They survived only because the Bank of England gave them special loans. Following the war, the banks became independently successful again. After the Second World War broke out in 1939, they started losing business.

International securities were the break that restored the City's fortunes. The Eurobond market started in London in July 1963 and received a competitive boost thereafter when the United States introduced compulsory US interest equalisation tax, which drove issuers away.

The fortunes of sterling have been a more broadly based factor in building up the City. In the late 1970s sterling rose sharply because of the North Sea oil bonanza and, in October 1979, the Conservative Government under Margaret Thatcher as prime minister abolished the exchange controls limiting the amount of currency that UK residents could exchange for another. This removed a restriction on the rise of sterling that had been in force since 1939. UK institutional investors started adding substantially to their overseas investments, although mostly through foreign brokers.

In the 1980s, the London Stock Exchange (LSE) was the unrivalled leader among European exchanges. In July 1983, it came to a historic agreement with the government to abolish fixed commission rates and single capacity in stockbrokers, a move intended to make them more competitive. The changes came into force on 27 October 1986, and were known as *Big Bang*.

The jobber had been a wholesaler of stock to the broker but was suddenly made obsolete. In came broker dealers, whose role merged the previous responsibilities of the jobber and broker, and market makers. Overseas securities firms could for the first time become members of the LSE, and trading on the floor of the Exchange was replaced with the screen-based Stock Exchange Automated Quotations (SEAQ) system.

At around the time of Big Bang, US banks were coming to London because the Glass–Steagall Act prevented them from conducting retail and investment banking business simultaneously. The popular perception of the City had been as a club of florid-faced ex-public school chaps with a penchant for long liquid lunches. With Big Bang, a new type of City worker, competitive and egalitarian, was stepping into key roles.

Information technology, including the electronic order book on the London Stock Exchange, has helped to make trading more prolific. In the London insurance market, the development of electronic processing of paperwork has helped to address, among other things, past failures to provide timely contracts.

To cope with these and other demands, including regulation, a growing product range and increasing internationalisation of the culture, financial services staff have to be flexible and also, often, to develop a specialisation. The equity salesperson or analyst may have little knowledge of the bond market while, for bond salespeople, the ignorance is about equities. Neither of these specialists may know much about the commodities markets or Lloyd's insurance.

At the same time, the various parts of the City are interlinked and an event in one market can create a chain reaction in another. Bonds issuance is supported by the swaps market, which enables some borrowers to swap their obligation for one that is more congenial. Derivatives hedging cannot exist without liquidity provided by speculators. Deposit accounts and various financial instruments are affected by foreign exchange movements, which are impacted by interest rate movements, in turn driven by inflationary pressures.

The macroeconomic numbers are under scrutiny by a vast army of City strategists and economists paid ample money to sit glued to their screens and bark out their opinions and forecasts. Securities analysts harness this and other data to prepare research that may assist, in particular, the lucrative investment banking divisions within the same firm, although recent regulatory developments have meant that the conflict of interests must be properly handled. How strategists and analysts communicate with the City is strictly regulated, but there are informal as well as formal channels.

The sophisticated way in which the FSA regulates the City helps its image abroad. Many banks in the City are foreign-owned, and the LSE attracts a large number of listings from non-UK firms. Managers of hedge funds, a relatively unrestricted form of investment vehicle, favour London as a location, but this may not continue because tax efficiency is strong in, for example, Dublin or Switzerland. The Lloyd's insurance market has kept a high international reputation in rocky times.

At the same time, some institutions have seen their roles diminished in some respects. The Bank of England no longer supervises the banking system and its main focus is now on monetary policy. Consolidation is frequent, as firms seek economies of scale and synergies to survive. In mid-2007, the London Stock Exchange agreed a merger with Borsa Italiana, the Italian Stock Exchange.

In financial services regulation, the UK and the United States make uneasy bedfellows, although the large US banks, for one, manage to straddle the two jurisdictions effectively. The UK principles-based regulatory regime puts the onus on firms to make their own interpretations, while the US regime is rules-based.

The UK is increasingly under pressure to conform to pan-European regulatory standards, including the Directives imposed on European states by the Financial Services Action Plan.

Markets are people

The City still has a reputation for being a world apart, and its workers do tend to enjoy better opportunities than may be available, for example, to metal workers in the North of England. Many are doing mundane work for above-average pay.

As the City has developed in size and international stature, it has demanded increasingly better-educated entry-level workers. In these days of programmed electronic trading, the demanding jobs are likely to be filled by mathematicians, economists and computer whizzes, many from France, Germany or Russia.

For bright university graduates, the City is often their first career choice. A good numerate degree, better still followed by an MBA, in either case from well-regarded institutions, can open doors, but the personality must be right. It is no secret that the front-line jobs in the City require heavy socialising and sales skills, and an ability to deal with clients, a criterion fully reflected in today's stringent recruitment process.

In the City, status comes from the size of the pay packet and bonus more than the intellectual demands of the job, although some fund managers prefer to see it differently. The City has its professional exams, and the programmes have become increasingly flexible.

Career openings are varied. The City has a small army of support staff ranging from IT professionals to settlement clerks, editors, newsletter writers, press officers, trainers and others. Some are more highly qualified than others and, for back-office processing, there are plenty of temps. Support services are increasingly being outsourced to cheaper locations such as India, which carries its own risks.

At the end of 2004, 316,000 people were employed in City-type jobs in London, up 5,000 on the previous year, according to a report by IFSL. But nobody's job is safe in the City. The large financial institutions are constantly reconstructing themselves, and may downsize their operations based on their own circumstances as well as market conditions.

The future

As the second edition of this book goes to press, the City is unlikely to overtake the US financial markets, the global leader, as talk was suggesting, because the overall gap remains huge.

London nonetheless remains attractive, not least because of a time zone overlapping with Asia in the morning and the United States in the afternoon. The City is open to foreigners, and it has a growing Islamic centre. English is the international language of business and London has a sound financial infrastructure and an acclaimed regulatory regime.

In April 2007, the Bank of England said that the UK financial system remained very resilient, although strong and stable macroeconomic and financial conditions had encouraged financial institutions to extend their risk taking, and the compensation for bearing credit risk was at very low levels.

Such risks are highlighted in the business pages of quality daily newspapers, or in the *Financial Times*. Read the press to keep up with events and learn about the City.

The next step

To understand the City requires you to grasp not just something about its individual activities but also how they fit together. This book aims to cover and to link the parts of the whole. In the next chapter, we will examine the role of the Bank of England.

2

The Bank of England

Introduction

In this chapter, we will focus on the Bank of England outlining its history, its role and operations. We will look at its open market operations and the role of the Bank's Monetary Policy Committee in keeping inflation to the specified level. We will conclude with a glance at the Bank's international liaison.

Origin

The Bank of England (www.bankofengland.co.uk) is the UK's central bank. It was set up as a private company in 1694 with the aim of helping the British government under William and Mary to raise cash to finance the war against Louis XIV of France. From the earliest years in its 300-year history, the Bank of England has been the government's banker. Sincc thc 18th century, it has also been a bank for other UK banks. As a result of the 1844 Act, the Bank of England gained the right to the sole issue of banknotes in England and Wales. It remained a privately owned bank until nationalisation in 1946.

Until 1997, the Bank of England was both the supervisor of banks and adviser to the government on monetary policy, tasks conducted from different departments. The banking crisis of 1973–75 revealed weaknesses in the informal supervisory approach, which led to the Banking Act 1979, and subsequently the Banking Act 1987, under which the Bank would authorise and, in a flexible way, supervise the banking sector.

The Bank of England's continued role as supervisor came under increasing scrutiny, particularly after the July 1991 collapse of Bank of Credit and Commerce International (BCCI). In October 1992, a report by Lord Justice Bingham found that the Bank had not pursued 'the truth about BCCI with the rigour which BCCI's market reputation justified'. But it did not recommend that the Bank should be deprived of its banking supervisory role.

The Bank of England has statutory immunity against negligence claims, but Deloitte, the liquidators of BCCI, brought an £850 million lawsuit against it claiming 'misfeasance in public office'. In November 2005, the case collapsed and the Bank was thoroughly cleared of any allegations of dishonesty in relation to its supervisory role of BCCI.

In 1995, Barings collapsed after its trader Nick Leeson had lost over £800 million through unauthorised trades in derivatives, and this triggered further consideration of the Bank of England's supervisory role. Under the regulatory regime of the time (discussed in Chapter 22), Barings, as a major investment and trading bank, had to seek authorisation from the Bank of England for its banking activities, from the Securities and Futures Authority for its securities dealing services, and from the Investment Management Regulatory Organisation for its investment management. The number of regulators perhaps made it difficult for any individual authority to supervise the diverse business of the bank.

Changes were inevitable. The Bank of England Act 1998, transferred responsibility for authorising the banks and supervision of the banking system from the Bank of England to the Financial Services Authority (FSA), a new single statutory regulator for the financial services industry. The Bank has retained responsibility for the stability of the banking system.

Role today

The Bank is responsible for the overall stability of the UK financial markets, and maintaining price stability. It also manages the UK's gold and currency reserves on behalf of HM Treasury. The Bank can intervene in the money markets and, in accordance with government policy, occasionally in the foreign exchange market. It also oversees payment and settlement services under the Settlement Finality Directive adopted in May 1998. All the clearing banks keep accounts at the Bank of England and use them to settle differences between themselves in the clearing system, exchanging cheques written by each other's customers, or moving credit.

The *Court* of the Bank of England consists of the Governor of the Bank of England, two deputy governors, and 16 non-executive directors, who oversee the Bank's affairs apart from the formation of monetary policy. The executive team is the Bank's senior management team. It consists of the governor; two deputy governors; five executive directors who are responsible respectively for financial markets, financial stability, monetary analysis and statistics, banking services and central services; and an adviser to the governor.

The Bank cooperates closely with the Treasury and the FSA and participates in many financial forums, but in accordance with the 1998 legislation, the FSA now supervises banks.

Monetary policy

The Bank of England and the government have traditionally cooperated on monetary policy – the setting of interest rates. The objective is to maintain monetary stability and to support the government's economic policies, including its objectives for growth and employment. As a central bank, the Bank of England can influence money supply by its interest rate decisions and open market operations, and by changing the level of bank reserves allowed to be held interest-free with the Bank.

Traditionally, the Bank of England advised on interest rate policy, and the decision on whether to change rates rested with the Chancellor of the Exchequer. But after the Labour Government won the May 1997 general election, Chancellor Gordon Brown, to the country's surprise, gave the Bank of England full responsibility for monetary policy, which became statutory when the Bank of England Act came into force on 1 June 1998. By this move, which meant independence for the central bank, the Labour Government answered concerns that government had a political agenda and so should not be given responsibility for setting interest rates and addressing inflation.

Inflation targeting

The chancellor, acting for the Treasury, defines price stability and sets the annual inflation target, and the Bank has the task of keeping inflation at the target set by the government. Its tool is the power to change the *repo* rate. This is the short-term rate at which the Bank of England lends to banks for repurchase agreements. It is for practical purposes synonymous with the term *base* rate. Under extreme circumstances, the government can instruct the Bank on interest rates for a limited period.

Inflation may be defined as a continued rise in price levels that diminishes the value of money and it is a necessary part of economic development. Experts cannot agree on the cause. Some cite cost-push inflation, based on rising manufacturing costs, and others believe in demand-pull inflation, based on demand exceeding supply. The monetarist view attributes inflation to a money supply that has grown too quickly, a view currently out of favour.

Business always has an underlying incentive to increase the profit margin and so create inflation, but this is hampered by the ability of competition to move in. Markets are more efficient than they were in the 1960s and 1970s, when employees routinely bargained through their unions for high wages linked to inflation expectations. Rising commodity prices contributed to the demand spiral. When inflation is high, prices become detached from value, and the economic outcome is suboptimal. Central banks such as the Bank of England traditionally fear that the inflationary environment could become embedded.

Inflation targeting, as practised by the Bank of England, has had a clear impact across the world in helping to keep inflation expectations low. But some critics suggest it has encouraged the public to take on more debt.

The Monetary Policy Committee

On the request of Chancellor Brown, the Bank has established a Monetary Policy Committee, known as the MPC, to make interest rate decisions. It consists of the Governor of the Bank of England, who is appointed for a five-year term by the Chancellor of the Exchequer, and two deputy governors, also appointed for five years, as well as the Bank's chief economist, the executive director of market operations, and four external members who have mainly been economists.

The MPC conducts two-day meetings every month to determine the appropriate interest rate used for lending money via the repo market (see Chapter 11), which is effectively the market's short-term interest rate. The Bank is mandated by the government to keep inflation at 2.0 per cent as measured by the Consumer Price Index (CPI), which may be used for making comparisons between countries in the eurozone and equates to the European Harmonised Index of Consumer Prices.

Before December 2003, the measure of inflation was RPIX, the headline offshoot of the Retail Price Index (RPI), and the target was 2.5 per cent a year. This is still published but may not be in the foreseeable future because it is no longer used much for practical purposes, although the RPI is still used for the indexation of pensions, state benefits and index-linked gilts.

If inflation should be more than 1.0 per cent above or below the 2.0 per cent a year CPI target, the Governor of the Bank must write an open letter to the Chancellor explaining why inflation has missed the target and what the Bank will do to bring inflation back within the inflation target parameters. The governor wrote such a letter in April 2007, which was the first since the government handed monetary policy control to the Bank in 1997.

In deciding on interest rates at its monthly meeting, the MPC considers a wide range of economic indicators and surveys, including the CPI, earnings growth, the Purchasing Managers' Index, producer prices, gross domestic product, retail sales, house prices and the performance of sterling. It considers the reports of its regional agents around the country.

In making up its mind, the MPC looks at its inflation forecast two years ahead; a change in interest rates can take this long to take full effect. If the economy has entered a fast-growth phase and employment is rising, the Bank may look to raise interest rates in an attempt to curb inflationary pressures. If the economy is in the early stages of a slowdown, the Bank may be less likely to raise rates. The MPC has kept the base rate unchanged more often than not over the past eight years, but this is not in itself a sign that the economy has been doing better or worse.

On the first day of the meeting, the MPC considers the briefings given the previous week by the Bank's economists; on the second day it considers and votes, announcing a decision by noon. The basis for decision making is a majority vote.

The minutes of the MPC meeting are published 13 days afterwards and are read carefully by strategists looking for enlightenment on the committee's thinking, including, most importantly, clues about likely changes in interest rate policy at the Committee's next monthly meeting.

In the June 2007 MPC meeting, Mervyn King, Governor of the Bank of England, had voted for a rate increase and, for only the second time in history, the governor was outvoted. If the governor was outvoted regularly, it would undermine his own position and the integrity of the MPC, according to Roger Bootle, managing director of Capital Economics, who is an adviser on MPC-related matters to the Treasury Select Committee, through which MPC members are individually accountable to Parliament. This awkwardness arises because the governor is not only an individual member of the MPC with one vote, like the other committee members, but is also the MPC chairman and its spokesman. On Bootle's observation, King, unlike the previous governor Eddie George, is the MPC's intellectual leader.

King is seen to be of the school of thought that the growth in money supply, significant in 2007, could at least have some useful forecasting value in terms of assessing inflation. The Bank's own forecasting model, the Bank of England Quarterly Model (BEQM), does not include an explicit role for money supply.

Quarterly inflation report

The Bank of England publishes a quarterly Inflation Report, which takes a retrospective look at recent progress and makes inflation and GDP growth forecasts.

Various economists, including a shadow MPC through *Times Online* (www.timesonline.co.uk), make interest rate predictions before the MPC meeting.

Knock-on effect

Once the MPC has changed the repo (repurchase agreement) rate, the retail banks tend to change their lending rates rapidly, often setting them at a margin above the base rate. Banks will vary their margin as a commercial decision, and may occasionally lend at the repo rate itself, which means that they will be lending money at the same rate at which they borrowed it.

Higher interest rates will usually have the broad effect of slowing consumer spending. They make it more expensive for companies to borrow, and this can slow their growth. A secondary effect is that investors may move from shares into cash because they can get a higher return on their deposit accounts, which can depress share prices.

Open-market operations

The Bank of England lends money to banks in the money markets. Through these *open-market operations*, the Bank covers any imbalance. It buys securities daily, both outright and on a repo basis. Repo means to buy securities from a bank and later to sell them back to it at a higher price. For more about the money markets and repos, see Chapter 11.

Lender of last resort

If a bank encounters liquidity problems, and this threatens to have adverse impacts across the financial system, the Bank of England can act as the lender of last resort. If a high street bank should fail and the public panicked and withdrew money *en masse* from the banking system, the Bank of England would have the power to step in to ensure that wider financial instability was avoided.

The criteria for intervention are intended to be stringent. In 1995, the Bank of England decided not to intervene to save Barings from going bust, taking the view that the event would pose no systemic threat to the UK banking system, and that a wholly market-driven solution was more suitable to address the bank's insolvency.

In other cases, the Bank of England has intervened. In 1890, the Bank, along with various commercial banks, rescued Barings after its bad debts in Argentina were three times its capital and threatened its solvency. In 1975, the Bank arranged a banking consortium to act as a lifeboat in a banking crisis precipitated by large exposures to the property sector.

In 1984, the Bank helped Johnson Matthey Bankers Limited, a London market maker in gold bullion, which had got into financial difficulties from its commercial lending exposures. If the operation had been allowed to fail, other bullion dealers would have joined the creditors, which would have diminished confidence in the London gold market.

In September 2007, the Bank of England agreed to provide Northern Rock, a mortgage lending bank, with 'as much funding as may be necessary'. The mortgage lender obtained three-quarters of its funds from wholesale markets, where lending had become much more difficult as a knock-on effect from US sub-prime mortgage failures (see Chapter 12).

Some commentators queried whether the crisis at Northern Rock, only the fifth largest mortgage lender in the UK, had justified intervention by the Bank of England, which on the Bank's own criteria should have been in the case of systemic threat. Others argued that the move was necessary for broader financial stability. Some thought that the Bank of England might have made things easier for banks generally if, like the European Central Bank (ECB) or the US Federal Reserve, it had injected liquidity earlier into the system.

The Bank of England's publicised support was met with a public panic, and hordes of customers withdrew savings from Northern Rock. A few days later the Chancellor offered an unprecedented and legally binding guarantee of all funds deposited with Northern Rock, something that it would not be able to extend to the entire banking system without having to print money on a scale that could lead to horrendous inflation.

Later in the same month, the Bank of England said it would pump a further £10 billion into the money markets at a three-month maturity, with penal interest rates, against a wider range of collateral, including mortgage collateral, than in its weekly open market operations.

Some commentators interpreted the move as a U-turn because the Bank of England had previously refused to inject substantial cash into the money markets to help banks cope with a drying up of liquidity. There was speculation whether the government had put pressure on the Bank to act, so compromising the Bank's independence, or whether the Bank of England itself had realised it was wrong.

Mervyn King's continued long-term role as Governor of the Bank of England came under brief trial by media. Shortly afterwards, King told a Treasury Select Committee that he had been stopped from acting quickly to prevent the Northern Rock panic because of four pieces of legislation that ensure transparency. He said he would have preferred to deal with Northern Rock by acting covertly as a lender of last resort, but was advised that the Market Abuse Directive (see Chapter 22) meant this action had to be made public. He told the Committee that he had hoped Northern Rock could be taken over, but this had not been possible because it would have taken too long. Acquisitions under the UK's Takeover Code take 60 days to complete.

King noted two pieces of current legislation that could contribute to public panic in the event of a banking liquidity problem. When a bank goes into administration, assets are frozen rather than transferred immediately to another institution, and the official deposit insurance (the Financial Services Compensation Scheme, covered in Chapter 30) can offer less than 100 per cent of funds to consumers.

The public panic before the Chancellor's intervention had perhaps been due to the discrepancy between the Bank of England's statement of unlimited support for Northern Rock and the limits on compensation. There is some feeling that it is time to shift towards a compulsory insurance system, as used in the United States, where rules of the Federal Deposit Insurance Corporation guarantee up to US $100,000. There is also talk of potential restructuring of the Bank of England's status as lender of last resort, with one suggestion being that the FSA and the Treasury should take responsibility for bailing out individual banks, leaving the Bank of England supporting main financial markets and institutions, where the true systemic risk lies.

International liaison

Globally, the Bank of England liaises with such organisations as the International Monetary Fund, and the Bank for International Settlements.

So far, the UK government's refusal to join the euro has kept the Bank of England in control of UK interest rates. If a referendum in the UK should decide in favour of joining the euro, and the transition was made, UK interest rates and monetary policy would rest with the ECB, which was established on 1 June 1998. The ECB is independent but must back the EU's general economic policies. It takes interest rate decisions on a majority vote, which, if applied to the UK, might not suit its economic conditions. The Bank of England, if it joined the single currency, might then conduct money market operations and foreign exchange intervention within EU policy limits in addition to providing assessments on the UK economy.

3

Commercial banking

Introduction

In this chapter, we will look at the activities of commercial banks, which take deposits, lend money, participate in the money markets and in foreign exchange and trade finance. We will look briefly at building societies. We will scrutinise how commercial banks raise finance, organise credit collection services, and address the issues of bad debt, capital adequacy and the Basel Capital Accord.

History

The original purpose of banks was to stash cash. The earliest bankers operated in Florence from the 14th century and conducted business from benches in the open air. The Italian word for bank is derived from *banco*, which means bench. If a bank was liquidated, its operation was broken up, hence the word *bankrupt*.

In the late 14th and early 15th centuries, some Italian merchants from Lombardy came to London, and set up as money lenders in Lombard Street, the part of the City of London where banking activities are still concentrated. British banking started in the 17th century, with rich merchants storing their money in the vaults of goldsmiths because these premises were secure. They were encouraged to seek safe custody for their assets when, in 1640, King Charles I seized private gold deposited in the Tower of London to pay an English army that he was raising against Scotland, where he was also king.

By 1677, there were 44 goldsmith bankers in London. They would provide a receipt for money deposited, which was initially used to regain the full sum but subsequently became assignable and so a primitive form of banknote. Clients could write a note directing money to be paid to another, the earliest form of cheque. A merchant would write an authority to his goldsmith to pay his tailor. The goldsmiths used cash and precious metals deposited to lend money to merchants, with the aim of receiving it back plus interest, following completion of a voyage. It gave rise to the phrase *when my ship comes home*. By offering such credit facilities, the goldsmiths were operating like banks.

Banking outside London and Italy was almost non-existent until the mid-18th century, but by 1810 it had grown to be represented by 650 banks. By 1900, London had become the world's largest banking centre with about 250 private and joint stock banks. During the First World War, the banking business expanded in size and scope. Banks, however, were subsequently hit by poor interwar trading conditions. During the Second World War, banks became subject to foreign exchange controls and lending priorities. In the 1950s, these were relaxed and banks expanded. In the 1970s, the government encouraged more active competition. From a comparatively few conglomerates, banks moved towards the broad provision of financial services that we have today. We have come a long way from the Victorian era when many small banks had provided limited facilities for a wealthy minority.

Today, investment banks cover not just investment banking (see Chapter 7) but also activities traditionally associated with commercial banking, including fund management, trade finance, leasing and factoring, venture capital, project finance, syndicated loans and foreign exchange. Convergence between the two types of banking has often been uneasy, and US politicians and financiers blamed it for the great crash of 1929. To prevent a recurrence, the US Congress passed the Banking Act of 1933, the Glass–Steagall Act, which separated the two types of banking. Recent opinion has been that securities trading need not harm commercial banking and, in 1999, Congress passed the Financial Services Modernisation Act, which eliminated the separation between the two types of bank.

Culturally, the entrepreneurial spirit of investment banking has sometimes been an uneasy bedfellow for the cautious commercial banking ethos. Investment bankers have been more likely to have a public school background and commercial bankers a grammar school education, but the dividing line has blurred.

Commercial banks today

Commercial banks are mainly involved in deposit taking and lending. Deposits build up when people leave surplus money in saving accounts. When banks lend money to their clients, it comes from other banking clients. In effect, what goes into one person's account as a loan must come out of another's. The banking system is said to be like double-entry bookkeeping.

Banks pay a small rate of interest on cash deposited, and lend out much of it at a much higher rate, making a margin on the difference. In common alone with the government, they keep bank accounts with the Bank of England. A bank must retain a required level of liquidity, and it can borrow or lend money wholesale on the money markets (see Chapter 11), dealing with other banks or perhaps multinational companies. Every night, a bank may offer surplus funds for overnight loans, or it may borrow funds, perhaps because a large number of customers drew down significant sums that day.

The banks will lend to consumers, which is retail banking, or to businesses and governments, which is wholesale banking. Companies borrow more than retail customers and negotiate a better rate, which the bank endeavours to offer through its money market operations. On a bank's balance sheet, deposits are liabilities because the bank owes money to customers. Any sums that banks lend, both from deposits and from wholesale funds that they have borrowed, are assets because they ultimately belong to the bank.

Retail banking has developed dramatically over the past three decades. The Royal Bank of Scotland's acquisition of National Westminster, and Barclays' acquisition of the Woolwich, as well as the merger of Halifax and the Bank of Scotland have made the industry more concentrated, according to the British Bankers' Association (BBA).

The system underwent a revolution from the 1990s, when traditional banks were forced to close branches. There was a trend towards centralisation as local industries collapsed, forcing workers to find jobs in the nearest town, where they would take their bank accounts. New cut-price providers of banking services, telephone-based and later internet-based, were springing up. The appeal of the new telephone-based banks is that they made personal banking possible from the office or home without the hassle of going into a branch.

In October 1989, First Direct, part of HSBC Bank, launched the first fully fledged, 24-hour telephone banking operation. It has targeted individuals across the socio-economic spectrum who prefer not to use bank branches and like to be in charge of their finances, a spokesman says. The service has obvious appeal for night workers. Internet banking is the latest variation and an internet-based bank is not just open all hours but also saves money on overheads, which it may pass onto the customer in the form of higher interest rates on deposit accounts and cheaper lending. But a *virtual* bank still has some overheads, including security costs. It appeals to broadband users who are at home and comfortable with technology, according to First Direct.

Egg, launched in late 1998 by the Prudential, was the first entirely internet-based bank and, like others that have followed, has a slightly quirky image. The largest proportion of its customers is in the 25–45 age grouping whose average income is a fairly high £30,000 per annum. Older customers are less likely to use internet banks, although some *silver surfers* break the pattern, an Egg spokesman says.

High street commercial banks today operate as mini-financial conglomerates. They can provide financial products, which may be *own brand*, or, if the bank operates on a multi-tied basis, from a number of providers (see Chapter 30). Banks sell savings products, and may own stockbrokers or have their own share-dealing services. They will have linked up with insurance groups or set up insurance subsidiaries, and they sell insurance more easily than insurers sell banking products. They provide a foreign exchange service, including travellers' cheques.

Banks in the UK have a reputation for being more user-friendly and flexible than those in continental Europe. They pay interest on credit balances in some current accounts, and an overdraft is easy to arrange. Some retailers such as Tesco have joined forces with banks to offer *own brand* banking services, although without chequebook facilities.

Banks offer a cashpoint card, which has a magnetic strip enabling owners to withdraw cash to a maximum sum from an automated teller machine, known as an ATM, in the high street. This card can also serve as a debit card, which is effectively an electronic cheque. Purchases made this way will be debited to the customer's account a couple of days after the transaction is made, in the same way that a traditional cheque would be. A credit card, on the other hand, will go across a separate account, with payments due monthly.

Banks issue credit cards in a highly competitive market. Transactions are processed through Visa or MasterCard. Credit card issuers profit mainly from interest charged to users, but also from fees that retailers pay. They must take into account bad debts, card thefts and fraud.

In 1999, Egg issued the Egg card, which paid 0 per cent on balance transfers and new transfers for nine months, meaning that users of another credit card could transfer their balance to Egg and pay no interest on it for this period. It was the first offer of this kind, but there are now around 110 zero-per-cent credit cards on the market. Many cards offer up to 56 days' free credit but only if the outstanding balance is repaid in full by the due date. The precise period of free credit will depend on the point at which the transaction is made or appears on the account.

At the end of 2006, the amount outstanding on credit cards was £31.2 billion, reflecting in net terms a £1.6 billion decline in lending, which almost exactly offset the £1.6 billion net increase in 2005, according to the BBA.

In 2006, consumer borrowing, either through personal loans or increased overdrafts, grew £2.3 billion, compared with growth of £4.7 billion in 2005, marking a more than 50 per cent growth decline, according to the BBA. This growth took outstanding consumer credit to £76.2 billion at the end of 2006.

Building societies

Let us now take a look at building societies. They are lending and saving institutions and they compete with banks. There are 60 building societies across the UK, with assets of over £305 billion. As mutual organisations, they are collectively owned by their members, and 50 per cent of their lending has to be from retail deposits. Unlike banks, they are restricted from raising money on wholesale markets to lend through commercial products.

The societies often offer better value products than the banks, particularly in the core areas of savings accounts and retail mortgages, because unlike banks they do not have to use around 35 per cent of their profits to pay dividends, according to the Building Societies Association. But bankers note that building societies may limit the availability of their offer to people living within a certain, relatively small, geographical area. Building societies have a total of 2,150 branches, employing almost 50,000 full and part-time staff, while banks have more than 11,000 branches, according to the BBA.

The Building Societies Act 1986 introduced demutualisation, which means conversion to an investor-owned company, and by the mid-1990s many societies had taken the plunge. Managers and directors favoured conversion into a bank to boost their own incomes, and *carpetbaggers* sought windfall profits by opening temporary savings accounts in the societies most likely to convert.

The downside was that borrowers from the newly formed banks could lose because the lending rates could rise. How far demutualisation replaced an out-of-date structure with a more efficient one is open to debate. It has enabled the converted entities to tap into traditional banking markets, including commercial lending and money markets, and there is no restriction on how they could raise money or on products offered, which has provided opportunities to gain scale to compete with banks.

In practice, the game has not always proved so easy. In July 1989, Abbey National was the first building society to convert to plc status and to be floated on the London Stock Exchange. The risks of corporate banking became apparent in 2001, after which Abbey National announced two years of significant losses, £984 million in 2002 and £686 million in 2003. In this case, the bank remained structurally solid and changed its business focus, shortening its name to Abbey. In November 2004, Abbey was acquired by Banco Santander Central Hispano, a Spanish financial group.

The Building Societies Act 1997 allowed traditional building societies, as distinct from the demutualised entities, to offer a wider range of banking products. Nationwide in particular has broadened its product range. But most societies have stayed with savings accounts and retail mortgages, offering the odd credit card or loan. Like banks, building societies may use the internet to offer savings account access to customers, or mortgage application access to independent financial advisers. Retail mortgage sales are sometimes carried out over the internet but most are managed through branches.

Building societies serve more than 15 million savers and over 2.5 million borrowers. They hold residential mortgages of over £200 billion, approximately 18 per cent of the total outstanding in the UK. On the savings side, they hold over £190 billion of retail deposits, accounting for 19 per cent of all those in the UK, but a much higher 37 per cent of cash individual savings accounts (ISAs) (see Chapter 30).

Now that we have seen the basics of how banks and building societies work, let us focus on how the banking system provides finance.

Raising finance

General

Banks provide uncommitted finance only to businesses. In this case, the bank will provide finance facilities, but is not committed to allowing money to be drawn at a particular time. The process is an agreement in principle. It could involve any form of finance, including a loan, perhaps in the form of a term loan.

Committed finance applies to business *and* personal accounts. It is when a bank commits itself to providing finance through a formal agreement or structured fee payment. The bank might say: 'We'll lend you £10,000 for five years, at a given interest rate, with fixed fees payable, and an agreed procedure if you fall behind with payments.' A committed facility need not be a loan, but could be a guarantee or a letter of credit. For example, if a local authority gives a contract for work, it may require a guarantee from the contractor's bank that if things go wrong, it will get its money back.

The overdraft straddles uncommitted and committed facilities. It is used both for business and personal accounts. A bank can arrange an overdraft quickly and informally; it will agree a limit, and the customer will pay only for money borrowed. Daily interest on the overdrawn balance may be set at a margin over the base rate or, typically for personal accounts, at a managed rate.

The syndicated loan

If a borrower wants more money than an individual bank will lend, a syndicated loan may be used to spread the loan across a number of banks. It will probably be for more than £50 million, and possibly for hundreds of millions of pounds. The bank awarded the client mandate may be either a commercial bank or an investment bank. If the borrower breaches its covenants under the loan agreement, the bank will be released from its commitment.

Project finance

A commercial bank may fund a large-scale infrastructure project through recourse lending. A recourse loan means that if the borrower should default, the endorser or guarantor of the loan has a secondary liability.

Investment banks may finance projects with non-recourse lending. Under a non-recourse finance arrangement, the lender does not seek repayment from the borrower personally, but is content with some other sources, for example, the stream of income from the asset.

In both recourse and non-recourse lending, the lender will require the project itself to repay the loan. It will assess the project's viability in terms of future cash flows, which may be guaranteed through a government contract to use the products or services generated by the project. The bank is likely to ensure it will be paid first by having a charge over escrow accounts into which income from the project must be paid.

Commercial banks provide some of the funding for projects in developing countries. Multilateral lending agencies – such as the European Bank for Reconstruction and Development – finance projects intended to benefit the infrastructure of less developed countries.

Asset finance

Clearing banks have broad businesses and investment banks are more niche-oriented, but either can provide asset finance. This has now overtaken bank loans as the main source of finance for capital purchases up to £100,000, according to the Finance & Leasing Association. The three main types are finance lease, operating lease and hire purchase. Asset finance can reduce pressure on the borrower's cash flow, enabling payments to be spaced out, and repayment terms may be customised.

Finance leasing is where the bank buys an asset and gives use of it to a company at an agreed rate over its whole economic life, with ownership usually remaining with the finance provider. The risks and rewards will have passed to the lessee. The lessee must treat this arrangement as an asset on its balance sheet, and it will be depreciated over its life. The bank can claim capital allowances on the assets it leases out, and will have a charge over them. For these reasons, it can offer the company a good rate of interest on the leased asset.

Over the life of the lease, the cost to the lessee is recognised in the profit and loss account (income statement) as both depreciation of the asset and a financing charge on the liability. The company must repay both the interest on the principal, which is the cost of the asset, and some of the principal itself. The repayments are known as the rental, which should cost the company less than borrowing to buy the asset directly.

At the end of the lease period, the asset's useful economic life is over. But the asset may still be useable, and the lessee may continue to lease the asset for a secondary term at a nominal rate. The company may, as an agent for the bank, sell the asset; if so it would receive the proceeds in the form of a rental rebate, after the bank had taken a cut. If the company kept all the money, it would mean that there had not been a true lease, and HM Revenue and Customs could react by removing the bank's capital allowances.

Operating leases, unlike finance leases, are for only part of the economic life of an asset. They do not provide the benefits of ownership, given that the risks and rewards of ownership have not been passed to the lessee, and are not assets on the lessee's balance sheet. Instead, their lease rental payments are charged to the profit and loss account as an operating cost. Companies prefer to classify a lease as an operating rather than finance lease, partly because none of the lease payments is classified as an interest charge.

Hire purchase involves finance for the whole economic life of an asset but ownership ends up with the client. The accounting treatment is similar to that of finance leasing.

Credit collection

Banks are involved in guaranteeing and collecting credit, as well as providing it. Let us see how they provide these services.

Trade finance

When a UK exporter of a product has found a buyer overseas, it commits itself to delivering the product and the importer commits itself to paying. The exporter shares its bank documents with the importer to confirm that the product has been put on transport for delivery and is of the specified quality, and the importer will either have funds in its account or will have made other financing arrangements.

The exporter will ask the importer to arrange a letter of credit (LOC) from the importer's bank. If the importer's bank agrees to issue the credit, it will send it to the exporter through the exporter's bank. The LOC will stipulate the documents required and any relevant timescales. At the time the goods are dispatched, the exporter will present the LOC to its bank together with the required documents. If all is in order, the exporter's bank will then pay the exporter under the terms of the LOC and claim reimbursement from the importer's bank.

Where an LOC is not involved, the collection of bills or documents works as follows. The exporter presents documents, usually with a bill of exchange, to its bank, with instructions to send these for payment to the importer's bank, of which the importer will have provided details. The exporter's bank will proceed accordingly, presenting the documents for payment. On the importer's authorisation, the bank will send the money to the exporter's bank, which will then credit the exporter's account, less any charges.

Factoring and invoice discounting

Factoring and invoice leasing are where a business sells its invoices to an invoice financier when they are issued. Invoice discounting is where the client maintains control of the sales ledger and factoring is where the invoice financier takes over. In either case, the bank pays the business up to 90 per cent of the invoice value in cash immediately, and the rest, excluding charges, following a set period or once the debt has been collected.

Funds advanced to businesses through factoring and invoice discounting in the UK amount to around £13 billion at any given time. Banks are responsible for around 70 per cent of the turnover, some operating the business through a subsidiary, separate from their main activities. The industry grew 12 per cent in 2005, and recent legislation has helped to persuade banks to move funding from overdrafts to invoice finance, according to the Factors and Discounters Association.

Bad loans and capital adequacy

General

A bank may make a specific provision on its balance sheet against a bad or doubtful debt, for example where an identified customer is unable to meet an obligation to pay a specified loan. There may also be a general provision; if, for example, a mine closes in a small town, people will lose jobs and the local bank will know that some loans will have to be written off, but not which ones specifically. The bank will raise a general provision against, perhaps, 10 per cent of the money borrowed.

In 2006, major British banking groups wrote off more than £6.6 billion in bad debts, up from £5.3 billion the previous year, based on lending to UK residents, according to the BBA. The main component reflects the write-off of £5.3 billion of loans to individuals, representing only 0.8 per cent of personal lending. This proportion may be expected to be small because, in value terms, 83 per cent of lending to individuals is secured lending on mortgages, where, if the loan goes bad, the lender may seize the collateral.

If a syndicated loan to a country cannot be repaid on time, banks may restructure the borrowing to avoid the country being declared bankrupt, which could lead to an international crisis and harm the global economy. If a default gets too deep, banks may feel forced to bite the bullet. In May 1987, Citicorp declared a US$3 billion provision against loans to third world countries, which amounted to public acceptance of a loss. Other banks then announced provisions against similar losses.

Historically, banking crises have occurred when too many customers have withdrawn cash in a panic, causing an immediate liquidity crisis. This is known as a *run* on the bank. See Chapter 2 for how it happened briefly at Northern Rock in September 2007. Banks need to have sufficient liquidity and capital to see them through such difficult times. In the UK, the Financial Services Authority now authorises and supervises banks, and it has set capital adequacy requirements for them based on best-practice recommendations of the Basel Committee for Banking Supervision (BCBS) (see below). But as events at Northern Rock, a lender of prime mortgages, showed, it is possible for a bank to be in difficulty through lack of liquidity without any immediate threat to solvency or any breach of capital adequacy requirements as they now stand.

The Basel Committee

The BCBS was set up in 1975 as a standard-setting body within the Bank of International Settlements (BIS), which serves as a bank for central banks in the interest of monetary and financial stability. The Committee consists of regulators and central bank officials from 10 major global economies known as the G-10 (plus Spain and Luxembourg).

Basel II was set up by the Basel Committee and published in June 2006. It is intended to reduce the possibility of consumer loss or market disruption as a result of prudential failure. To achieve this, Basel II seeks to ensure that financial resources held by a firm are commensurate with the risks associated with its business profile and internal control environment.

It is a more advanced version of Basel I, the first stage of the Basel Accord, which required banks to keep a minimum 8 per cent level of regulatory capital as a proportion of assets weighed by credit risk, and was subsequently amended a few times, including measures to cover market risk. Basel II retains the same minimum capital-to-assets ratio, and the buffer capital in the banking system must not be permitted to fall below levels required under Basel I. All solvent banks hold more than the minimum capital, but the framework encourages better risk management.

Under Basel II, banks may use a more advanced way of measuring their risks and, if so, they may have lower capital charges than banks using the simpler approaches. In practice, only a few major banks are interested in this approach.

A perceived benefit of Basel II is that as a result of greater risk aversion, institutions can price more keenly. But critics say it is too complicated and expensive, and may benefit larger banks more than smaller ones. Banks may be reluctant to lend to small businesses because they represent a greater security risk, and the strict requirements for covering risk may inculcate a false sense of security.

In the EU, Basel II was made law by the Capital Requirements Directive (CRD) (see Chapter 22), which allows for national discretion in a number of areas of implementation, perceived both as a strength and a weakness. All firms subject to the CRD must have adopted the new regime by 1 January 2008.

In July 2007, US federal banking agencies said they had agreed on how to implement Basel II in the United States, a move that would enable them to issue a single Basel II capital rule by the end of September in that year. The agencies approved a proposal that the Basel framework should be adjusted if there was a 10 per cent drop in aggregate capital among the major banks. The core banks must use the advanced approach to measuring capital requirements. There will be a three-year transitional floor period in the United States, with a maximum cumulative capital reduction of 5 per cent in 2009, 10 per cent in 2010 and 15 per cent in 2011. Only from January 2012 will US banking capital be subject to Basel II with no floor, as for banks outside the United States.

4

Introduction to equities

Introduction

Much of this book is about institutional investors, which are responsible for the vast majority of investing by value. In this chapter, which focuses on equities, we will assume the perspective of the private investor.

We will look at the mechanics of the stock market, including how nominee accounts work, and indices. We will focus on the different types of stockbroker.

Shares

Shares are a type of security that represents ownership in a company. Equity is often used interchangeably with stock or share, which signifies the investor's share of ownership. Once a company is quoted on the London Stock Exchange (LSE), or any other exchange or trading facility, including abroad, you can usually buy and sell shares in it, which is most often done through a broker. Shares can rise or fall in value, which is reflected in a fluctuating share price. The price is set as a spread between a buying price, which is above mid-price level, and a selling price, which is below it.

Many companies quoted on exchanges pay a dividend, which in the UK is paid twice a year, and this represents a payment from corporate profits to shareholders. The share price is likely to rise a little as the dividend day approaches, and will fall subsequently. Dealings on or after the ex-dividend date will be at a lower price because it excludes the dividend entitlement.

By owning a share, you are a part-owner of the company, and may attend an annual general meeting (AGM). The AGM is a statutory requirement and it offers you as a shareholder the chance to review the company's activities. You also have voting rights.

If you are a private investor, you will often need to hold your shares for at least several months, and perhaps some years, to gain profit from your investment. Traders go in and out of stocks within a much briefer period and so base their investment decisions on more short-term factors.

Shares are now usually held in electronic form through nominee accounts, although the old-fashioned paper share certificates are still used to a limited extent. Investors have their shares registered in the name of a nominee company but retain beneficial ownership. The account is run by their broker. Investors do not lose access to shareholder perks and voting rights, but it is up to the nominee company to provide them with the relevant information. Dividends are paid and regular account statements are provided.

Since February 2001, the industry standard for settlement of shares held in nominee accounts has been T + 3, meaning that both counterparties to a trade agree to *settle* a trade three business days after the trade date, although market makers, as opposed to the electronic order book, can offer some flexibility. For paper share certificates, it is T + 10.

Some private investors dabble on a one-off basis in the stock market but for those with a more sophisticated approach, the conventional wisdom is to build a diversified portfolio, investing in a number of companies, each in a different sector. This way, the risk is spread. If one share falls in value, the others may outperform, balancing out overall performance.

On a broader scale, investments may be diversified across assets and countries. Bonds are less risky assets than equities, and cash deposits are the safest asset class of all. Commodities and property will broaden the spread. Geographically, Western Europe is a more stable environment in which to invest than emerging markets such as China and India, but it has less growth rate potential.

Investors take long and short positions in shares and other assets. A long position is where they own a share and expect to sell their position in the future at a profit. If they go short, they will sell a stock they do not own with the aim of buying it at a lower price before settlement, so making a profit on the price difference.

The rolling settlement system makes it difficult for private investors to go short on shares. But they can take a short position using contracts for difference, covered warrants, or spread betting (see Chapter 9). In 2002, terrorist groups were suspected of having raised funds by taking short positions on various stocks before and after the 11 September 2001 terrorist attacks on New York, but this was never proven. In October 2002, the Financial Services Authority issued a discussion paper on short selling. It considered it a legitimate activity but thought more transparency would be helpful, and, in the years since, it has not changed its position.

If an investment bank has a net short position in a stock, it may borrow from a lender to deliver the securities on the agreed settlement date. From the buyer's perspective, there is no practical difference between borrowed and owned stock. If the bank has a net long position, it may lend the stock to borrowers for a fee.

As a result of short trades, stock lending flourishes in bull markets, and improves market liquidity. Stock lending figures, available from Euroclear UK & Ireland and other sources, provide only a very loose indication of short selling levels as other factors must be considered as well.

Market indices

If you want to see how the broad market, or a part of it, is performing at any given time, you will look at market indices. The indices can serve as a benchmark against which to buy or sell individual shares or a portfolio.

The most widely quoted index is the FTSE 100 Index, which covers the largest 100 stocks listed on the LSE by market capitalisation (share price multiplied by number of shares in issue). FTSE 100 companies, referred to as blue chips, each have a market capitalisation that may be several billion pounds or more, with wide variations, and the index represents about 80 per cent of the UK market.

The FTSE 250 Index includes the next 250 stocks by market capitalisation behind the FTSE 100. It represents 17 per cent of the UK market capitalisation. Companies on the FTSE 250 are large enough to survive hard times, but have more room for growth than the blue chips.

The FTSE 100 and the FTSE 250 together cover 95 per cent of the whole UK market and make up the FTSE 350 Index. An even broader measure of the whole market is the FTSE All-Share Index, which includes the 700 largest shares on the LSE.

Companies too small to be included in the FTSE 350 may be in the FTSE SmallCap Index. Stocks in the FTSE 350 and the FTSE SmallCap Index make up in its entirety the FTSE All-Share Index (see previous paragraph). The FTSE Fledgling Index consists of companies too small to be included in the FTSE All-Share Index, but all of them will have achieved a full listing on the LSE, with a market capitalisation that can be as little as £500,000, but is usually at least a few million pounds.

Smaller companies may choose to be listed on the LSE's Alternative Investment Market (AIM), and these are represented in the FTSE AIM Index. Some smaller companies are PLUS-quoted (see Chapters 7 and 16). Very young companies may be unquoted as they would more likely be seeking venture capital. Institutional investors do not always give a lot of attention to small stocks because they are hard to trade in large quantities. The banks and stockbrokers research them less. But specialist funds focus on small stocks.

Small company shares are a favourite hunting ground for private investors, often guided by tip sheets (see Chapter 21). Stockbrokers note that the stocks are volatile, have many more losers than winners and are not particularly liquid, which tends to cause problems in a market crash.

Bond prices often move in broadly opposite directions from share prices, although they sometimes move in line, and bonds are considered a less risky investment. Chapter 11 explains how government bonds work. The UK Gilts Indices are calculated by the FTSE Group and are based on all eligible British government securities, divided into conventional gilts and index-linked gilts. There are also corporate bonds, which are slightly lower risk than government bonds, as discussed in Chapter 12. In the UK, these are represented and measured in the FTSE Sterling Corporate Bond Index.

Now that we have seen how shares work, and how indices track the market, let us take a close look at stockbrokers.

Stockbrokers

There are three main types of stockbroker. The advisory broker gives advice and the discretionary broker makes decisions on its clients' behalf. Together, these two cater for around half of all private clients. The third type of broker is execution-only. Let us look at each.

Advisory

Advisory stockbrokers advise clients on which stocks to buy or sell, and when, and execute the trade. Some specialise in certain types of stock such as small growth or high-income blue chips. The service is about getting the balance right between having the clients involved in decisions and protecting them from making mistakes. Levels of expertise vary widely, and success may depend partly on the relationship between the broker and client.

Discretionary

Discretionary brokers or fund managers take full charge of an investor's portfolio, and execute the trades. They make buying and selling decisions on the investor's behalf for a fee.

Some discretionary firms have produced unfortunate results, particularly in market downturns. Some allocate too high a proportion of cash into risky assets such as equities because it pays them more in commissions, or overtrade portfolios.

The broker is not always to blame. The client may have indicated that it has an appetite for risk when it started the relationship. Even so, investors should make it clear that they are watching. They should ask about investment decisions, request frequent statements, and check that the broker at least cuts losses and runs profits.

Execution-only

The execution-only broker offers no advice to investors but simply executes their orders online or by telephone. This reduces staff and other costs, and they pass the savings on to the investor. The trend towards online services, along with industry consolidation, has contributed to a steady reduction in the average commission and fees per transaction, according to Compeer, the benchmarking and research services specialist.

For practical purposes, in dealing with such brokers, private investors should be self-reliant and pick their own stocks. They will need to research companies and sectors in order to select shares, skills also needed to watch what an advisory or even a discretionary broker is doing.

The next step

In the next chapter, let us look at the most important data used for measuring the performance of the market and of individual shares.

5

How to value shares

Introduction

In this chapter, we will see how to value shares. We will see how analysts work. I will define key financial ratios such as earnings per share and the P/E ratio, as well as discounted cash flow. We will focus on what influences the market, including the biggest movers, company results and trading volumes.

Analysts' forecasts

The City is more influenced by analysts' *forecasts* for a company than by results, which are based on the past. The share price is typically based on what the company is expected to do in one to two years' time, and this perception can change.

If an analyst at a prestigious bank changes a stock recommendation from *hold* to *buy*, this will affect the share price on the day as traders react. A change in the share price target will have some impact but less. The share price may overreact up or down, and will later even out. Reuters, the online news and data service, reports analysts' changes in recommendations and price targets in real time but the full service is for subscribers and is expensive.

In the business pages of *Times Online* (www.timesonline.co.uk), you may enter a company name to find, where available, a consensus brokers' opinion, as part of financial data provided by Hemscott. A chart shows how far along the scale from *strong buy* to *strong sell* a given stock is placed. If the opinion is exactly between the two, it reads a *hold*.

For more about how analysts work, see Chapter 20. Let us now see how you may borrow from analysts' techniques and value stocks.

Ratios

Financial ratios enable a quick assessment of a company against its own past or its peers'. To understand what they mean, it is helpful to know how they are made up, but you do not need to calculate them yourself. In the business pages of *The Times* some of the key ratios and statistics are included under the two pages headed 'Equity prices'. You will find here a list of companies quoted on the London Stock Exchange under alphabetical sector headings representing broad categories of business. The first heading is 'Banking & finance', and the last one is 'Utilities'.

Against the names of companies, of which those in the FTSE 100 Index (the 100 leading stocks) are in bold, the first column covers the high and low of the share price in the past 52 weeks; the bigger the gap, the more volatile are the shares. In Monday's edition, a column for the company's market capitalisation (share price multiplied by number of shares in issue) is provided instead.

The next column has the company's name. It is followed by the share price, which is at yesterday's closing mid-price – halfway between the buying and selling price, based on the most competitive quote. To the right is a column headed by a plus and minus, showing any difference in pence between yesterday's and the previous day's close. On Mondays, the share price change shown is weekly rather than daily.

Further to the right is the yield, which is the dividend, divided by the share price, multiplied by 100. The higher the yield, the higher the income payments to investors as a proportion of the current share price. Some sectors such as utilities are high yielding, but growth companies typically have a low yield.

The earnings per share (EPS) is the ratio that City professionals follow most widely. It is the listed company's profits after tax divided by the number of shares in issue.

The City likes to see the company's EPS steadily rising over the years. It is worth checking out the last five years of figures to see how far this has been achieved. Be aware, however, that, despite recent standardisation of accounting practices across Europe, accountants have some discretion on how they allocate profits, which affects the EPS. They will try to present the company in a favourable light.

Obtain the EPS, and its annual growth in recent years, from a company search on the business pages of *Times Online* (www.timesonline.co.uk). Bear in mind that earnings can be greater than cash flow because they can include items other than pure cash. In accounting terms these items may be categorised as earnings, although the money may not yet have been paid to the company. As the City saying has it, profit is a matter of opinion and cash is fact.

To compare cash flow with earnings, the ideal approach is to compare the cash flow statement with the income statement in the annual report and accounts, which is usually available on a listed company's website. If net cash generated from operating activities on the cash flow statement is materially less than net operating profit on the income statement, there has been creative accounting at work, as Jim Slater put it in his book *The Zulu Principle*.

Earnings per share divided by dividend per share provides dividend cover, a figure that you will be able to calculate from data provided on individual companies in the business section of *Times Online*. Dividend cover says how easily a company can pay a dividend from profits. It only applies to those stocks that pay dividends, which excludes some of the small growth stocks. A company in good financial health should be able to pay its dividend, assuming it has one, comfortably from current earnings. If not, it may have to use its reserves to keep up the payment. As a rule of thumb, when dividend cover is less than one, there may be cause for concern.

Let us return to *The Times* share price tables, where the last column is headed 'P/E'. This is the price/earnings (P/E) ratio, which is widely used and shows how highly the market rates a company. At *Times Online*, it is called PER. The P/E ratio is the current share price, divided by the earnings per share in the most recent 12-month period. It moves in the opposite direction to the yield.

If a stock has a P/E ratio higher than for its peers, the market rates it highly. The shares may be overpriced but could shoot higher, based on demand exceeding supply in the short term. If the company or market has a setback, the crowd euphoria can reverse and the share price could revert to a level closer to fundamental value.

If the P/E ratio is low, the market is not attaching much value to the stock's prospects, often for a good reason. But in the case of a less widely followed stock, a low P/E ratio suggests possible overlooked value.

If a technology company, for instance, has no earnings per share because it has not yet broken into profit, it will have no P/E ratio, and other valuation methods will have to be used, such as price-to-sales ratio (available at *Times Online*).

The professionals use several ratios at once, and other valuation tools, to build a composite picture of how a stock is performing. In the case of small growth companies, a P/E ratio is more useful when considered in conjunction with profit growth. If a stock has a P/E ratio of 20 and is growing at 20 per cent a year, this may represent good value, but if the annual growth rate is only 5 per cent, it could look expensive. The PEG (price/earnings/growth ratio) is the P/E ratio divided by earnings growth and so covers both these factors. It is included under company headings at *Times Online* and can be useful in valuing small companies.

The return on capital employed (ROCE) is a measure of management performance. It is calculated as profit before interest and tax, divided by year-end assets less liabilities, expressed as a percentage. Analysts favour a rising ROCE that is higher than in peer companies.

To value property companies, investment trusts or composite insurers, the share price/net asset value (NAV) per share may be used. This is the company's total assets less its liabilities, debentures and loan stocks, divided by the number of shares in issue.

Gearing represents a company's level of borrowing, or the relationship between debt and equity in its capital structure. It is most commonly expressed as debt capital as a percentage of total capital funding (that is, of debt capital plus equity capital). The higher the gearing, the greater the risk, but, as a rule of thumb, more than 50 per cent is potential cause for concern.

For capital-intensive companies with large borrowings, such as in telecoms, a useful figure is earnings before interest, tax, depreciation and amortisation (EBITDA). In this type of company, EBITDA arguably presents a more realistic valuation than conventional earnings, which are calculated after interest and tax.

However, EBITDA is not recognised by accountants. Because it excludes tax, there is an obstacle in comparing stocks based on this valuation across international borders when the respective countries' tax regimes differ, although this avoids what is seen as a distorting factor in making the comparisons.

Analysts had used EBITDA to value WorldCom, a US telecoms group, which in July 2002 made a Chapter 11 bankruptcy protection filing a month after it had revealed a US$11 billion accounting fraud. Analysts then stopped using EBITDA as a stand-alone stock valuation tool, but still have it as a weapon in their armoury.

Analysts value companies using the enterprise multiple, which is enterprise value (EV), consisting of a company's market capitalisation plus debt, divided by EBITDA. The EV/EBITDA ratio takes debt and cash into account, which the P/E ratio does not, and it is used to find attractive takeover candidates, helpfully showing how much debt the acquirer would have to take on. Like the P/E ratio, the lower the enterprise value, the better the value of the company, although the ratio tends to be higher in high growth industries, and comparisons should be made against the sector.

The most widely used tool of analysts, and arguably one of the most dangerous in the wrong hands, is discounted cash flow analysis.

Discounted cash flow analysis

Discounted cash flow (DCF) analysis translates future cash flow into a present value. It starts with the net operating cash flow (NOCF). You find this by taking the company's earnings before interest and tax, deducting corporation tax paid and capital expenditure, adding depreciation and amortisation, which do not represent movements in cash, and adding or subtracting the change in working capital, including movements in goods or services, in debtors and creditors, and in cash or cash equivalents. This is the year's NOCF. It can be calculated for future years, and reduced in value to present-day terms by a discount rate.

Weighted-average cost of capital (WACC) is often used as the discount rate. This represents the cost of capital to the company. It is the average of the cost of equity and debt, weighted in proportion to the amounts of equity and debt capital deemed to be financing the business.

The cost of equity, which is part of WACC, is the expected return on equity, which is most often measured by the Capital Asset Pricing Model (CAPM). The CAPM finds the required rate of return on a stock by comparing its performance with the market. It expresses this return as equal to the risk-free rate of return plus the product of the equity risk premium and the stock's beta. The beta measures the sensitivity of a share price to movements in the general stock market.

The CAPM stipulates that the market does not reward investors for taking unsystematic (company-specific) risk because it can be eliminated through diversification. The model is theoretical and is based on various assumptions, including no taxes or transaction costs. Share buyers require a higher return than debt providers to compensate for the risk, and for the fact that the company must give priority to debt repayment over paying dividends.

The cost of debt, the other part of WACC, is more transparent. It is commonly estimated as the redemption yield on the company's bonds, and interest rates on loans and overdrafts.

DCF has proved itself a flexible tool in the hands of analysts wishing to create valuations sometimes out of thin air but it has lost credibility since the market crash of March 2000.The problem has been more about how DCF is used than with the underlying concept. You only need to change one or two of the parameters and you will get a different figure for DCF, and this leaves it open to manipulation.

To make an accurate forecasting scenario more likely, analysts may plot DCF models using different discount rates and different cash generation scenarios to present alternative valuations. The aim must be to present a prospective picture, including variables, and not to be too dogmatic, although investors crave specific numbers.

Now we have looked at some stock valuation techniques, let us turn our attention to what influences the market.

Market influencers

The market is influenced by sector and economic news, particularly of events in the US market the previous day or in Asian markets overnight. It discounts what is known or thought will happen in the future. Investors focus particularly on the biggest movers, company results and trading volume. Let us look at each.

Biggest movers

You can obtain yesterday's main risers and fallers on the stock market from some financial websites, including from some stockbrokers. This gives you a valuable indication of what is driving equities. Shares that soared yesterday are likely to have overdone it and may drop back today, or they may continue up – but not forever. As an investor, you need to check out the reason for the price movement so far, and assess how far it is discounted in the current share price.

Company results

The share price moves in anticipation of results. When a company reports results and they are as expected, there will not be much price movement. But if the results have a surprise element in them, it can affect the share price, particularly if there is a shock profit warning. In such a case, analysts will take time to forgive the company for not having given them a steer, and may be loathe to give it a high valuation.

Company results are reported as news stories in the financial pages of the national press. Useful tables accumulate the figures in one place. In *The Times*, company results are reported in the table headed 'Results in brief'. Against the company's name and (in brackets) the sector, you will find the year or half year covered – for example 'Yr to June 30', or 'HY to August 1', the pre-tax profit or loss, the dividend per share (if none, 0p) and payment dates. The pre-tax profits and dividends for the same period last year are given in brackets.

The rise or fall in the share price over the past year is never the full story, and some understanding of the company's strategy will help to put the new numbers in perspective. A company may have cut expenditure to increase profits now, at the expense of the long term, or conversely, it may have invested in an expensive advertising campaign, which reduces profits now, but will raise them later.

Trading volume

Trading volume can say a lot about the depth of a market move, indicating how likely it is to last. It may be defined as the number of shares traded in a stock or, alternatively, as the number of shares traded, multiplied by market capitalisation.

The LSE provides in the statistics section of its website (www.londonstockexchange.com) a monthly figure for the number of bargains in individual securities. Divide it by the number of trading days in the month for a daily average. As a rule, if the share price moves significantly on strong volume, it means the change is backed by plenty of investors, but if it is on thin volume, the backing may be from only one or two big traders, and the price change may prove more fickle.

Some technical analysts see underlying volume as important, but the consensus is that it takes a secondary place to share price movements.

6

New share issues

Introduction

In this short chapter we will take a look at the markets available for companies that want to issue shares. Most of the markets we will cover are on the London Stock Exchange. Read this with Chapter 7, which explains how investment banks bring companies to market.

Capital raising

A company that is looking to raise cash should consider which route is most suitable at its stage of development. If it is a young company, it may seek venture capital or borrow from the bank. A larger company may prefer to issue equities (shares) or debt.

A company may issue equities and bonds, a form of debt, on the Main Market of the London Stock Exchange (LSE). For international companies there is a choice here of a primary or secondary listing. Away from the Main Market, the LSE offers the Professional Securities Market, the Professional Fund Market and the Alternative Investment Market. PLUS Markets has set itself up as a rival to the LSE. Let us take a closer look.

The Main Market

The LSE's Main Market is the world's most international market for listing and trading of public equity and of debt, including bonds. In 2006, there were 83 new equity issues on the Main Market, raising more than £18 billion, and 712 further issues raising more than £14.5 billion. The investor reach is global as non-UK-based funds buying UK equity exposure are attracted to Main Market securities.

Companies listed on the Main Market have a market capitalisation from around £5 million up to £200 billion, which will typically be for an international group with a multiple listing, although not all of the trading will necessarily take place on the LSE.

The Main Market on the LSE is tiered. It offers a primary or a secondary listing for equities and debt securities. Let us look at each.

A primary listing requires a company to meet the highest standards of regulation and disclosure in Europe. It requires *superequivalence*, which means that the standards are over and above those required for admittance to EU-regulated markets. The company must have three years of audited accounts, and 75 per cent of its business must be revenue-generating. All UK companies joining the Main Market are required to take a primary listing.

Companies with a primary listing must comply with the UK Listing Rules, which means that they must comply with the Combined Code, which is the UK's corporate governance system (see Chapter 25), or explain why they do not. Primary listed companies are eligible to be included in the FTSE UK Index series, which helps to build greater liquidity for Main Market companies by providing investors with benchmarking of stocks, sectors and the market.

A secondary share listing does not in itself mean that a company has a listing in another market. Unlike a primary listing, it does not need three years of audited accounts; the accounts must instead cover the company's life or three years, whichever is shorter. The secondary listing requirements are part of the UK Listing Rules.

A company may have a secondary listing either in shares or in global depositary receipts (GDRs), which are certificates listed and traded in London that represent ownership of the company's shares on its domestic exchange. GDRs are also available on the Professional Securities Market (see below).

The requirements for GDRs and secondary listed shares are broadly similar, but GDRs are often preferred by international companies because on the LSE they are traded on a dedicated order book, the International Order Book (IOB), which is not open to retail investors and which is used by professional investors interested in foreign companies. In 2006, IOB trading exceeded US $289 billion, executed from almost one million trades. Neither secondary listed shares nor GDRs may be included in the FTSE UK index series, but they can be included in other indices. For example, the 10 leading Russian GDRs on the IOB form a distinct index, the FTSE Russia IOB.

Professional Securities Market

The Professional Securities Market is open to issuers listing debt convertibles or depositary receipts in London as an alternative to the Main Market. It enables issuers to follow a wholesale regime irrespective of the type of denomination of security. They may use their local accounting standards rather than go through the costly procedure of preparing International Financial Reporting Standards (IFRS), as required on the Main Market.

This market was introduced to address concerns surrounding the Prospectus Directive, implemented in the UK in July 2005, and to help keep London's pre-eminent position as a listing venue for the specialist securities covered.

The Specialist Fund Market

The Specialist Fund Market (SFM) is for specialist investment managers that want to access London pools of capital in a flexible way and is closed to traditional trading companies. It is designed to appeal to managers of large hedge funds, private equity funds and certain emerging market and specialist property funds seeking admission to a public market in London.

These funds are looking for institutional investors but not for a wider investment base. A separate market has been created for these funds because they may be unsuitable for retail investors due to characteristics such as high gearing, concentrated risks, variable liquidity and sophisticated corporate structures. These features may also make them ineligible for inclusion on the Main Market.

Opening on 1 November 2007, the SFM will have filled a specific gap identified by London's legal and investment banking community, given that in June 2007 the Financial Services Authority's (FSA) UK Listing Authority indicated it was abandoning its two-tier listing regime, consisting of its Main Market and a lighter 'directive minimum' regime for overseas funds (see Chapter 19, under *Split capital investment trust*). The lighter regime had attracted claims of inadequate investor protection from some investment trusts and traditional fund managers.

Investment funds may list on the Main Market under Chapter 15 of the Listing Rules and, at the time of writing, the FSA was consulting on relaxing this regime to make it more attractive for overseas funds to list.

The Alternative Investment Market

The Alternative Investment Market (AIM) was created by the LSE in 1995 to meet the needs of small growing companies and is a high-risk/high-reward market. Typically companies on the AIM will have a market capitalisation of anywhere from £2 million upwards; the largest may be up to £500 million, although they would almost certainly not be that size on joining the market.

Disclosure requirements are less rigorous than on a full LSE listing. A start-up company can go to the AIM without three years of IFRS accounts, but if it has a track record, it must show the accounts. If an AIM company wants to make an acquisition of less than 100 per cent of a company, it need not first obtain shareholder approval.

The LSE has been promoting the AIM as a secondary stock market listing in London for non-UK companies that wish to retain their local market main listing. It has focused on, among others, the Benelux region, China, Australia, India, Russia and Kazakhstan.

More than 2,500 companies have been admitted to AIM and more than £34 billion has been raised collectively. It is a sign of AIM's maturity that 57 per cent of its shares are held by institutions, up from 41 per cent the previous year, as revealed in an August 2006 Growth Company Investor survey.

The regulatory framework of AIM hinges on the Nominated adviser, or Nomad, which brings the company to the market and is responsible for its behaviour afterwards. A company has a direct line to its Nomad, which is in turn regulated by the LSE.

On 20 February 2007, the LSE announced some regulatory changes for the AIM. A separate rule book has been introduced for Nomads, which codifies best practice. The Nomads have greater responsibility than before for assessing a company's suitability, its business plan and its management, and it is easier for the LSE to discipline the companies. For natural resources companies, a competent person's report must be carried out.

AIM companies are subject to enhanced disclosure requirements, which include a requirement, from August 2008, to display core management and financial documents on websites.

PLUS

Away from the LSE, PLUS Markets Group provides two markets. The first is the PLUS-listed market, which is in regulatory terms equivalent to the LSE's Main Market, and the second is the PLUS-quoted market, which is in regulatory terms equivalent to the AIM, although each is much smaller than its longer-established competitor.

PLUS Markets Group has been a recognised investment exchange (RIE) since July 2007 (see also Chapter 16), which has made possible the PLUS-listed market. The RIE status enhances the group's cross-border status and reputation, according to Nemone Wynn-Evans, PLUS Group's director of business development.

PLUS is introducing a much broader range of primary market products and service offerings, including for investment trusts, REITs (real estate investment trusts) and other structured products, where it would compete with the LSE's Main Market. Its PLUS-listed market opened to cater for these issuers in August 2007.

The group's PLUS-quoted primary market specialises in small to mid-cap companies. It is slightly longer established than the PLUS-listed market and it used to be part of the old Ofex business, which it took over, completely restructuring the market and, by October 2006, changing the name to bring it into line with its PLUS branding. The group offers itself as a listing destination for primary issues with an admission process designed to keep costs proportionate to the size of the company and fund raisings. For example, in October 2006, Quercus Publishing floated on PLUS, raising £2.8 million from institutional investors.

Before it achieved RIE status, PLUS was viewed as only in competition with AIM. Under RIE, its PLUS-quoted market continues to compete in this space. Companies on AIM with a market capitalisation of less than its average £50 million can find it hard to make their voices heard, according to Wynn-Evans. 'Companies on PLUS can garner greater profile than their size might suggest.' In addition, joining PLUS can be very cost-effective for smaller companies as its regulatory framework helps to keep costs proportionate to the size of the company and/or its fundraising. PLUS-quoted stocks have an average market capitalisation of £20 million.

Some companies may not raise cash through an initial public offering (IPO) but want their shares to be traded, perhaps to obtain a valuation for acquisition purposes or to value employee share options. Around 200 companies are PLUS-quoted with their listing on the PLUS primary market, as at May 2007.

7

Investment banking

Introduction

Investment banks raise money for clients in the capital markets, and they advise on mergers and acquisitions. Investment banking is also known as corporate finance, and this chapter explains how it works. Read it in conjunction with Chapter 6, which covers new issues.

Overview

In the lucrative area of investment banking, the procedures for getting together a syndicate of banks, running a book and underwriting are broadly similar for issuing equities, on which this chapter is mainly focused, and debt. Banks are increasingly merging their equities and bonds origination activities. Investment banking also includes mergers and acquisitions advice, covered at the end of this chapter.

Elsewhere within the investment bank, traders deal with other banks directly or through money brokers, trading securities for themselves, as proprietary traders, and for investors. The salespeople manage investor accounts.

The initial public offering

If a company is going to issue its shares on the Main Market, it may launch an initial public offering (IPO). Ernst & Young has defined an IPO in its *Global IPO Trends 2007* as 'a company's first offering of equity to the public'. London Stock Exchange (LSE) statistics refer to a company's first offer of shares on its market as an IPO, even when the company has issued shares on another market.

INVESTORS CHRONICLE
AIM INVESTMENT AWARDS 07
BROKER OF THE YEAR
Ready to face your potential?
Brewin Dolphin is the Investment Bank of choice for companies who are looking to grow into their potential. That's why we were voted AIM Broker of the Year 2007.
Brewin Dolphin
Investment Banking
For straightforward commercial advice, call Graeme Summers on 0191 279 7531 or visit www.brewindolphin.co.uk.

BREWIN DOLPHIN INVESTMENT BANKING

Brewin Dolphin is a respected and emerging force in UK Investment Banking as a specialist strategic advisor to small and medium-sized quoted companies (up to £1 billion market capitalisation) on the Official List (OL) or the Alternative Investment Market (AIM) of the London Stock Exchange.

Over the last 12 months Brewin Dolphin has raised over £500m of capital for its clients of which there are 131, and has worked on transactions with a total value of more than £1.4 billion.

The core sectors in which Brewin operate include Business Support Services, Consumer, Healthcare, Human Capital Management, Industrial Services, Oil & Gas, Renewables and Technology.

Corporate Client services offered by the Investment Bank's Corporate Advisory & Corporate Broking team include Mergers and Acquisitions, Flotations, Secondary Fundraisings, Debt Advice, Public to Private transactions and Trade Sales.

Like most credible investment banks the corporate headquarters are within the City of London. However, Brewin also benefits from a unique regional spread of operations with significant presences in Edinburgh, Glasgow, Leeds, Manchester and Newcastle.

Brewin Dolphin's Investment Banking business has grown consistently over the last few years based on a very simple model. It concentrates on key industry sectors that it knows well and focuses on high quality growth companies in those sectors. As a result, Brewin has been able to add value to both its corporate clients and its institutional clients, assisting both in making significant returns.

A selection of transactions in recent years is summarised below:

- £453m Official List float of eaga PLC, raising £220m
- £58.0m AIM IPO of Caretech Holdings PLC, raising £26m
- £30m secondary fund raise for China Gold Mines Plc
- £28m AIM IPO & £25m secondary raise, of Vertu Motors PLC, followed by the £65m acquisition of Bristol Street Motors
- Reg Vardy plc £505m sale to Pendragon plc
- European Motor Holdings plc £263m sale to Inchcape plc
- Synergy Healthcare plc £160m hostile bid for Isotron plc
- Advising Dobbies plc on £155m sale to Tesco plc
- Go Ahead Group plc – multi million pound share buyback programme

In the year ending 30 September 2007, the business enjoyed record performance based on its growing reputation for focus, integrity, diligence and a commitment to working in the client's best interests over the medium to long term.

Like any successful business, none of the above could happen without the ability to attract and retain industry-leading people and Brewin Dolphin has more than its fair share in all of its disciplines.

How is the Investment Banking division structured?
The business is organised into 2 parts divided by a 'Chinese Wall' to ensure that price sensitive information relating to a company is kept away from the market.

The Corporate Advisory & Corporate Broking team is the part which interfaces most with the corporate client. People working here are classed as 'permanent insiders' and have a deep knowledge of the client company and its strategic plans for the future. The team offers expert advice on strategic transactions to private and public client companies. This includes Initial Public Offerings (IPOs), private equity, acquisitions and disposals, takeovers, debt advice and financial restructurings. We also help our clients by carrying out strategic reviews and assessing their optimal equity and debt capital structures.

The Equity Capital Markets team incorporates Institutional Sales & Trading and Research. As the name implies, this team interfaces mostly with the equity capital market, serving over 100 fund managers who manage and invest billions of pounds of money on behalf of institutions' pension funds, hedge funds or retail investors. The team provides high quality, sector-focused research on over 140 small and mid-cap quoted companies for investors and also transacts significant volume of share trades in the companies it recommends.

Like its own business, Brewin's client companies are spread across the UK and they like the personal service they get, being not just City-based but also typically located on or near their own patch, as the following testimonies demonstrate:

"Brewin was appointed following an extensive beauty parade of leading City advisors as a result of their sector expertise and track record. The team set out their views on valuation during this process and delivered on them." Farouq Sheikh, Executive Chairman, Caretech Holdings Plc.

"We have been impressed by the advice and commitment from the whole team - sales, research, corporate broking and corporate finance – an excellent and integrated service." Gordon Banham, Group Chief Executive, Hargreaves Services PLC.

"Brewin delivered on its promises. At IPO, Morson achieved a valuation premium over the MBO completed just six months earlier." Ged Mason, Group Chief Executive, Morson Group plc.

"Brewin Dolphin has a reputation in the support services sector which is second to none. The team carried out extensive due diligence and came up with a valuation for our company which they comfortably delivered on." John Clough, CEO, eaga plc.

Whilst Brewin Dolphin does not actively seek awards, it is highly encouraging that the business has enjoyed some significant recent accolades including 'Best AIM Broker' as voted by fund managers (Financial Times 2007), 'Best Small Cap Analyst Team' across the whole of Europe (AQ Research 2007 – based on the value added by research recommendations on absolute return to investors).

If you are a private company considering a flotation or trade sale or an existing small or medium sized quoted company and would like to speak to someone regarding Brewin Dolphin's Investment Banking services please call:
Graeme Summers on 0191 279 7531 or
Mark Brady on 0845 213 1000
email: firstname.secondname@brewin.co.uk

Brewin Dolphin
Investment Banking

Note for Editors : Brewin Dolphin Investment Banking is a division of Brewin Dolphin Ltd, which is the principal operating company of Brewin Dolphin Holdings PLC which is listed on the Official List and traded on the Main market of the London Stock Exchange of the UK Listing Authority. Brewin Dolphin Ltd is authorised and regulated by the Financial Services Authority and is a member of the London Stock Exchange.

Brewin Dolphin Ltd is also the UK's largest independent private client investment manager with £21 billion of funds under management, of which £10 billion is managed on a discretionary basis.

Opportunities

An IPO is used particularly by large issuers. Let us see how it works.

Beauty parade

The IPO starts with the *beauty parade*. One bank, or two jointly, as selected by the issuer, will land the lucrative job of preparing the company for its IPO.

In choosing between candidate banks, the issuer looks for a track record in floating similar companies. There are other criteria. For example, Mike Lynch, chairman of the software company Autonomy, told me it has appointed banks as book runners in its capital-raising initiatives primarily on the basis of how well they understand the business, and partly on the bank's geographical distribution power.

A bank cannot become a book runner if there is an unresolved conflict of interest, which could arise if it is launching the IPO of a rival company. If two banks are selected as joint book runners, any historic conflicts will come under scrutiny in the selection process. In practice, many IPOs and secondary placings are handled by banks that have a corporate relationship with the issuing company.

The book runner takes lead responsibility for placing the newly floated shares with investors and, in a sizeable deal, may organise backup from a syndicate of other banks. The bank at the top of the syndicate may have the status of global coordinator and other banks within it may have key roles such as lead manager or manager.

A method of selecting the book runner for an IPO, known as competitive IPOs, has arisen by which banks compete for a mandate on the basis of how easily they can gain indicative support from investors for the proposed flotation. There has been some regulatory concern that analysts may be under pressure to provide positive research about the issuer as an investment opportunity, thus compromising their independence in an undeclared way.

Pre-marketing

In a pre-marketing phase, the book runner meets with potential investors and presents the investment case for the company it is bringing to market. It ascertains the indicative price of the company's shares upon issuance and sets parameters within which it believes the new issue should later be priced. The banks often make this indicative price range public. Analysts away from the deal may say that the range is too high or too low against company fundamentals or peer ratings. The press may take a view, based on analysts' comments.

The book runner may occasionally move the indicative price range up or down. If so, it means that it had not properly anticipated demand. If the shift is downwards, which becomes more of a possibility in volatile markets, the risk is that the book runner may ultimately postpone the offering.

The book build

The book build is based on investor interest that the banks have drummed up during the pre-marketing phase. The banks build an order book through a road-show, which, in the case of large issues, travels across continental Europe and the United States as well as the UK. Banks in the syndicate organise group presentations and, outside the visiting schedule, may use video conferencing. The company's chief executive, finance director and head of investor communications address potential investors alongside the book runner's corporate financiers and analysts. One-to-one presentations will be organised by the banks with *tier-one* clients, which are the biggest and most important.

A traditional book build lasts two to three weeks, but can be longer in difficult market conditions. The pressure is then on investors to subscribe to the IPO. Most orders are confirmed two days or less before the book closes.

Once the IPO date has been declared, the entire process becomes highly susceptible to market news and conditions. The financial spread-betting firms may run a bet on the future price of a popular pending new issue. They will have set unscientifically a *grey market* price that may be quoted in the press and sway investors. This can become a self-fulfilling prophecy, although usually only a few punters will have bet.

Underwriting

When a company is brought to the market, it is typically underwritten. The underwriter is an investment bank that guarantees a given price for a given number of securities to the issuer in exchange for a fee. The riskier the deal, the larger is the underwriter's fee.

Underwriting fees on US transactions average between 6.5 and 7 per cent of the amount raised, compared with between 3 and 4 per cent on European exchanges, according to *The Cost of Capital: An International Comparison*, an Oxera study in June 2006, jointly commissioned by the LSE and the City of London.

Pricing

The issuer and book runner set the issue price ideally at the maximum level acceptable to institutional investors. If the deal is oversubscribed, the price may have been too low, but some oversubscription is likely in a successful IPO because, to ensure adequate share allocation, investors tend to request more shares than they want. This in itself helps to create demand, including in early secondary-market trading.

When pressed, major investment banks have admitted that the criterion for pricing the deal is not value but demand, which can partly be created. It is influenced not just by market conditions but also by perceptions of interest that the issuer, book runner and PR initiatives have been able to whip up.

With retail investors involved, a book runner may price a new issue higher. This is partly due to the extra take-up and the publicity it generates, but also because the price will usually then be more sustainable in early secondary market trading, helping to safeguard the reputation of the book runner, which is particularly useful if it had overpriced the issue in the first place. Retail investors often hold new issues long after they ought to have sold, partly because they are inadequately advised.

In the business pages of *The Times*, you will find a table headed 'Recent issues'. It includes stocks recently issued on the stock market, including the AIM, with yesterday's closing price, and any rise or fall on the day.

Early secondary-market trading

In good market conditions, a deal will typically reach a small premium, perhaps 10–15 per cent, over the issue price in early secondary-market trading. This creates demand for the shares, fuelled further by the oversubscription for the issue. If the free float is small, meaning that the shares are tightly held by company directors and few are available to the public, demand may quickly exceed supply and the share price may soar.

Institutional investors who bought shares during the IPO process may snatch a profit by selling the shares early in the first days or weeks of secondary-market trading. Such 'flipping' is often the best way to make money quickly from new issues, contrary to the buy-and-hold strategy often recommended to retail investors.

The book runner may welcome some flipping from favoured institutional investors because it needs liquidity to establish value in the shares and to meet the demands of buyers. After a few weeks the shares are likely to lose their initial momentum and, at least for a period, to slip below the offer price.

In poor market conditions, new issues are infrequent. If they happen, the shares may start trading at a discount to the issue price.

Specialist types of share issue

Accelerated book build

In an accelerated book build, the bank takes a selling company's shares in a listed company onto its books, and offers them to its investor clients. It will sell the shares in the course of one day or, exceptionally, over two or three days. This compares with several weeks for a conventional book build, and allows less time for market conditions to deteriorate. In a declining market, institutional investors respond favourably to this form of capital raising.

Bought deal

The bought deal is where a bank buys securities itself from an issuer and resells them in the market. The bank will have assumed all the risk by itself and so must have confidence in the deal. Issuers are often attracted to a bought deal because it gives instant liquidity.

Rights issues

If a UK company wants to raise more than 5 per cent of its existing market capitalisation, it must use a rights issue. The company will issue new shares to existing shareholders pro rata to their existing holdings. In a '1 for 5' rights issue, shareholders will have the right to buy one further new share for every five they hold. The process takes perhaps six to eight weeks, twice the length of a conventional share offering.

Through a rights issue, shareholders have an opportunity to acquire new shares without paying their stockbroker a commission. They do not have to buy and, if they are to do so, must be convinced that the company will use the cash properly. If the rights issue is to pay off debt, shareholders should assess the chances of success before they subscribe.

The issuing company will usually appoint an underwriter, generally a major bank, to the deal, which guarantees full subscription (see above under 'Underwriting'). If the issue fails, the underwriter will take up the rights. Some rights issues are not fully underwritten, which can be a high-risk strategy for both the issuer and the underwriter.

Once the rights issue is under way, the share price can fluctuate, which may happen more in uncertain markets or if the issue is for a purpose that may not benefit shareholders, or if it is not underwritten. Hedge funds may trade the underlying shares, which can cause havoc with the price.

The new shares in a rights issue will be priced lower than the market value of the existing shares. In difficult markets, the discount might be as high as

40–50 per cent, which is known as a deeply discounted rights issue and is more likely to attract subscription.

Following a rights issue, the overall share price will find a balance based pro rata to the price of the old shares and of the cheaper new shares, in proportion to the number of shares in issue of each. It is often slightly lower than before the rights offering. For capital gains tax assessment, HM Revenue and Customs considers the new shares were acquired at the same time as the original ones.

Shareholders not interested in a rights issue may sell the rights to which they have not subscribed, known as *nil paid* rights, to other investors. After they have received the proceeds, and the share price has adjusted down as a result of the rights issue, they will be in a cash neutral position.

Unsubscribed rights are known as the rump. The book runner will later sell them to new investors in an accelerated book build (see above).

Placing

In a placing, the broker issues a company's shares privately to institutions, at least some of which are its own clients. This form of capital raising is often used to raise small amounts, and may be enacted through a broker or investment boutique rather than an investment bank. Retail investors are not usually given the opportunity to buy.

Placing and open offer

A placing and open offer occurs when the placing (see above) takes place simultaneously with an open offer to existing shareholders. This dual approach is used to place shares in already quoted companies. The shares are placed provisionally with institutions but subject to clawback by shareholders that may exercise their right to take up shares under the open offer. Sometimes key shareholders will have undertaken to take up some shares.

A placing and open offer can be a quicker and more reliable way to raise cash than a rights issue, particularly in difficult markets. The amount raised must be below the size threshold at which a rights issue becomes compulsory (see above) and so a placing and open offer tends to be for small capital raisings, typically under £50 million.

Introduction

An introduction is where the company joins the LSE's Main Market without raising capital. The process requires no underwriting fees and little advertising. It is sometimes used as a preliminary to future capital raising.

Bond issues

When interest rates are low, listed companies may find it cheaper to raise money through corporate bonds (see Chapter 12) than through equities. If a company issues bonds, it may have to pay a coupon of 6 per cent, but if it issues equities it may have to give shareholders a 10 per cent return.

In the UK and some other developed economies, interest on bonds issued is tax deductible against the issuing company's profits. Let us assume that the bonds pay a 6 per cent coupon. Based on a 30 per cent corporation tax (main rate for 2007–08), the true cost of servicing the bonds would be 6 per cent × 0.7 = 4.2 per cent.

Companies sometimes issue bonds and use the cash raised to buy back shares from investors. The downside of bond issuance is the risk of taking on too much debt in relation to equity, which is known as 'high gearing' and gives the issuer a riskier profile with the credit rating agencies. Generally, banks have easier access to capital than companies and are more highly geared. Debt issuance is likely to be the second largest liability on a major bank's balance sheet, behind cash deposits.

The bond issuer cannot skip paying the coupon, as is possible with dividends on shares. It also must repay the principal on maturity, but can refinance by issuing new bonds.

Banks, like companies, invest cash in bonds, across the risk spectrum and in all major market currencies. Some bonds will be included on the asset side of the balance sheet, where in terms of risk weighting under Basel II (see Chapter 3), they are more attractive than loans.

Issuers of bonds usually offer a fixed rate of return, which is what investors prefer. But if the bonds fall in value, investors may feel they have lost out. This is why investors use the swaps market, which enables them to swap fixed for floating rates. The majority of the swaps market consists of interest rate swaps (see Chapters 8 and 11).

Mergers and acquisitions

Mergers and acquisitions (M&A) is the area where investment banks are often compared and judged. They will advise a company planning a takeover or that is a likely bid target, and may help it to raise capital for the purpose.

The prospective buyer of a quoted company can be another company, from Europe, the United States or elsewhere. Alternatively, it can be a private equity firm, which is able to acquire a listed company and take it private. Private equity has more resources to make acquisitions than quoted companies, and is not similarly encumbered with the need to make merger synergies, according to analysts.

To finance an acquisition, a company may use the capital markets. The acquirer pays for a target company's shares either with cash, its own shares or a combination of the two. If appointing an investment bank as an M&A adviser, the company will make the choice itself, choosing the one with the best ideas. For smaller transactions particularly, there is a growing trend for companies to use in-house M&A advisers, perhaps ex-bankers, and avoid using the investment banks. In 2006, European M&A transactions without external advisers reached US $453 billion, which was 28 per cent of the total, according to data provider Thomson Financial.

An investment bank's fee for M&A advice is up to 2 per cent of the deal's value, diminishing as the deal becomes bigger. The bank is only paid if the bid proceeds, and the bidder may withdraw, perhaps after it has concluded a due-diligence inspection or a rival bidder has muscled in. If a bank is advising a company making an acquisition, it may also raise capital for it, which is more lucrative.

Should the investment bank be acting for a target company, it may fend off the bidder with the intervention of a *white knight*, a congenial rival bidder, or may block the deal with a *white squire,* a significant minority shareholder. As a twist on the theme, the bid target may make a counter bid for the bidder.

If a takeover is to go ahead, the predator must obtain more than 50 per cent of the target company's voting shares. Once its stake has reached 30 per cent, it must make a formal offer to all shareholders. If some shareholders decline to take up an offer, a buyer can acquire their shares compulsorily if holders of 90 per cent of the voting shares have accepted.

The Panel on Takeovers and Mergers, an independent body, supervises and regulates takeovers with the aim of ensuring fair treatment for all shareholders. The Panel now has statutory powers.

M&A drives UK equity markets

M&A talk was the biggest share price driver for FTSE 100 companies in the bull market of 2006 and continued into the first half of 2007. Even if the market turns down, M&A interest will remain because investment banks have large deal pipelines that they will not quickly dismantle.

Bid rumours may never become reality but, particularly on a quiet day, they may boost the share price of a potential target company, and sometimes the entire sector. The share prices of companies seen as likely bid targets will rise in value, but if nothing happens sellers will emerge, sending the share price back down. The bid speculation is likely to recur on a quiet day, particularly if some analyst has decided to fan the flames. On the flip side, bid speculation can depress the bidder's share price if it is felt the deal would not be beneficial at the price mooted.

Bid talk recurs in some sectors, such as banking and insurance, and among utility companies and building companies, both of which have been helped by deals in the sector. The cash-rich mining sector has long been a source of bid speculation, and in July 2007 Rio Tinto announced a planned US $38 billion takeover of Alcan, a Canadian aluminium group. Other areas where the bid talk became a reality are in steel making and cigarette making.

There is doubtless more to come. Industrial group Hanson, airline British Airways and hotel group Intercontinental are among many that attract speculative bid talk. On days of slow trading, talk about retailer clothing Next as a bid target resurfaces.

It is important to note that M&A does not always produce the expected benefits. Sometimes, the integration of two companies can be problematic and not all deals enhance shareholder value, at least in the short term.

Disclosure and regulation

When acquisitions take place, it is hard to assess their value creation due to significant goodwill expenditure, coupled with under-reporting of intangible assets and a general lack of disclosure, according to Intangible Business, a brand valuation consultancy.

The FTSE 100 reported about £40 billion spent on acquisitions in 2006, and over half of this expenditure was put down to goodwill, according to a survey by Intangible Business. One conclusion was that the International Financial Reporting Standards (IFRS) 3, the accounting standard for business combinations, had failed in its objective of showing investors how their money was being spent on acquisitions.

Across European borders, takeover activity remains subject to national barriers, which so far the Takeover Directive has not succeeded in removing. In early 2007, the European Union said that only 17 of the 27 member states had transposed the Directive, which came into force in May 2006, or had adopted necessary framework rules.

For details of suspicious share transactions before M&A activity, see Chapter 22, under 'Market Abuse Directive'.

8

Introduction to derivatives

Introduction

In this chapter we will define derivatives and see how they work. We will examine the distinctions between on-exchange and over-the-counter markets, and the various products, as well as clearing and settlement, and issues related to hedging and speculation. In later chapters, we will focus on related areas.

Cash and derivatives

In the cash market, trades are in an underlying investment: for example Microsoft stock or British Airways bonds, or 100,000 barrels of oil. Cash is paid for assets and delivery is made. In derivatives, there is a financial or paper transaction, not on the underlying asset but based on its value, and that can turn into a deliverable. The recent demand for derivatives has grown far more than for cash products, according to market sources.

Derivatives include four basic transactions: spot, forward, option and swap. More complex terminology may be used, depending on which of the asset classes are involved.

The asset classes are credit fixed income, financials, interest rate market, equity and commodities. Credit fixed income includes credit derivatives, bonds, commercial paper and loans; financials include foreign exchange and forwards; interest rate markets include interest rate swaps and options, and deposits, as well as forward rate agreements and overnight index swaps.

Of the rest, equity covers the stock market; commodities include soft commodities such as food, feedstuffs and beverages, including grains, pork bellies, shrimp, wines, wheat and corn, as well as hard commodities, which are industrial raw materials such as oil, gas, electricity, nuclear fuel and metals. For more on commodities, see Chapter 13.

Within all these asset classes, you will find two types of trading: on-exchange, which takes place on an exchange, and over-the-counter (OTC) which is a customised transaction off exchange. We will look at the distinction in more detail later in this chapter.

Both on and off exchange, trades in the money markets (see Chapter 11) may be either in the underlying instrument such as shares or bonds, or their derivatives, which are based on the underlying instrument.

Let us now take a look at the four main types of derivative transaction, any of which may be used for either taking a position or hedging.

Four types of derivative transaction

Spot

When a derivative is spot, the price at which you trade is known to you now, and you buy and take delivery. The transaction timescale is typically short. It is expressed as T + 1 or T + 2, which is the trade date plus the number of business days until settlement. For example, trades in foreign exchange (covered in Chapter 14) are T + 1: you trade today, and transfer the money and receive your purchase the next business day.

Forward

On a forward transaction, the price at which you will trade is set in the future. If you trade a forward on an exchange, it is called a future. If you trade a forward on the OTC market, it is called a forward.

For futures, there could, for example, be a March delivery that stipulates delivery of 1,000 lots of an underlying commodity on 23 March. As a trader, you will either reverse out of the future before that date, or there will be delivery of the underlying instrument. On the forward market, you will choose the day of delivery.

A brief case study best shows the distinction between forwards and futures. Let us assume that you will need to exchange one billion dollars on 23 March because, on 24 March, you are required to pay for a factory. If you buy a future on an exchange and delivery is on 23 March, this fits exactly with your requirement. But if the exchange contract expires on 15 March, you will receive the money earlier than you need, or if it expires on 15 April, you will receive it later. Either would be an imperfect hedge.

On the OTC market, you can avoid this because the contracts can be tailor-made. You may buy a three-month forward on 23 December and receive payment on 23 March. If, alternatively, you ask the bank on 6 January for a forward to 23 March, you can get it, although this is a *broken date* because it is not over a standard period and it will cost more due to both the decreased liquidity and the need to find a counterparty.

Option

An option is a right. It is not an obligation, which distinguishes it from a forward or a swap (see below). If you have an option to buy euros at £1.50 in three months, and the price rallies to £1.55, you will be pleased to exercise at £1.50 and make 5p profit less expenses per option held.

The risk with OTC trades is that if the entity that wrote the option is no longer viable, you cannot exercise it, and no clearing house will take on the responsibility of completing the transaction. Once no clearing house is involved, you need to look at credit risk much more carefully.

For OTC options and similar, banks have a team of specialists assessing the creditworthiness of counterparties and clients. For a detailed explanation of how options work, see Chapter 9.

Swap

To see how swaps work, let us imagine that company A and company B each need a loan of £100 million. Company A can only get a variable (i.e. floating) rate loan from its bank but it wants a fixed rate to avoid exposure to a rate rise, which it believes will happen. Company B, conversely, can only get a fixed-rate loan of 4 per cent, but it wants a variable rate to avoid exposure to a rate decline, which it believes will happen. If rates should fall, the loan interest would become cheaper, enabling the company to retain a higher proportion of its profits.

An interest rate swap gives each company the chance to achieve strategically what it wants. Company A will swap its variable-rate loan with the fixed-rate loan of company B. Even after paying charges, both company A and company B benefit.

From a company perspective, swaps can save money. If you are a mid-sized company and you embark on a 10-year investment project in Japan, let us assume that you need to borrow yen, the local currency, at a fixed rate to cover the cost of the project. Let us say that nobody in Japan has heard of you, and so you can have a 10-year loan at a high fixed rate or at a lower floating rate. You may take a floating rate loan and instruct your bank to arrange a 10-year swap, which gives you fixed interest cash flows. The overall cost will be lower than for a 10-year fixed-rate loan.

Sometimes, companies can negotiate 10-year fixed-rate loans at a very low fixed rate, but actually require floating-rate money to meet short-term commitments. A company may borrow the money by issuing a low fixed-rate 10-year bond (see Chapter 12) and swap it for a floating rate.

Banks trade swaps with each other, typically acting for clients, which are increasingly hedge funds. In about 50 per cent of cases, the banks will use a broker. Contractual terms have given rise to problems in the past as it was easy to cancel the contract if conditions were not met. The International Swap Dealers Association has since introduced full *two-way* agreements by which, if there is a default, swap counterparties will net swap agreements.

The swaps market has developed from nothing in 1982 to a level that dwarfs the bonds and equities markets together. The notional global amount outstanding of interest rate swaps and options and cross-currency swaps grew by 18 per cent to US $250.8 trillion during the first six months of 2006, according to a 2006 mid-year market survey by the International Swaps and Derivatives Association. The notional amount of credit default swaps grew by 52 per cent to US $26.0 trillion.

On-exchange versus OTC derivatives

An exchange-traded contract has the advantage of being standardised, which makes it much cheaper and means that you can move a large deal quickly, with very little price impact. There is no counterparty risk when you are dealing with the exchange. An OTC contract, unlike its exchange-traded counterpart, is negotiated between both parties to the contract. It is more flexible than the contract traded on exchange, but is less transparent and harder to value.

The main use of exchange-traded derivatives for professionals is for hedging, according to market sources. For example, a bank that buys a government bond may automatically hedge it in the futures market. Products tend to start on the OTC market, and it is only after several years of established maturity that they are mimicked in the on-exchange markets, where a lot of liquidity in one place is needed.

On-exchange trading in financial derivatives in London is focused substantially on two main exchanges. One is Euronext.liffe, the third largest derivatives exchange in the world. The exchange, which moved from floor to electronic trading in 2007, is the largest in Europe by value of contracts. The other main exchange is Eurex, a European exchange owned jointly by SWX

Swiss Exchange and Deutsche Borse, on which over half of all trading is derived from London.

From data provided by Euronext.liffe and the London Stock Exchange, the value of daily turnover in exchange-traded derivatives in London is 25 times greater than in exchange-traded equities.

OTC derivatives are a market only for professional investors, and market estimates suggest it is about four times the size of the market for exchange-traded derivatives. Banks prefer to use the OTC market because they do not compete with the man in the street and, when trading on their own book, will use it more often than exchanges.

The distinction between exchanges and OTC markets is becoming less clear, and the launch of futures contracts on credit derivatives on Eurex is an example of how exchanges compete with OTC markets, according to Michel Prada, chairman of French financial services regulator Autorité des Marchés Financiers at the Global Bond Market Forum in May 2007 in Paris.

Trades in OTC derivatives are made on the phone, often via inter-dealer brokers, and electronic services are not yet used extensively. The process of confirming trades can be laborious, and there have been moves to automate the process, as well as regulatory concerns about the backlog of unconfirmed trades.

Given that many of the contracts are bespoke, there may be similar deals at different prices, depending on the margin put up as collateral or the counterparty's creditworthiness. The *Best Execution* requirements of the Markets in Financial Instruments Directive (MiFID) (see Chapters 16 and 22) are not always applicable to OTC markets, where bonds as well as derivatives are traded. The client of an OTC trade may trade on an agency basis, with Best Execution, or ask for a quote and decide whether to enter a transaction with his dealer without Best Execution.

Some member states have argued unsuccessfully that equity transparency provisions should apply to all financial instruments. The EU Commission was mandated to report to the European Parliament and Council, by October 2007, on possibly extending these provisions to bonds and derivatives, a move the industry does not see as necessary or desirable.

The UK is the most important OTC marketplace as measured by booking location, according to the May 2007 edition of *International Financial Markets in the UK*, published by International Financial Services, London (IFSL). The UK's share of world turnover rose from 27 to 43 per cent between 1995 and 2004.

A wide range of financial institutions, including commercial and investment banks, securities houses and commodity dealers actively trade in OTC markets. In the UK, the average daily turnover in OTC currency and interest rate derivatives was US $643 billion in April 2004, up from US $275 billion in April 2001, according to the Bank for International Settlements. This compared with US $355 billion in the United States, up from US $135 billion over the same period. The 10 largest UK institutions accounted for 80 per cent of total reported turnover in April 2004, up from 74 per cent in 2001. The institutions most active in interest rate derivatives markets were not necessarily active in currency derivatives.

Interest rate derivatives (see Chapter 11) and credit derivatives (see Chapter 12) are the largest categories of OTC derivatives, but there are many others. The demand for any one type of OTC derivative may fluctuate. In 2000, the energy derivatives market crashed, partly because of supply and demand dynamics, and partly because of market manipulation by, among others, US energy company Enron. The credit derivatives market is being heralded as the equivalent to an early stage interest rate market, but time will tell whether it develops on a similar scale.

The growth that some OTC derivatives markets can achieve is demonstrated in the niche area of freight derivatives. Shipping represents 10 per cent of City activity and the notional value of trading in forward freight agreements rose from US $2.5 billion in 2001 to US $30 billion in 2005, according to industry estimates. This market is based on the freight costs of transporting cargo by sea. Ship owners and charterers use freight derivatives to hedge against market volatility and some large investment banks now take a position. The Baltic Exchange provides benchmark price data.

The banks are constantly inventing new OTC derivatives products, the latest of which is property derivatives. Until recently, property was the largest physical market left that did not have associated derivatives. If a group hopes to open an operation in Hong Kong with 3,000 people in a year's time and property prices are rising, it may be well advised to buy now. But this would require the work of finding and leasing a building and, if the group later decided not to move to Hong Kong, it would need to resell it. The bank would find it easier and more flexible to buy a property index option.

Turnover on London-based derivatives exchanges in 2006 was 1,048.2 million contracts in 2006, up from 981.4 million in 2005, according to IFSL. Globally, based on notional value of contracts traded, the largest exchange in the world is the Chicago Mercantile Exchange in the United States, followed by Euronext.liffe and Eurex.

Clearing and settlement

There are two ways to clear and settle derivatives: central counterparty clearing and bilateral settlement.

On-exchange futures and options trades are cleared through a clearing house acting as central counterparty, which takes on the risks associated with the trade. Trader A has no time to assess whether trader B is an acceptable credit risk. The central counterparty eliminates not only the credit risk but the delivery risk as well.

A clearing house can only clear trades entered into by or given up to its clearing members. So, a broker, if itself not a clearing member, would have to give up the trades to a clearing member to enable the delivery of central counterparty clearing services.

Clearing members, generally banks, must place collateral with the central counterparty, in each case perhaps tens of millions of pounds, to protect against default by any other clearing members. They receive some interest on the money, but are not able to have full use of it.

Eurex Clearing clears and settles derivatives business on Eurex. LCH. Clearnet undertakes this role on Euronext.liffe, the London Metal Exchange (LME) and ICE Futures (see Chapter 13), as well as some equities derivatives on EDX London. Metal forward contracts on the LME are settled by exchanging warrants, which are records of physical metal ownership in LME-approved warehouses.

In an OTC environment, there has traditionally been no central counterparty, so traders A and B must assess their counterparty's credit and delivery risks. If they are satisfied, the deal is bilaterally settled; if not, the deal does not get done.

If an acceptable OTC counterparty is found and the trade is bilaterally settled, the buyer and seller are anonymous until the broker has put them together. The deal is the responsibility of the two counterparties, and the broker simply matches them. The broker identifies them post-trade, which may not be a disadvantage. Bilateral settlement is used for interest rate and credit derivatives, currency options and most spot and forward transactions. It typically involves payment over the period of the contract, and a possible transfer of collateral.

In some of these markets, the potential loss is so great, and movements are so volatile, that no entity is willing to be the central counterparty. In foreign exchange futures and options, there has not been enough demand for central counterparty services, according to a clearing house.

But increasingly OTC environments are seeking the introduction of a central counterparty. LCH.Clearnet clears most 'plain vanilla' interest rate swaps through its clearing service Swapclear. It operates Repoclear, which clears 50 per cent of repos, including OTC.

Hedging and speculation

Warren Buffett, regarded by his admirers as the world's most successful investor, has famously described derivatives as *weapons of mass destruction*. A few large scandals have left the public with much the same impression and some companies flaunt the fact they do not use derivatives. The professionals are unimpressed. Without derivatives, companies are not using a cheap and effective way of hedging their position. Hedging has the effect of insurance. It is at the other end of the pole from speculation, for which the very same types of derivative may be used. If a company takes a 4 per cent variable loan, it should hedge itself against the risk that the rate could soar to 12 per cent, failing which it is vulnerable to the full hit.

A company's treasurer will assess the cost of using forwards or options, and will deal directly with a bank to arrange an appropriate derivatives strategy. For example, in the third quarter of 2005, after Hurricane Katrina, the price of fuel was soaring, but discount airline easyJet was not hit badly because it hedged with options against short-term fluctuations in the fuel price. EasyJet also hedges against movements in the dollar, a currency in which aeroplanes, spare parts and fuel are denominated.

Some of the big corporate scandals in 2005, including Enron, WorldCom, Ahold and Parmalat, made no ripple in the market because the financial risk was hedged with derivatives, according to City brokers. When a company invests in derivatives, it is across a range of them, which reduces the risk of systemic failure.

Let us not underestimate the role of speculators. The economic rationale behind the earliest futures was to hedge against price risk, and speculators have always taken second place but they are the key liquidity providers. They make hedging possible and sometimes advisable.

The Financial Services Authority performs a useful function in authorising individuals in client-facing roles and monitoring the procedures and risk controls of entities. It aims to reduce systemic risk. Banks are now more sensitive to internal risk and have tighter procedures, including 'know your client'.

Problems and fraud

The problem with derivatives is not in the product itself, but in how it is sold or managed. If a company is to trade in derivatives, it must understand their value. Software data will calculate the *value at risk*, known as VAR, which is how much the company is willing to lose at any time. The VAR changes daily. Banks have thousands of loans on their books, both receiving and giving. They need good systems and procedures to determine VAR, and this is an underlying complexity.

There are always rogue traders, or treasurers of companies who do not behave responsibly. An overzealous derivatives salesman could go to an unaware company treasurer and say: 'Swap your fixed rate for a variable rate loan. Nothing will happen to rates.' If rates then go from 4 to 12 per cent, the company would have problems.

Swaps have not always been used responsibly. In the 1980s, the London Borough of Hammersmith and Fulham lost money when it used interest rate swaps to bet on interest rates, and sold 'swaptions', which are options to enter a swap at a fixed rate.

Pure fraud happens, as when trader Nick Leeson brought down Barings Bank using various deceits to cover for his derivatives gambling losses, but it is infinitesimal compared with the amount of trading. For more on the Barings collapse, see Chapter 2.

9

Derivatives for retail investors

Introduction

Retail investors use derivatives for speculating and hedging in the same way as professionals, but have less access to over-the-counter products. They trade in much smaller sums and have a narrower range of products at their disposal. In Chapter 8, we saw how derivatives work. In this chapter, we focus on those that are relevant for retail investors, which are options, futures, warrants, contracts for difference and spread betting.

Options

Options may be over the counter (OTC) or exchange traded (see Chapter 8). If you are a retail investor, a traded option on exchange is accessible. It enables you to bet on the movement of individual shares, or of indices, currencies, commodities or interest rates, or may be used for hedging. Through an option, you have the right to buy or sell a security at a pre-determined price, the exercise price, within a specified period.

The option is geared, which means that the underlying share or other asset is under control for the comparatively small upfront cost of the premium, which is the market price of the option. The premium is a small percentage of the option's size. For every buyer of an option, there is a seller, also known as a writer.

An option buyer on completion will pay an initial margin, which goes to the writer of the option. This initial margin is calculated to cover the worst loss in a day that could arise. The option buyer must regularly top up the initial margin to any extent that his or her position has declined in value to an uncovered level.

If the investor does not exercise the option, the premium that he or she has paid will be lost to the writer. But if it is exercised, the writer must provide the underlying financial instrument at the exercise price. One side will gain and the other will lose, but neither has the odds intrinsically in its favour.

You can buy a *call* option, which gives you the right, but not the obligation, to buy the underlying security at the exercise price. If the asset price is more than the exercise price of the option, the difference represents the option's value, and the option is *in the money*. If the asset price is less, the call option is *out of the money*. If you buy an option deep *out of the money* and the underlying price moves a lot, the premium could move in absolute terms much less, but in percentage terms more proportionately.

As the buyer of a *call* option, you will make money if the price of the underlying share moves up so that it becomes higher than the exercise price plus the premium that you have paid. In this case, you could sell the option and realise the profit on the options trade, but it is usually simpler to trade it as a profit.

You can buy a *put* option, which gives you the right, but not the obligation, to sell a security at the exercise price. If the exercise price is higher than the underlying security's current market price, the option is *in the money*. If it is lower, the option is *out of the money*. You will make a profit if the option price falls to below the level of the exercise price plus the premium that you have paid.

The extent to which the underlying stock's value surpasses the option's exercise price is known as intrinsic value. An option only has intrinsic value when it is *in the money*. The time value of an option is its total value less intrinsic value. The more time an option has until it expires, the higher this figure is likely to be, as the price of the underlying stock has more chance of changing in the option buyer's favour.

The premium consists of both intrinsic and time value, both of which can change constantly. These are factors used in the Black–Scholes model, which was developed in 1973 and is widely used in financial markets for valuing options. Other factors used in the model are volatility, the underlying stock price, and the risk-free rate of return. But Black–Scholes makes key assumptions that are not always tenable, including a constant risk-free interest rate, continuous trading and no transaction costs.

Equity options tend to come in the standard contract size of 1,000 shares. To find the cost of an option contract, multiply the option price by 1,000. If a call option is priced at 70p, it will cost £700 per contract. The contract size may vary if the underlying company is involved in a capital restructuring such as a rights issue.

The options on Euronext.liffe, the London-based exchange, have expiry dates grouped three, six or nine months ahead. A first group of companies has the expiry dates of January, April, July and October; a second group has February, May, August and November; and a third group expires in March, June, September and December. In any given month, options for only a third of the relevant companies will expire. When, for instance, a contract expires in March, a new one is created for expiry in June.

Options on stock market indices, known as index options, are essentially contracts for difference (CFDs) (see below). They are riskier than equity options as they often trade for larger amounts, perhaps several thousand pounds per contract against several hundred pounds. They are also more volatile.

The interest rate option enables traders to speculate on or hedge against interest rate risk. The price level of a contract is derived by subtracting the interest rate from 100. An interest rate of 5 per cent means that the contract is 100 – 5 = 95 per cent. Settlement is on a value per fraction of a percentage change in interest rates. Because of the price structuring, the higher the interest rate rises, the further the contract price declines, and the reverse.

Futures

Futures are a binding agreement to buy or sell a given quantity of an asset at today's price by a specified future date. The market has become increasingly open to private investors and it has made available some small-sized contracts and packaged futures products.

The futures market started in the United States in the early to mid-19th century, when mid-West farmers sold their future crops at a fixed price in Chicago. By this early form of commodity futures, the farmers had a guaranteed sale and a certain profit. The traders who bought from the farmers were speculators who hoped that the crops would be worth more on the sell date than they had paid.

Today, futures could be on commodities such as cocoa or coffee, or, since the 1970s, on financial futures. The trader who goes long or short on a contract will put up an initial margin rather than the entire value of the contract, and it may have to be topped up, on the same principle as for options or spread bets. The trader can place a stop loss to sell an offsetting contract at a price that has fallen to a specified level or, should the market have fallen too rapidly to enable this, at the best price available.

In theory, a trader can run a futures contract to expiry, but in practice, will usually trade it. If you have bought a contract, you will sell it, or if you have sold, you will buy. For details of commodities futures, see Chapter 13.

Financial futures are based on a financial instrument such as a bond, share, index, interest rate or currency, and the agreement is to exchange a cash sum reflecting the difference between the initial price of the underlying asset and its price on settlement. Interest rate futures enable buyers to hedge against adverse movements in interest rates by buying a future to offset it. Contracts on indices or on interest rates cannot go to delivery, and any buyer or seller who does not close the position is closed out by the clearing house. Most major bond futures contracts can go to delivery.

Warrants

Covered warrants are an exchange-traded packaged derivative mainly for retail investors, and have been popular for some years in continental Europe. The London Stock Exchange (LSE) introduced them in late 2002 in an early move to obtain a significant presence in derivatives after its failed attempt the previous year to buy the London International Financial Futures Exchange (LIFFE). So far, covered warrants in the FTSE 100 index have proved the most popular in a market that has been slow to take off.

The covered warrant is a security and not a contract. As with options, traders in covered warrants pay a small premium, which is the amount they pay for the right to buy or sell the underlying asset, and the warrants are split into calls and puts. As time passes, the covered warrant becomes less valuable, which is reflected in a declining premium. Every covered warrant is normally traded before its maturity date and is *covered* because the issuer covers its position by simultaneously buying the underlying stock or financial instrument in the market.

Covered warrants are expensive compared with some equivalent derivative products and cannot be shorted, but the spread (the difference between the buying and selling price) is often narrow, and the packaging is user-friendly. The LSE says: 'In theory, private investors could go straight to the banks and get a similar product created for them over the counter. In reality, they would not have the knowledge to get the product specified for them, and the banks wouldn't issue anything at such small values.'

Unlike in CFDs or financial spread betting (both covered later in this chapter), the trader cannot lose more than 100 per cent of his or her money, and at the end of the term, covered warrants that are *in the money* are automatically closed out on the investor's behalf. No stamp duty is payable on purchase, and owners will receive no dividend from the underlying share. Capital gains tax is payable.

Some warrants are traded on the Central Warrants Trading Service (CWTS) platform, which is part of SETS, the LSE's electronic order book, and the product may generally be traded via retail service providers (RSPs). For more on trading systems and RSPs, see Chapter 15.

The covered warrant should not be confused with the conventional warrant, a product that may be used to buy a specified number of *new* shares in a company at a specified exercise price at a given time, or within a given period. Companies like to issue conventional warrants because they do not need to include them on the balance sheet. They are not part of a company's share capital and so have no voting rights. Sometimes the warrants are packaged as a sweetener to accompany a bond issue. They tend to rise and fall in value with the underlying shares, sometimes exaggerating the movement. Capital gains tax is payable on profits.

Financial spread betting

To take a spread bet is a way to trade on the movement of stocks, indices or other financial instruments. You may bet on futures, or sometimes on the underlying cash products. Spread bets are accessible even to the least sophisticated traders, and on small sums of money. The market is over the counter and the party issuing the bet is always the counterparty. The firms are regulated by the Financial Services Authority, which has cracked down on some misleading advertising from the industry.

The financial bookmakers are execution-only, which means they cannot advise you on how, or whether, to bet, although they may offer data and working examples. Traders who use spread betting firms are almost entirely male, with a leaning towards the 25–35 year old age group, and those who work in information technology.

As a trader, you may place a bet based on your belief that a share price, an index, or interest rates will move up or down. Spread betting and CFDs (see under the next heading) make it possible to take a short position, which is a position that will profit if the underlying instrument goes down. Short selling is effectively closed to private investors in conventional share trading, due to the short standard settlement period.

Spread bets are geared and, as a trader, you need to put up only an initial margin, perhaps 10–15 per cent of the underlying value, but will need to top up the amount should the trading position move against you, on the same principle as for options or futures. You will gain or lose as a percentage of the underlying.

Because of the gearing, price movement can quickly wipe out the margin or more, or can make a large profit.

You can take a spread bet on a wide range of financial instruments, but shares and indices are the most popular. These can include US traded stocks through American Depositary Receipts (certificates issued by a US bank representing shares in a foreign stock that is traded on a US exchange). Some bookmakers offer a grey market in pending popular new share issues (see Chapter 7). Bets are available on foreign exchange, treasuries, commodities and other products, allowing multiple exposures. The spread betting firm may hedge its own position, using futures or CFDs.

As a trader, you may nominate a unit stake, which on a small transaction is typically £2–£5 for a single point, and may take a very large position on putting up the required margin. The difference between the price at which you place a bet and that at which you close it out is your profit or loss. If you have made a gain, the firm will deposit it into your account.

Traditionally, spread bets have been on futures and options that, by anticipating movements, are likely to move faster than the underlying share price. In 2002, CMC Markets started rolling spread bets where the basis for pricing a spread bet is the cash price of the underlying instrument, and other large bookmakers now offer a similar product, at least on large stocks and indices.

In all cases, you will pay neither fees nor commissions to the spread betting firm, but spreads are at its discretion. Critics say that spreads on futures bets are too opaque and enable dealers to change them as it suits them for individual trades, making CFDs more effective. The industry's typical advice is that, when you ask for a two-way quote on the telephone, you should not reveal whether you are a buyer or seller.

Rolling cash bets have a much tighter spread – the difference between the buying and selling price –than forward bets (that is, bets on futures), and it can be the same as when you buy directly in the cash market. A rolling cash bet on Vodafone has a spread of a quarter of a point at the time of writing, which is the same as on its shares.

Spreads, even as narrow as this, are one way in which spread betting firms make their money. A second way is through overnight lending charges to traders on rolling cash bets, which are based on 100 per cent of the underlying money. The daily charge is typically LIBOR (London Interbank Offered Rate – at which banks can borrow from other banks) plus perhaps 2 or 3 per cent, which is divided by 365, representing days of the year.

It is a small daily sum but, on an aggregate basis from all customers, it makes a profit for the spread betting firm. If you take a short position, it is the *firm* that pays interest on overnight positions. The firm pays no interest on deposit accounts where the margin is placed, or perhaps, if the margin is sizable, a low rate, which means it can use the money so saved more profitably.

If you take a spread bet on futures rather than on the cash price, you will not have to pay overnight borrowing charges, but the spreads are larger, covering *cost of carry* as well as expenses and the firm's profit margin. If the underlying shares will go dividend before the forward dealing date, the forward price is reduced accordingly.

Spread betting, like other derivatives, may be used for hedging but it mostly attracts speculators. You cannot enter a bet with one firm and close it with another, but you can enter two bets simultaneously with different firms. Canny speculators have two or three accounts with financial bookmakers in an effort to get the keenest prices.

Investment banks, aggravated by the disproportionate impact of spread bets on new issues, have dismissed the industry as betting. The point is open to dispute. In an interview with the *Daily Telegraph* on 14 May 2007, Clive Cooke, chief executive of City Index, a major spread betting firm, said that he did not consider spread betting to be betting, but rather trading and money making.

To take out a spread bet has two clear advantages over investing directly in the stock market. Traders pay no stamp duty on purchases, and profits will be free of any applicable capital gains tax. The tax advantage is the only significant reason why some switch from spot trading foreign exchange to spread bets given the spreads are the same, financial bookmakers say.

Spread betting firms will apply a stop loss for traders free of charge. A financial instrument can fall too fast to apply the stop at the set percentage level. The reliable solution is to use a *guaranteed* stop (unavailable on traded options), but traders will pay a premium for this in the form of a wider spread. Some traders also use a limit order to close a profitable bet at a predetermined level.

There are 400,000 financial spreadbetting accounts open, with an annual 25 per cent growth rate, according to a June 2006 paper authored by two academics of Cass Business School. Financial bookmakers specialise. If a trader wants to place a more unusual bet, it may be sensible to go to IG Index (www.igindex.co.uk) or for a low-size bet, Finspreads (www.finspreads.com).

How much further the industry can expand depends partly on whether it can overcome the stigma attached to betting, say traders within firms. It is unlikely that spread betting will reach beyond the UK in the foreseeable future because of difficulties in online gaming legislation in other countries. In contrast, CFDs have an international presence.

Contracts for difference

The contract for difference (CFD) is a contract between two parties to exchange the difference between the opening and closing price of a contract, as at the contract's close, multiplied by the specified number of shares. It provides you with exposure to the price movement in, among other things, a stock or index without ever owning the underlying instrument. If the price of the underlying shares goes up or down, you, as a trader in the CFDs, will make or lose money on the movement.

Like spread betting, CFDs are an over-the-counter market, which means the counterparty is the product issuer. But unlike spread bets, the CFD aims to replicate all the financial benefits of share ownership except for voting rights. As a trader, you are entitled to dividend payments and, depending on your broker, will have full access to corporate actions, including rights issues and takeover activity.

CFDs are offered by spread betting firms, CFD market makers, specialist brokers and online dealers. The market now accounts for more than 20 per cent of trading by volume on the LSE. CFDs have expanded their coverage to include almost any market or any kind of asset. There are CFDs based on indices, currencies and commodities and in all UK stocks with a market capitalisation (share price multiplied by the number of shares in issue) of over £50 million, many US and European stocks, and in all major world indices.

The market attracts institutional investors, particularly the hedge funds (see Chapter 19), and enables them to take a position in equities without revealing their identities. By direct market access through brokers, the traders often obtain keener prices than through spread betting firms acting as market makers, but the deal will have to be of a specified minimum size.

In recent years, private investors have become increasingly involved in CFDs but, unlike spread bets, this product is open only to experienced investors. As with other derivatives, the CFD is traded on margin, which is required to be high for stocks outside the FTSE 100, and low for indices.

As a trader with a long position in a stock, you will pay a financing charge (perhaps LIBOR plus 1.5 per cent) for the outstanding amount above the margin, pro rata to the annual rate. If you have a short position, the firm will pay you the interest (perhaps LIBOR minus 2.5 per cent) for this. If you close out the CFD intraday, financing payments will not apply.

The CFD has no settlement date, unlike futures and spread betting where the contract on expiry must be rolled over to the next one. As in spread betting, there is no stamp duty payable on a CFD purchase but, after it has been held for about 60 days, the amount saved this way compared with owning shares is eroded by interest payments. From this point, it makes no economic sense to continue holding a CFD unless it is significantly increasing in value.

Unlike in spread betting, you are liable for capital gains tax on profits beyond the annual exemption level (£9,200 in 2007–08), but you may offset losses against future liabilities.

10

Wholesale market participants

Introduction

Wholesale markets cover short-term interest rate instruments, credit, foreign exchange and commodities, in both cash markets and derivatives. In this chapter, we explain the role of market participants, which are banks, investors and inter-dealer brokers.

Banks

In City jargon, banks are on the *sell* side, which means that they sell to funds, investors and other customers, who are on the *buy* side. The banks employ traders in derivatives, money market instruments, foreign exchange, bonds and equities.

The traders complete transactions with traders in other banks, sometimes for their own bank, which is proprietary trading, and sometimes for a client, in which case they will sometimes use an inter-dealer broker (see below). Traders will specialise in a particular area. For example, traders will work on the short-term interest rates (STIR) desk, where they will trade repos, cash, certificates of deposit, forward rate agreements and very short-term interest rate swaps. The products are all driven by interest rates and the dealers will try to arbitrage between them.

The banks described as first-tier, which denotes a large size, are the main participants. The second-tier banks are not so large. Third-tier banks offer banking facilities to corporate customers but are in their turn customers of the larger banks. Hanky Panky Bank in Lithuania, for example, may have a client that knows local fish farming and wants to hedge its business with derivatives. The bank will not have a foreign currency book so will offset the risk by working through a bigger bank.

The banks will have their own strengths and weaknesses, often for historical or geographical reasons. For example, Royal Bank of Scotland is strong in the freight derivatives market because it has a long track record in providing services to the shipping industry.

Investors

Investors who buy products are the *buy* side. They could be companies, investment funds, pension funds, hedge funds or insurance companies (see Chapter 18).

Inter-dealer brokers

Banks do not always use inter-dealer brokers, particularly in liquid markets. On swaps, banks deal directly with each other for about half the time but for the rest use a broker as intermediary, according to market sources.

If traders use such a broker, they can buy or sell anonymously, which can be useful if the seller does not want the buyer to know the price of a previous deal, or whether one was done at all. If it was known such a deal was done more cheaply, it would set a precedent.

The inter-dealer brokers will serve mainly first-tier and sometimes also second-tier banks. They will trade in a number of products, including derivatives, money market instruments, bonds and foreign exchange. They used to be known as money brokers due to their involvement in the money markets. The interdealer brokers do not lend or borrow, or take a principal position. They charge a small commission and arrange the deal, much like estate agents.

At large firms, the individual brokers are organised so that distinct groups cover specific areas of the market. One desk is for credit derivatives and another for interest rate derivatives. The desks are situated next to each other in an open-plan style. This enables brokers sitting at one desk to communicate with those sitting at another, which is useful because, for example, bond trades may affect credit derivatives trades. At the large interdealer broker ICAP, there is a desk for foreign currency and over-the-counter (OTC) foreign currency options, and products are separated into currency clusters, so, for example, a dollar-based cluster will include desks for repos and other products in dollars.

The brokers will shout at each other across desks, which, coupled with sound from telephone speakers, creates a buzz on the trading floor. It is useful for one desk to know what trades are being done on another because they may have a knock-on effect.

Markets are becoming more electronic, which means that trading is faster and more automated and picks up opportunities that might otherwise have been missed because of the complex mathematical calculations dealers would have had to make under time pressure.

In the highly liquid inter-dealer market for on-the-run US Treasuries (the most recent batch of Treasury securities of a given maturity), more than 99 per cent of trading is now done on electronic platforms. Repos, another highly liquid market, are traded electronically.

Electronic platforms efficiently extend beyond the trading floor to the back office via straight-through processing, which is also now used in markets where voice trading prevails. Trades are routed through to clearing and settlement by straight-through processing, with integration into the risk management system, feeding real-time updated information to the trader about his or her position and the day's profit or loss in a given position.

The less liquid the market, the more likely it is that a voice broker will be used. For example, OTC options are less liquid, and such tailor-made products lend themselves more easily to voice broking than electronic trading. The broker is paid on commission for deal execution, the amount reflecting how easily and quickly deals go through, which can vary enormously.

In the chapters that follow, we will look at interest rate products, credit products, commodities and foreign exchange. Banks trade these from one floor, although separately.

11

Interest rate products

Introduction

In this chapter, we will focus on money markets, interdealer brokers and debt securities, including certificates of deposit, commercial paper, bills of exchange and floating rate notes. We will look at the repo market and government bonds, as well as interest rate derivatives.

Overview of money markets

Money markets are wholesale cash markets where governments, banks and companies can lend or borrow short-term money, and where the lending is high volume and low risk.

It is corporate cash flows that determine how much use is made of the money markets, and when. If a local authority lender borrows on the 15th of the month and pays salaries on the 26th, it will lend the cash on the money markets between these dates.

From May 2006, the Bank of England implemented its new framework for sterling money markets. The old system was too complex and led to too much fluctuation in market interest rates compared with the official Bank Rate.

Under the present new system, the main aim is to stabilise short-term rates at the policy rates. Banks have always used money held with the Bank of England to maintain liquidity for paying deposits on demand. But since the reform date, the banks have been, for the first time in history, paid interest – at Bank Rate – if they maintain an agreed level of reserves with the Bank of England on average over the maintenance period between one monthly monetary policy meeting and the next.

As a result, banks have an incentive to put money with this system rather than square their books in the open market as much as possible at the end of every day, as in the past. The result, unlike before, is a flat curve over the period.

Banks also have access to lending and deposit facilities at the Bank. The rates on these form a 'corridor', which narrows on the final day of the maintenance period to 25 basis points above and below Bank Rate. This too reduces incentives to influence market rates.

Open market operations (OMOs), where the Bank lends money to banks in the money markets and sometimes borrows from them (see Chapter 2), partly by way of repo (see below), aim to satisfy the system's targeted level of reserves over the maintenance period as a whole. As before, the aim is not to implement interest rate policy.

This is a very simplified explanation of the new framework. For further details, visit the Bank of England's website at www.bankofengland.co.uk. Look initially under news releases for the date 18 May 2006.

Debt securities

Borrowers can issue debt securities, including commercial paper, floating and fixed-rate notes and certificates of deposit, through the money markets. Some securities are issued at par, which is face value, including certificates of deposit, money market deposits, and interbank deposits of at least £500,000. Other securities are issued at a discount to face value, including treasury bills, bills of exchange, local authority bills and commercial paper.

The Debt Management Office (DMO), established in April 1998 as an executive agency of HM Treasury, sells one-month and three-month treasury bills (T-bills) on the government's behalf every Friday in a tender offer to banks, and six-month bills about once a month. The T-bill is issued in sterling at a discount to face value, and the face value is later repaid, the difference being interest equivalent.

The T-bill is traded less than it was because developed countries such as the UK and United States are able to borrow for longer periods, which is cheaper based on the inverted yield curve that reflects a decline in bond yields as the maturity extends into the future. Issuance is consequently more likely in bonds than in T-bills.

The euro bill is similar to the T-bill but is issued in euros. The Bank of England issues £900 million a month in three and six-month euro bills, which helps it to fund euro liabilities.

The certificate of deposit (CD) is a money market instrument distinguished by its maturity date and its fixed interest rate. A bank or building society issues the CD, which certifies that the CD holder has deposited the money with it. The issue is typically for at least £50,000 with a five-year maturity, and need not be repaid until maturity. But the CD is highly liquid and can be sold on before maturity if the lender needs the cash. If the CD is traded, market conditions will influence its value and investors may receive more or less than the amount originally invested.

The local authority bill is a discounted short-term loan, issued by local government bodies in the money markets as a non-tradable instrument, with a maturity of up to six months. The market is far weaker in the UK than in the United States.

Companies issue debt instruments. Commercial paper is an unsecured short-term loan issued at a discount to face value, which undertakes to repay at the face value, the difference being the interest equivalent. The minimum denomination is £100,000. The loan has a life of up to one year, but it can be rolled over. It is a bearer note, which means that ownership is transferred only in paper form, and whoever physically holds the note on maturity receives the repayment.

The bill of exchange is a promise to pay for goods sold in a specific transaction. A company owed money draws up a bill and presents it to the debtor company, which signs it to acknowledge its debt, for which a payment deadline may have been specified. The company that drew the bill may hold it or sell it to a third party that will collect the debt. A bank, known as an accepting house, may have put its name on the bill of exchange, so accepting responsibility for paying the bill on maturity. Bills of exchange were originally bought by discount houses, which no longer exist, and this form of debt security is no longer as widely used as it was.

A company may issue a floating rate note as an alternative to bonds. The note is a debt security that pays regular interest through a floating rate coupon, reset typically every three or six months in accordance with LIBOR or another standard money market rate, that typically has a five-year maturity. If a bank lends at floating rates, it is useful to have borrowed likewise to match it. A fixed-rate note pays interest regularly through a fixed-rate coupon, with a higher rate than on a floating rate note of the same maturity.

These financial instruments have in common that they pay a return expressed as an annual interest rate or an equivalent as a discount to maturity value.

Repos

The repo (see also Chapter 2) means a sale and repurchase agreement and is effectively a short-term secured loan in the money markets, sometimes between banks and the Bank of England, and sometimes between financial institutions without involving the Bank directly.

The popularity of the repo reflects the overwhelming shift in the money markets from unsecured towards secured lending, where bigger sums may be borrowed. The trend has been driven by the 1990s banking crisis in Japan, and recent banking problems in Germany, according to brokers.

Let us look at how the classic repo works in the UK. Sometimes a bank borrows money from the Bank of England for a stated period, perhaps 7, 14 or 28 days, and provides collateral, usually in the form of government bonds. The banks are sitting on large portfolios of mainly government bonds, which they need to hold for reserves, and which have low yields but high collateral value.

The Bank of England will take the UK government bond, or any other type of eligible security, from the bank and will lend money against it as part of its OMOs. It will return this collateral to its owner at a future date at a specified higher price that includes the rate of interest on the money.

The collateral is almost never called on, but it provides the Bank of England with the security it needs, and is typically 2 or 3 per cent more than the loan. For £100 loaned, the collateral may be £103, and the £3 difference is known as the *haircut*. The Bank of England cannot recall a default on repos.

The reverse repo is the opposite transaction to a repo, involving buying the bond and selling it back on termination of the transaction. Every repo is a reverse repo as well.

A debate rumbles on about how far central banks, in selecting bonds as collateral in the repo market, should differentiate between risk profiles. Bonds issued by the Italian government currently have a lower credit rating, as set by the large credit rating agencies, than those issued by the German government. This implies that Italy has a higher chance of defaulting on debt than Germany. But the European Central Bank accepts the bonds of both countries equally as collateral, which some feel should not be the case.

Through OMOs in sterling money markets, the Bank of England determines and implements repo rate changes. The Bank may deny liquidity to the banks, which will mean credit is harder to obtain and interest rates will rise.

Besides the classic repo there are sell/buy-back repos and securities lending. The sell/buy-back ratio is the sale of a bond on the value date and a purchase of it for value on a forward date. The buying and selling price are different, whereas in the classic repo, they are the same, only with interest built in.

Securities lending is a temporary exchange of securities for collateral and is not technically a repo. Institutional investors will lend their bonds for a fee to enhance the income from their fixed interest portfolios. The borrower must provide cash, securities or a letter of credit as collateral to the lender.

Interest rate derivatives

Interest rate derivatives are the main instrument in the OTC derivatives market. They enable companies that have made large borrowings to protect themselves against adverse interest rate movements, and are a major part of the money markets.

In the global OTC derivatives markets at the end of June 2006, interest rate contracts had a notional amount outstanding of US $262.3 trillion, which was more than 70 per cent of the total amount for all OTC derivatives, according to a Bank for International Settlements (BIS) survey, *OTC Derivatives Market Activity in the First Half of 2006, November 2006.*

Among interest rate contracts, swaps (described in Chapter 8) had by far the largest notional amount outstanding, at US $207 trillion, according to the BIS survey.

Behind repo transactions, the second most prominent type of trade in the money markets is the overnight index swap, where fixed rates are swapped for floating rates, with the floating rate set according to the Sterling Overnight Index Average (SONIA), or the Euro Overnight Index Average (EURONIA). The indices track actual market overnight funding rates, and are provided by the Wholesale Markets Brokers' Association (WMBA).

The forward rate agreement (FRA) came to the market in the 1980s and is a contract between counterparties to pay or receive the difference between a floating reference rate and the fixed FRA rate agreed in advance. It is for a single forward period only, while the swap is an agreement for many forward periods. A number of FRAs are the equivalent of a swap.

The FRA is sold with a bid–offer spread and some banks will buy FRAs at one rate and sell them at another. Banks tend to prefer the FRA, which is OTC traded, to the future, which is exchange traded, according to interdealer brokers. The FRA is a medium with which banks are familiar, is easy to trade through brokers, and is flexible in terms of the delivery date.

Banks with a low credit rating find FRAs expensive and instead look to cover interest rate exposures through futures, where the same institutional pricing is available to all the banks. The futures market tends to be aligned with the cash market through arbitrage.

The interest rate forward has been used less than the FRA because it is based on real money, which means that it has been recorded on the balance sheet. This type of contract, sometimes called a 'forward for an exchange', is when two counterparties agree to borrow or lend a fixed cash sum at an agreed rate for a specified period starting on a future date.

In the past, swaps and FRAs, when used for hedging, have been off the balance sheet, allowing a deferred profit or loss. Now, International Financial Reporting Standards (see Chapter 26) require that all derivatives are accounted for at fair value on the balance sheet and marked to market through the profit and loss account.

For details of how the interest rate option works, see Chapter 9.

Government bonds

Bonds are short to long-term debt vehicles. As an asset class, they are more stable than equities, although they show much lower long-term gains. Pension funds and insurance companies (see Chapter 18) are the largest traditional investors because bonds can help to match their liabilities more precisely than equities or other instruments. Rates on annuities (see Chapter 31) are linked to bond returns. Mutual funds, central banks and high net-worth individuals favour bonds.

In September 2006, the outstanding value of bonds from UK issuers was £1,854 billion, up 10 per cent on the end-2005 total, and more than three times the amount 10 years earlier, according to the May 2007 edition of *International Financial Markets in the UK*, published by International Financial Services, London (IFSL).

In the UK, there has been a movement away from government into non-government bonds, the IFSL report said. International bonds claim a 66 per cent share of total outstanding value of UK bond issuance, up from 32 per cent 10 years ago, while the share of UK government bonds is 23 per cent, down from 47 per cent. Corporate bonds (see Chapter 12) and financial bonds account for the remaining 11 per cent.

A minority of bond issuers are supranational issuers (ie, bigger than some governments) such as the World Bank and US agencies that use the money raised to finance the housing market. Since 1999, non-government bonds have accounted for more than half of the total outstanding value of bonds issued in the UK, the IFSL report said.

The DMO issues gilts, which are UK government bonds, in the wholesale market so that the government can fund its annual net cash requirements and make gilt redemptions (the amount paid back to investors when gilts mature). National Savings and Investments offers retail savings products to the retail market, and the Bank of England issues foreign-denominated government bonds.

Gilts are considered as risk-free as you can get; the government has never defaulted on its debt obligations. They are classified according to when they mature. Gilts maturing in 1–7 years are classed as short term; if they mature in 7–15 years, they are medium term; if they mature in more than 15 years, they are long term.

There are about 50 gilts currently in issue, of two main types: conventional and index-linked. Conventional types, which account for approximately 75 per cent of the gilt portfolio, are fixed coupon, which means that they pay a fixed amount of annual interest. There are three older double-dated conventional gilts, which means that the government may repay the principal at any time between the two maturity dates given; they account for less than 0.3 per cent of gilts in issue.

About 25 per cent of UK gilts are index-linked, which means that they are guaranteed to keep pace with inflation. The principal amount is increased if the Retail Prices Index (RPI), a measure of inflation, should rise, and the interest rate would rise accordingly because it is applied to the principal. On the gilt's maturity, the principal is repaid at the increased amount.

Holders of conventional fixed-coupon gilts require a higher yield than holders of index-linked gilts to compensate for the greater risk.

About 0.71 per cent of gilts are undated, which means that redemption is at the government's discretion. Because these are the oldest gilts in issue they have low-rate coupons. The government has little incentive to redeem such borrowing while it is cheap, and investors can retrieve their capital only by selling to other investors.

In the first years of the DMO's operations, the size of the gilt market fell as gilt redemptions exceeded gross issuance, but in 2002–03, new issuance turned positive as the government's financial requirements started to increase. The gilt market reflects this trend by its size, its nominal value by the end of March 2007 being £442.9 billion, up 59 per cent from the £278.8 billion level in March 2002. Average daily turnover in the gilt market has risen 168 per cent from £5.7 billion in 1999–2000 to £15.3 billion in 2006–07.

Yields and redemption

Bonds pay interest through a coupon, which is the annual rate of interest on the bond and is stated as a percentage of the nominal value. The coupon will have been decided by the level of interest rates in the market at the time of the bond issue.

If a bond offers a 3 per cent coupon, it will pay £3 a year in interest for every £100 of nominal value. Gilts pay the coupon in two instalments.

On redemption of a bond, the bond issuer repays the principal sum at nominal value or par, which in the case of gilts is £100. In practice, the bond will have started its trading life at par, or close to it. The market price may deviate from nominal value at any time in the bond's life.

The dividend yield that investors receive from buying a bond on the secondary market can vary from the coupon because it consists of the return expressed as a percentage of the bond's price, which can fluctuate from the nominal value. The yield can be expressed in different ways.

The current yield is the annual interest of a bond, divided by the current bond price. It is also known as the running yield, flat yield, simple yield or annual yield. The higher the bond price rises, the lower the current yield will be, and, conversely, the lower the price falls, the higher the yield.

The gross redemption yield, also known as yield to maturity, is widely used to compare the returns on bonds. It is the current yield plus any notional capital gain or loss at redemption.

In the period between interest payments, interest accrues on a daily basis. A buyer of bonds pays not just for the financial instrument but also for any income accrued since the last interest payment. This is cum (with) dividend. If he or she buys it ex dividend, it is the seller who will have retained the right to the pending interest payment.

Gilt prices may be quoted either clean, where accrued interest will need to be added to the bargain because it has been excluded, or dirty, where an interest adjustment is made to the clean price. The bond issue may be timed so that capital repayment will coincide with anticipated income from specified projects. An exception is the undated bond, which is not redeemed.

Conventional gilts are repaid at their nominal value and so the price moves towards this level as the redemption date approaches. This is the 'pull to redemption' or 'pull to par'. As interest rates go down, bonds rise in value, and when interest rates are up, the price of bonds falls. But the closer bonds are to maturity, the less influence this will have in comparison with the pull to par.

On this basis, long-term bonds, particularly if undated, are more exposed to interest rates because redemption is further off. If you think interest rates will go down, you should buy long-term bonds. The yields are generally higher to compensate for a perceived greater risk, despite the inverted yield curve discussed earlier.

A bond may often be callable, which means that the issuer, usually a company, may redeem it before maturity. If interest rates should decline, the issuer is likely to call the bond and reissue it at a lower rate of interest. The investor would then be left with money to reinvest in a world where interest rates are low. To compensate for this *reinvestment* risk, the callable bond will often pay a high coupon.

12

Credit products

Introduction

In this chapter, we will cover credit products, as distinct from the interest rate products covered in Chapter 11. We will focus on corporate bonds, international debt securities, junk bonds, asset-backed securities, zero-coupon bonds and equity convertibles. We will consider credit derivatives.

Overview

Credit products are integral to financial markets and help to fuel merger and acquisition activity, which, as we saw in Chapter 7, can keep equity market activity high. A predator will often finance a company takeover partly out of cheap debt, which has helped to keep credit markets buoyant.

Credit products may be seen as parts of a larger whole. For example, credit default swaps, a form of credit derivative, have a direct influence on the price of bonds, a link on which we will touch later in this chapter.

The risk with debt is that it may not be repaid. The development of complex financial markets and the spate of loan agreements without individual covenants suggest a need for caution about how much you lend, Mervyn King, Governor of the Bank of England, said in his June 2007 Mansion House speech.

In mid-2007, default problems had arisen with US sub-prime mortgages, which are mortgages for those with a patchy credit history, and this hit collateralised debt obligations (CDOs), which package up these mortgages and trade them. Hedge funds and other asset managers invest in these CDOs more than in the underlying assets.

The fear was that there would be a spillover into other areas of financial markets, including collateralised loan obligations and synthetic CDOs, both discussed later in this chapter. As the second edition of this book goes to press, that has not happened and there is a more optimistic school of thought that the spreading of risk through packaging it up in these various ways actually makes the framework more robust.

For more on these crises, see below, under 'Asset-backed securities' and under 'Collateralised debt obligations'. For details of regulatory concerns about the UK, as opposed to the US, sub-prime mortgage market, see Chapter 28.

Bonds

Let us take a look below at some types of bonds available, mainly but not exclusively corporate ones. Consider also UK government bonds, where there is effectively no credit risk, as covered in Chapter 11.

Corporate bonds

Corporate bonds work similarly to government bonds, and in Chapter 11 we referred to their share of the UK market. They have a risk of default and thus are not equivalent to government bonds and so they pay slightly higher interest. The yield may be 60 bps above that of gilts (bps are pronounced 'beeps' and are basis points, each of which is a hundredth of a per cent).

Large companies issue corporate bonds to raise cash without using up conventional credit sources. Small or medium-sized companies do not find this economically viable. Smaller corporate bond issues are not necessarily very liquid, and this market depends on dealers committing capital.

Corporate fixed interest bonds can be secured on specified assets, which is reassuring to investors as an insurance against insolvency. They can also be unsecured, which is most usual for international bonds (see below), in which case they have higher yields to compensate for the greater risk. Restrictive covenants may be in place to set a borrowing limit.

Investors in corporate bonds face price risk linked to interest rates, as applies to government bonds, and credit risk, which is the likelihood that the bond issue will fail to pay interest or repay the principal. The credit rating agencies (see box below) try to measure this risk, which depends on the underlying company's financial status.

The higher the credit rating, the less interest the issuer will have to pay, a principle of credit that applies also to short-term financial instruments. Highly rated bonds are unlikely to default, although the agencies do not always agree on their ratings. On corporate bonds, there is also liquidity risk, which is measured by the size of the bond's spread (the difference between bid and ask price).

'Junk bonds' is an unflattering term for those bonds classified by the rating agencies as sub-investment grade. Corporate bonds may have fallen to junk status due to a deterioration in the issuer's financial performance. Junk bonds pay a high yield to compensate lenders for the credit risk of the issuer, just as banks lend on credit cards at a rate reflecting default experience. Their promoters call them high-yield bonds.

Junk bonds from two companies that have the same yield may perform differently. Various forms of junk bond have been used to finance takeovers, and the product has a poor reputation. Junk bonds are not acceptable as collateral for repo trades (see Chapter 11).

Credit rating agencies

The credit rating agency rates the creditworthiness of a bond. The higher the rating, the better the credit terms a borrower will receive. The major agencies are Standard & Poor's, Moody's Investment Services and Fitch Ratings.

The rating is a paid-for service, which has called into question its independence. If a company does not buy a rating, some agencies have been known to publish it unsolicited, even if based on incomplete information.

In rating a company, the agencies have access to non-public information and they estimate only the default risk. The criteria used vary slightly between agencies, but include social and political risk, the regulatory environment, and the level of Westernisation of the borrower's country. Critics say that the agencies react to events rather than anticipate them.

The agencies do not always agree on their ratings, even after allowing for differences in grading structure, but bonds highly rated by the major agencies are unlikely to default. If an agency reduces its rating on a bond, the price is likely to decline.

So far, credit rating agencies have resisted regulation, saying that they do not need it because their business depends on the trust of the companies that pay for a rating. They have a code of conduct, published in December 2004 by the International Organisation of Securities Commissions.

International debt securities

London has a large market in trading international debt securities, which include Eurobonds and foreign bonds. The Eurobond is a tradable bond with a maturity of at least two years, denominated in the currency neither of the issuer nor of the country where it was issued, and it is listed on an exchange, which distinguishes it from a loan.

The Eurobond market started in 1963 when President John F Kennedy imposed a compulsory interest equalisation tax on interest that Americans took from stocks and bonds that foreign entities had issued. It led to a move of dollar-denominated debt business from the United States to Europe. In 1974, the US requirement for this tax was abolished, but by then the Eurobond business had become established in London.

Large companies as well as banks, governments and financial agencies issue international bonds to borrow cheaply in a foreign market. Book runners in London are estimated to account for about 60 per cent of the primary (issuance) and 70 per cent of the secondary (trading) market in Eurobonds, according to International Financial Services London (IFSL) in its May 2007 edition of *International Financial Markets in the UK*.

Eurobond issuers need good credit ratings because this type of bond is unsecured. The larger Eurobond issues are global, and are sold to high net-worth individuals as well as institutions. Investment banking methods are used to sell Eurobonds, rather than the commercial bank methods used to sell syndicated loans. A lead bank will run a syndicate of banks to underwrite the issue. A group of selling banks that need not be underwriters will retail the bonds to investors.

In practice, Eurobond issuers raise cash in the fastest and cheapest way, cherry-picking floating or fixed rate and currency. Some issues are more liquid than others. Taking the advice of investment banks, Eurobond issuers will exchange the money flows for those that they really want through the swaps market. More than two-thirds of Eurobond issues are swapped, according to industry surveys.

Eurobonds pay interest gross, which gives time for the gross interest to be invested before tax is paid. They tend to be held in book-entry form by the international central securities depositories, Euroclear Bank and Clearstream Banking Luxembourg. Ownership records vary according to whether the Eurobonds were issued in registered or bearer form.

Globally, net issues of international debt security markets reached US $2,733 billion in 2006, up from US $1,850 billion in 2005, with the UK contributing US $414 billion, up from US $362 billion, marking a decline in UK market share from 20 to 15 per cent, according to the May 2007 IFSL report.

The United States gained in market share from 11 to 18 per cent over the same period, leapfrogging the UK as its net issues rose from US $205 billion to US $505 billion. Spain, France, Italy and others lost market share, while the Netherlands and Ireland gained.

Zero-coupon bonds

Zero-coupon bonds do not pay interest in their life. Investors buy them at a deep discount from par value, which they receive in full when the bond reaches maturity. The bonds give investors predictability, but the price swings easily with interest rate changes and the market is fairly illiquid. If investors should sell before maturity, they may not make a profit. Gains are subject to capital gains tax.

Equity convertibles

Equity convertibles are bonds with an embedded stock option. The holder may convert the bond into a given number of shares in the underlying company. If the company does well, its shares will rise in value but its bonds will not improve as much, and the holder will want to convert. If the company does badly, the holder will prefer to stay in the bonds, and if it goes bust, bond holders are repaid before shareholders.

The issuer of an equity convertible will offer a lower level of interest than on a conventional bond because of the conversion option. The option could be one of various kinds, including a US option, which you can exercise whenever you want, or a European option that you can exercise on maturity.

An exchangeable bond gives the holder the right to convert a bond issued by one company into the shares of another.

Covered bonds

Covered bonds are investment-grade full-recourse debt instruments issued by banks and collateralised by a cover pool of assets consisting of mortgage loans and/or public sector debt. In case of default, bond holders have an initial claim against the issuer as well as a preferential claim on the cover pool of assets.

The claim on the issuer is a main advantage that the covered bond has over the asset-backed security (see below). With securitisation, the investor only has access to the underlying assets, put into a special purpose vehicle and, if there is a loss, the lower-rated tranches of those assets will take a hit. See 'Asset-backed securities' below. Covered bond issues, in contrast, have one tranche, which is usually triple-A, and is protected by generous collateralisation.

No default on covered bonds has been recorded since they were first issued in the late 18th century, and the bonds offer a yield that is sometimes greater than on government bonds.

The Capital Requirements Directive (see Chapter 22) requires a legal framework to be in place in the issuer's jurisdiction before a lower risk rating on covered bonds can be obtained, which would mean they will not attract high regulatory capital charges. The UK, like the United States, Italy and the Netherlands, does not yet have a national legal framework in place. Instead it has a 'structured covered bonds' regime in which it uses contractual agreements to replicate issuance under a legal framework. In July 2007, the UK government said it was to publish proposals for a new covered bond regime, which it said would help lenders to finance long-term fixed-rate domestic mortgages of up to 25 years.

Asset-backed securities

Asset-backed securities (ABS) are bonds backed by assets such as mortgages or credit card receivables, including US sub-prime mortgages, a market that in mid-2007 was experiencing defaults. The bonds are issued in different classes of risk and return, and the classes are rated by the credit rating agencies.

The issuer of the ABS pays interest to investors from the income arising from mortgage or finance payments. If some of this income stops because mortgage or credit card owners default on their obligations, it is investors who will have assumed the risk. The bonds are sliced into tranches of differing risk. Investors in the lowest class of bonds will first suffer from a loss, followed by investors in the higher classes of bonds.

Collateralised debt obligations

With tightening bank regulations, banks are finding it useful to transfer risk off their balance sheet to other investors, and collateralised debt obligations (CDOs) of asset-backed securities are a way to do this. Let us take a look at these portfolios of debt, which Sir Howard Davies, the former chairman of the Financial Services Authority (FSA), once dubbed 'toxic waste'.

The CDO packages up bonds that are backed by pools of mortgages and other kinds of debt, including leveraged loans used by private equity to fund buyouts. The CDO is sold to investors and the income from its assets is used to pay them. Investors are exposed to the risk of default and, if a default is big enough, it cascades up the scale to include the higher classes of bonds in which they are invested.

Some CDOs, known as CDO squared, package bonds from other CDOs and they reslice and resell the risk.

The synthetic CDO is a type that is uncollateralised, involving an issue of securities on which the return is decided by reference to a portfolio of debt obligations that does not physically exist. The credit exposure and return are synthetically created by the issuer executing a credit default swap with a counterparty, which pays a monthly fee equivalent to an interest margin on the loans. If the portfolio suffers a credit event, the issuer must pay losses, which, beyond a given level, are passed to investors.

If the buyer of CDOs fails to meet margin calls on funds it borrowed to invest in them, the lender may seek to sell the collateral for the loan, which consists of the CDOs. Higher margin requirements could lead to forced selling of CDOs or investor redemptions.

By mid-2007, investment banks that lend money to hedge funds to buy CDOs had been raising the margin requirements. At about this time Florida-based United Capital Asset Management suspended redemption in its Horizon funds, which were significantly invested in US sub-prime mortgage assets. Two hedge funds owned by US bank Bear Stearns came close to collapse because they failed to meet margin calls on CDOs made up of risky US sub-prime mortgages. Some banks that were their creditors threatened to sell off at auction the underlying sub-prime mortgages that they had held as collateral but it became clear that a quick sale would fetch poor returns. In June 2007, it was announced that Bear Stearns had agreed an emergency $3.2 billion (£1.6 billion) loan for one of the funds.

The crisis at the Bear Stearns hedge funds has led to widespread concerns about how CDOs of asset-backed securities are priced. The market for CDOs is not particularly liquid, and huge sell-offs of bonds can cause a significant repricing. This can be triggered by downgrades from the credit rating agencies, a process that was starting to happen in mid-2007. Many CDOs are not marked to market, which means losses are not shown for long periods of time.

Collateralised loan obligation

The collateralised loan obligation (CLO) is a form of CDO. It is an asset-backed security constructed from securitised loans. The CLO creates pools of the debt and sells it as securities with different levels of risk to investors. CLOs offer a higher yield than similarly rated fixed-income investments.

Some leveraged loans bought by the CLO are 'covenant-lite', which means they have fewer or no maintenance contracts, making them like bonds. There is no requirement for the borrower to meet certain financial ratios at regular times, as set out in maintenance contracts. Only incurrence tests apply, which specify criteria that must be met during given events such as extra borrowing, or buying another company. The United States is leading the flow of 'cov-lite' deals.

Credit derivatives

A credit derivative is an off-balance-sheet arrangement that permits one party to transfer a credit risk in an asset it may or may not own to a guarantor, without selling the reference asset. The asset could be a portfolio of assets, and so there may be a portfolio credit derivative, as well as a credit derivative. Effectively, the party transferring the credit risk pays a premium for protection against a counterparty default.

The market for credit derivatives started to grow in the late 1990s and has been higher than expected, with the range of products diversifying. The range of users has expanded from just bank lenders hedging their risk to include fund managers and insurance companies. Hedge funds have contributed to the industry's growth by their arbitrage activity.

The global market size of credit derivatives has grown from US $180 billion in 1996 to US $5 trillion in 2004 and an estimated US $20.2 trillion in 2006, and will reach an estimated US $33 trillion by 2008, according to the British Bankers' Association's (BBA) *Credit Derivatives Report 2006.*

The London market share had dipped from 45 per cent to below 40 per cent over the period. But this level of market share shows that London remains attractive as a key centre for trading in credit derivatives, according to the BBA.

Credit default swap

The single-name credit default swap (CDS) was the first credit derivative. It is a bilateral over-the-counter contract in which the seller agrees to make a payment to the buyer in the event of a specified credit event on a reference entity, in exchange for a fixed payment or series of fixed payments. Credit events will be specified in the contract and may include restructuring, default or bankruptcy.

The basket CDS is a group of CDS contracts where the reference entity is more than one name and the credit event will be a default of some combination of the credits in the basket. The bank can sell protection on this basis more cheaply than for the names individually. Protection against default by the first name in the basket is more expensive than against subsequent names.

Greater correlation between bonds in the basket increases the price of protection because the number of defaults is likely to be higher and protection at every tranche level would be quite expensive. The basket of bonds may be standardised, allowing 'index' trading.

In 2003, the CDS accounted for 51 per cent of credit derivatives' market share, which made it the most popular credit derivative. In 2006, it remained the most popular product, although its market share had fallen to 33 per cent, according to a BBA report.

Banks are the largest users of the CDS, and use it to hedge their loan book. Hedge funds use it to short the market and in arbitrage, as well as for hedging purposes. Investors in corporate bonds, including fund managers and insurance companies, can buy a CDS as a hedge against a default by the bond issuer. They will pay quarterly premiums to the bank selling protection. If there is a default, the buyer will give his or her bonds to the seller of protection and will receive their full value.

A credit default swap index is a standardised credit security and so may be more liquid than credit default swaps, which are traded over the counter. It can be cheaper to use an index for hedging bonds than it would be to use a variety of CDSs for the purpose.

Unfortunately, like any free-ranging financial instrument, the CDS is not always a reliable hedge. In the two Bear Stearns hedge funds that came close to collapse in mid-2007, as discussed earlier, credit default swaps, mainly through an index, were used as a hedge, and should have provided some protection against a decline in the value of bonds held, but in March of that year, both the bonds and hedges deteriorated at the same time, according to a Bear Stearns note to investors.

The CDS market is so liquid that it is now seen to provide a market price for the credit risk of the reference entity and so it influences the bond market. The CDS market may be influenced by CDOs, particularly synthetic CDOs, which are in high demand.

Back-office issues

Some back offices have struggled to keep up with product innovation in credit derivatives. A problem has arisen when contracts are non-standardised, or when the standards used by two parties differ. This has led to negotiation about which party's contract will take the lead during a lock-in period.

One of the problems was that hedge funds (see Chapter 18 and 19) were investing more in the front office, which brings in the money, than in back-office technology, according to Robert Benedetto, manager of financial services practice at consultant BearingPoint. It is arguably in their interest to avoid progress in clearing up the backlog of credit derivatives settlements because they benefit from the arbitrage opportunities thrown up by the present inefficient market.

Electronic trading platforms have helped towards resolving the back-office issues. In its *International Regulatory Outlook December 2006*, the FSA said good progress had been made in this area, and that the focus was shifting to embrace equity and interest rate derivatives as well.

The future

In mid-2007, warnings from the Bank of England about credit risk to borrowers as well as lenders, and long-standing caution from the FSA, coupled with defaults in the US sub-prime mortgage sector, led to some sharp reactions, including some criticisms of the rating agencies that gave the bonds issued high enough ratings to sell. The Bank for International Settlements, the ultimate bank of central bankers, warned that years of loose monetary policy have fuelled a credit bubble, and that the global economy is vulnerable to a 1930s-style slump.

Some issuers pulled debt sales, concerned about the potential lack of demand, and there was talk of a threat to market stability. Central banks round the world pumped money into banking systems to combat a broadening credit crisis. There was a flight to 3-month US treasury notes.

However, there were also views that the problems related only to short-term volatility, and that sub-prime mortgages are, after all, only a small part of the debt market, and that packaging up risk in CDOs actually makes the framework more robust.

13

Commodities

Introduction

Commodities are a growing source of portfolio diversification for mainly institutional investors. In this chapter we will see how commodity derivatives work and how they are traded.

Overview

Commodities, from metals to agriculture products, are a volatile asset class, correlated with the dollar, and a driver behind the performance of many stocks. A commodity is 'something that hurts when you drop it on your big toe, or smells bad if you leave it out in the sun too long,' according to a June 1983 definition in US investment journal *Barron's*.

Commodities comprise a derivatives-driven market, with only precious metals normally owned physically. The market for commodities derivatives is at an earlier stage of evolution than for financial derivatives. There are options on commodities although, in this chapter, we will focus mainly on futures. Industry wisdom has it that the financial derivatives market is 15–20 times the value of the underlying cash market but in commodities this is reversed, and the physical market is 15–20 times bigger than the derivatives.

Over time, commodity derivatives are expected to catch up with their financial cousins, and traders use both markets for speculating and hedging. Commodities rise and fall in value depending on supply and demand. Commodity futures prices are ultimately aligned to those in the underlying industry, but the basis differential – the difference between the future's price and the underlying commodity – will fluctuate during the contract's life.

Short-term fluctuations can arise because of panics or euphoria based on events affecting supplies. Traders take huge positions, which can have a manipulative effect.

As a speculator, the trader buys a future committing to buy a commodity at a given price. If its value rises above the price paid, the trader may close out the position with the opposite contract, which is committed to selling the contract. By trading before expiry in this way, the trader invariably avoids physical delivery of the underlying commodity, and may also sell short, which is to seek to gain from a downward valuation of the future's price.

The trader in commodities may pay the full amount at the start, as when buying a stock, or can pay on margin, which is when the trader pays only a small amount of the amount traded, but will top it up if the position goes against him or her to a level not covered by the initial margin. The highly geared nature of this trading position means that the trader gains substantially in relation to money put up if the future rises in value, but can quickly lose everything if it declines.

Hedging activity may run parallel to the buying and selling of raw material. For example, a car manufacturer may buy futures contracts on the London Metal Exchange to lock in the price that it pays for metal as a buyer. Once the futures position is financially closed out, the hedge will offset any adverse claims that may have arisen in that physical purchase of the metal. A buyer may also hedge sales of metal.

The prices for some commodity futures are included in tables under 'Commodities', a section in *The Times* published Tuesday to Friday. The spot price, which is the present delivery price, is sometimes given. For futures prices on commodities, delivery months vary. For example, crude oil has 12 contracts a year and cotton has six.

The futures price on the earliest of the delivery months, called the front month contract, is closest to the spot price, but will be slightly higher to include interest, dealing charges and, where relevant, the cost of storing the underlying commodity. If the gap between the futures price on the front month contract and the spot price became too wide, traders' arbitrage would reduce it.

The number of derivatives contracts traded on the exchanges has mushroomed in recent years, partly due to electronic trading. But exchange trading is yet to catch up with the over-the-counter (OTC) derivatives market, a market strictly for professionals, where trades are carried out by telephone, often using inter-dealer brokers.

The notional amount outstanding of OTC commodity derivatives globally in June 2006 was almost US $6.4 trillion, which had risen steadily from under US $1.3 trillion in June 2004, according to the December 2006 Bank for International Settlements quarterly review.

Pension funds are the main institutional investors in commodities. In the UK, they are less keen on commodities than, for example, in the Netherlands and Germany. Two of the biggest declared commodities investors are Sainsbury's, and Hermes, owned by the BT Pension Scheme.

Most commodities investors put their money in index funds, of which the largest is the Goldman Sachs Commodity Index (GSCI), which Standard & Poor's acquired in February 2007. The GSCI, which is heavily weighted towards energy, rose in value from US $4–5 billion in 2001 to US $60 billion in early 2007. Index funds can only take a long position, which means they cannot profit from a declining market by taking short positions, and they are not geared.

Backwardation and contango

Index funds will roll contracts at periods that the market can often predict. If the market is in backwardation, the forward price (agreement to buy or sell at an agreed future point) is lower than spot (agreement to buy and sell immediately and settle for cash). Index funds will gain because they sell high and buy low.

If the market is in contango, the forward price is higher than spot, and index funds will lose money because they sell low and buy high. In early 2007, some commodities had switched into contango, which made it arguably a bad time to start investing in commodities.

Some index funds are looking at rolling futures contracts differently to reduce the contango effect.

Retail investment in commodities is negligible. But private investors can invest in managed funds that invest in underlying companies such as energy or mining companies, or directly in the companies themselves. This does not always achieve the same result as investing in pure commodities because a lot of corporate factors unrelated to commodities must be taken into account. Spread betting (see Chapter 9) is a way to trade commodity derivatives.

Private investors can also invest in exchange-traded commodities (ETCs), a product recently launched on the London Stock Exchange, where the maximum loss is 100 per cent of your premium. The ETCs are open-ended asset-backed securities, offering a choice of index trackers (following an entire index of commodities with its particular balance) or individual securities. They are quoted in US dollars, which carry a currency risk for UK investors.

Let us look at the main types of commodity traded, and, for on-exchange trading, which exchanges are used.

Hard commodities

Hard commodities are the product of extractive processes. They include energy, and metals. Let us take a look.

Energy

Energy is the largest market in commodity derivatives, covering electricity and gas contracts in the OTC derivatives market. The energy market has grown in recent years, partly due to the deregulation of electricity generation in the United States and Europe and the trading in an increasing range of energy-related financial instruments. Investment banks and hedge funds are now active in the market, as well as oil and gas producers and consumers.

Some countries want to reduce their dependence on crude oil, but there is a lack of cost-effective substitutes. There are fears that there is not enough cheap oil left in the world. Experts do not agree on the true resources of oil producing nations, and a perceived world shortage sends the oil price soaring.

Natural gas is seen as environmentally superior to oil, and it becomes attractive when oil is priced too highly. Russia is the world's largest natural gas producer but is seen as an unreliable supplier due to its unspoken political agenda, as well as its lack of investment in the industry.

ICE Futures, which was known until October 2005 as the International Petroleum Exchange (IPE), is Europe's leading futures and options exchange for energy products. Nearly three-quarters of its worldwide business is in Brent Crude. Also traded on this exchange are gas, oil and, from February 2006, West Texas Intermediate crude contracts.

In April 2005 the IPE had ended face-to-face, or open outcry, trading in favour of electronic screens and had become a fully electronic exchange, trading many more contracts in late 2005 than Nymex Europe, a rival exchange run by the New York Mercantile Exchange, which started a London open outcry operation in September 2005.

Non-ferrous metals

The London Metal Exchange (LME) is the world's leading non-ferrous metals market and its three core services are hedging, pricing and physical value. The Exchange provides futures and options contracts for metals and futures contracts for plastics, which enable the physical industry to hedge against movements in the price of raw material.

The Exchange's largest contract is for primary aluminium. Of the six metals traded, the second largest contract is for copper (Grade A), which has applications in housing, construction and many other areas of activity. In recent years there has been an increased demand for copper from China, India and other developing nations. Chile and the United States are the major producers.

The other contracts traded on the LME are zinc, tin, lead and nickel, plus two aluminium alloy contracts. There is also a metals index future. Futures contracts can be traded any day from cash (two days forward) to three months ahead; they can then be traded weekly, followed by monthly.

In December 2006 the Exchange launched 'LMEmini' contracts for copper, aluminium and zinc. LMEminis are smaller than standard contracts, in five-tonne lot sizes, cash-settled and only traded electronically and via the telephone.

Since May 2005, two global plastics contracts for polypropylene and linear low-density polyethylene, have been traded on the LME in low volumes. In 2007, the LME was introducing major changes to these contracts to improve liquidity, including the introduction of regional contracts and a move from monthly to daily contracts, as for metals. The LME is to start trading in steel futures contracts from April 2008.

Trading on the LME is conducted in lots rather than tonnes. Each lot of aluminium, copper, lead and zinc is 25 tonnes, but nickel is traded in 6-tonne lots. In 2006, the LME saw trading volumes up almost 10 times on the 1988 level, to over 78 million lots traded. LME prices are quoted in dollars per metric tonne but can be cleared in sterling, euros or yen.

Three trading platforms are in use at the LME: open outcry, telephone-based or electronic systems, with different levels of membership and access. Only the 11 ring-dealing members (category 1) are able to trade by open outcry on the 'ring', a market open from 11.45 am to 5.00 pm and the process that sets the official physical prices in metals and plastics for the day.

Category 2 members typically include large financial institutions such as ABN AMRO, HSBC and UBS. They may trade by telephone, which is a 24-hour a day market, or electronically via LME Select, open from 1.00 am to 7.00 pm. A metals company wanting to hedge would select a member firm on the basis of the level of trading and access to the market it requires and of its business model and internal processes.

The LME contracts are highly liquid and are usually settled financially but, if required, they are backed by ultimate delivery of the underlying metal or plastic. To facilitate this, the LME has more than 400 approved warehouses.

The LME regulates the market and the Financial Services Authority (FSA) oversees the conduct of LME member firms. Following the Sumitomo copper trading scandal in 1996, where a rogue trader unsuccessfully tried to corner the world copper market through buying up copper to boost its price, the LME radically restructured its approach to regulation and compliance to prevent any future manipulation of the market. The Exchange introduced lending guidance requiring the holders of dominant positions to lend back to the market at agreed rates, ensuring that trading of the nearby dates remained orderly.

In the future, the Exchange plans to expand into the over-the-counter (OTC) market, ranging from metals that it does not yet trade to other derivatives, Martin Abbott, chief executive at the LME, told CNBC Europe in January 2007.

Precious metals

Precious metals, unlike non-ferrous metals, are often owned physically. They are traded away from the LME. The most prominent of the precious metals is gold.

Gold

Gold is a basic store of value against inflation, depreciating currencies, revolution and war. It differs from other metals in that it does not have industrial uses. It is mainly bought for jewellery, and volatility has proved limited compared with most commodities. If the dollar weakens, gold, as a dollar-denominated currency, becomes more in demand, although more expensive for buyers holding other currencies.

London has had a market in gold for centuries; since 1717 there has been a *de facto* gold standard, and from 1816, a legal gold standard. From 1934, the United States adopted a gold exchange standard, requiring it to buy gold at US $35 an ounce. In the 1960s, a consortium of central banks was dealing in gold through London in attempts to curb speculative price movements. It did not always work. In 1968, central banks replaced this intervention with a dual system of central-bank dealing, to maintain the US gold price, and free market dealing. In 1971, the United States devalued the dollar and ceased its link with gold.

The majority of global gold trading is through OTC transactions, which are flexible and subject to the agreement struck between the counterparties, although there are also standardised exchange-traded futures and options, including through London terminals of the COMEX division of the New York Mercantile Exchange.

London is the main centre for the 24-hour a day OTC market, and the lowest transaction size is typically 1,000 ounces. Most OTC trades are cleared through London, and most major bullion dealers round the world are members or associate members of the London Bullion Market Association. Trading is done by telephone and electronically. The market is most liquid in the London afternoon, which is when it is morning in New York and both markets are open.

The reference price for the day's trading is a 'fix', which is done twice a day during London trading hours. There is a bidding process in which the gold price adjusts until orders are all matched and the price is fixed. From 5 May 2004, gold-price fixing ceased to take place at NM Rothschild and instead started to be conducted daily by telephone at 10.30 am and 3.00 pm, London time. There are five gold-price fixing members: the Bank of Nova Scotia-ScotiaMocatta, Barclays Bank, Deutsche Bank, HSBC Bank USA and Société Générale. The chairmanship of the gold fixing rotates annually among its members.

The basis of settlement is delivery of a standard London Good Delivery Bar. The clearing process is a system of paper transfers, avoiding the security risk and cost of physical movement.

The gold price quoted in the international market is the spot price – for delivery during the two days after the transaction date – in US dollars per troy ounce.

Other forms of transaction in gold, notably forwards, futures and options, will be settled against a date further in the future than the spot settlement date. The forward or futures price is a function of the underlying spot price and the prevailing interest rate in the money markets plus insurance and storage.

The forward premium will usually be quoted as a percentage of the underlying price. Gold is nearly always in a contango, meaning at a premium over the nearby price, because of the ready availability of above-ground stocks, which can be borrowed at low interest rates. A backwardation may happen during a price squeeze, but is extremely rare.

Silver

Silver is a more practical metal than gold but is similarly a store of value. The metal has been used as money for longer than gold, and in more countries. It is used in, among other areas, technology, photography and electronics, as well as in jewellery and silverware, and industrial demand is rising. It is the best conductor of metals, although copper is preferred for this because it is cheaper.

The metal is in demand from investors, including hedge funds, and through the iShares Silver Exchange Traded Fund, which was started in April 2006.

Platinum

Platinum comes mostly from South Africa. It is used in industry and, to a lesser extent, in making jewellery. It is a rare metal but supply is at least equal to demand. It has attracted speculative traders, including a few hedge funds, and is volatile.

Palladium

Palladium is derived from nickel mining in Russia and Canada, and is also produced in South Africa. It is found in the same ores as platinum but is less useful in some machinery, including diesel engines. It is half the weight of platinum, so is used to make lighter jewellery. The metal has attracted trading from hedge funds. Unlike for gold, there are no significant above-ground stocks in palladium, which means supply can run scarce, driving up demand.

Soft commodities

Manufacturers use soft commodity futures to ensure that farmers deliver raw material such as sugar or wheat at a fixed price when required, and the farmers also use futures.

Soft commodities are affected by climate issues, and factors such as drought and frost. As with hard commodities, the price benefits from strong demand from China and elsewhere. The price in the developed world tends to be inelastic, which means that price fluctuations make little difference to demand.

On Euronext.liffe, the London-based international derivatives arm of NYSE Euronext, the markets in soft commodities are much smaller than those in crude oil futures. But cocoa, Robusta coffee and white sugar futures on the exchange set the global price benchmarking for the underlying physical markets, and are actively traded by managed funds, other institutional investors and a range of short-term investors.

The products are also traded on the Coffee, Sugar and Cocoa Exchange (CSCE) in New York, owned by the New York Board of Trade, in contracts sometimes strongly correlated to Euronext.liffe, which provides arbitrage opportunities. Coffee, sugar and cocoa are not the only soft commodities but are widely traded. Let us take a look at each.

Coffee

Coffee is produced by over 40 countries, and there are two main types. There is Arabica, which is the most widely produced, and Robusta, which is the stronger. Coffee commodities are traded in a free market by speculators as well as coffee growers and exporters, and the United States is the largest consumer.

Euronext.liffe has a Robusta coffee contract, and the New York Board of Trade has an Arabica coffee contract.

Sugar

Sugar is produced in 110 countries, and about a third of it is exported. Euronext.liffe operates the main white sugar futures market and the New York Board of Trade operates the main international raw sugar futures contract as well as a domestic one.

Demand for sugar is strong, partly because of its use as fuel to power converted cars. Supply is shrinking, partly because of a curtailment in European subsidies.

Cocoa

Cocoa is grown in Africa, Asia, Brazil and the Caribbean, and production depends partly on weather and prices, and the growing policies of countries. A cocoa tree takes seven years to grow, and each cocoa fruit on the tree has around 40 beans.

Over 80 per cent of the world's production is now deliverable against the Euronext.liffe contract.

The investment case for commodities

Commodities are promoted to investors with the tag of portfolio diversification and high returns. There is a perception of high risk, largely based on the fact that commodity derivatives are often traded on margin.

The case for diversification of a portfolio by investing in commodities is strong. A 2006 paper by Gorton and Rouwenhorst shows that between 1959 and 2004, a portfolio of 34 commodities made returns negatively correlated with stocks and bonds, suggesting that commodities are an ideal form of diversification.

The case that commodities give high returns is more controversial. It is agreed that commodities are driven by supply and demand and that, when they are out of kilter, investors can make a profit. The commodities portfolio scrutinised in the Gorton and Rouwenhorst paper generated an average return and volatility compared with stocks.

But over a shorter, more recent period of years, it is commodities that have overpowered stocks. Commodities expert Jim Rogers points out in his book *Hot Commodities* (see Appendix 2 for details) that the Rogers International Commodities Index, which he founded, was up 254 per cent eight years after its start on 1 August 1998, while the Standard & Poor's index of major US stocks was up 32 per cent. He noted that commodities had outperformed bonds over the period and that the Lehman Long Treasury Bond Index was up only 67 per cent.

When the dollar is weak, energy and metal prices tend to rise, although the effect can be lagged, and when it is strong, they fall. Soft commodities seem unaffected by the dollar movement. Generally, stock prices can fall to nothing, but this does not happen to commodities.

As at mid-2007, commodities, despite some short-term fluctuations, were rising. The cynical view was that this was a speculative bubble but there is a case that it is a demand-led bull market, which Rogers believes is long term. His case is that China is becoming economically strong and that its 1.3 billion population is the major source of high demand for commodities. The counter-argument is that much of China's growth reflects a shift in manufacturing location from the West to China, most Chinese people are very poor, and that China will increase its own production of commodities, following which it will negotiate lower prices when it imports commodities from abroad.

The other case for a boom in commodities – less fashionable at this time – is that they are supply led. One indication of a shortage of supply is decreasing LME stocks in some metals. In April 2007, copper, lead and nickel were particularly low, although they had been lower in the past. 'But LME warehouse stocks constantly change as material comes on and off warrant, and stock levels and trends will differ according to the metal and its particular market fundamentals,' a spokesman said.

Cycle theory suggests that commodities have outperformed stocks in a regular 18-year cycle, and in mid-2007, there was much talk that commodities were in a super-cycle, which perhaps the market had discounted. But if there have been cycles in the past, it does not in itself mean they recur in the same form.

Regulation

By the time this second edition of the book is in your hands, the Markets in Financial Instruments Directive (MiFID), implemented from 1 November 2007 (see Chapter 22), will have introduced for the first time a legislative regime for some firms trading commodity derivatives.

The European Commission is to complete a review of some aspects of that regime in 2008, and the FSA has said that these developments may affect the future of commodity derivatives markets.

14

Foreign exchange

Introduction

London has the largest foreign exchange market in the world. In this chapter, we will look at how it works, including main currencies and transaction types, and its participants.

Global overview

Foreign exchange is an international market where currencies are traded quickly and exchange rates fluctuate rapidly. It is unregulated and it has no physical location, but business is conducted from financial market centres around the world. A trader who has bought into a currency will often invest the amount in high-interest-paying liquid securities, which means foreign exchange has a knock-on effect on other markets.

The market is driven mainly by speculative flows, and after that by trading from governments, central banks and companies. Foreign exchange, like derivatives, is used for hedging.

There are 170 currencies in use worldwide, but most are not very liquid. The US dollar is by far the most widely traded currency, not least because the United States has the biggest and most liquid bond markets, and commodities are priced in dollars. The US dollar is the global reserve currency and an invoice currency in many contracts. However, many believe that, in 10 years' time, the dollar will no longer have this status.

The euro, introduced at the start of 1999, initially in non-physical form, has enabled eurozone member countries to trade with each other directly without the need to exchange their currencies. London was able to increase its share

of foreign exchange markets because transactions in sterling no longer had to compete with those in a variety of European currencies.

Currency traders see the next most important currencies as perhaps the Swiss franc, sterling and yen, and then the Australian dollar. Next in priority are currencies such as the New Zealand dollar and the Norwegian kroner, followed by emerging markets, and the less popular currencies such as those in Arab countries.

In the City

Foreign exchange is the most liquid of the financial markets in the City, and the largest. In 1979, exchange controls were abolished, which made it easier for companies to export money. By this stage, there were many dealers working in banks, and the infrastructure was in place for foreign exchange trading. The foreign market in London expanded.

London's market share of global currency trading was around 32 per cent in April 2006, more than in New York and Tokyo combined, which made it the world leader, according to International Financial Services, London (IFSL). The third largest player is Japan, with 7.6 per cent.

The UK has increased its market share over the last two years while the United States and Japan have lost ground, the statistics show. In the UK, there is more trading in dollars than in the United States, and more trading in euros than in all the eurozone countries combined.

In April 2006, the average daily reported traditional (spot, outright forward and FX swap) foreign exchange turnover was US $942 billion in the UK, up 19 per cent on October 2005, according to a survey by the Foreign Exchange Joint Standing Committee, established under the auspices of the Bank of England.

Average daily reported UK turnover in other OTC foreign exchange instruments (FX option and currency swap) was US $87 billion in April 2006, up 18 per cent on October 2005, the survey showed. Combined average daily turnover was US $1,029 billion, 39 per cent higher than in April 2005.

Foreign exchange has developed into an asset class (a type of investment, such as equities or bonds) over the past decade, partly because it is uncorrelated to any other asset class, according to IFSL. Pressure on fund managers to deliver greater returns from their assets has led them to look outside traditional asset classes. Many foreign exchange trading platforms allow very high gearing (borrowing in relation to cash put up as margin) which is barred from derivatives exchanges; for example positions of 100 times capital are permitted.

The Bank of England oversees, but does not regulate, the foreign exchange market. It may intervene in it, either openly or through an intermediary, when the government or a financial authority wishes to influence exchange rates.

The participants

Dealers

The sell side consists of banks that make a market or enable client foreign exchange business, with dealers working for them, and their customers make up the buy side .

The banks have access to the primary markets, whose activity heavily influences prices in secondary markets. The 10 largest banks account for about 75 per cent of turnover in London's FX market, and the smaller banks trade with them rather than with each other.

The dealers are traders in the large commercial banks, which run day and night shifts. They operate like dealers in money markets, OTC derivatives and bonds. They buy and sell currency for clients, quoting competitive real-time spreads on portals, which are online markets. They may hedge this exposure, and will take speculative positions for themselves.

A dealer of one bank will deal directly with those in the trading room of another. Dealers make money from the spread, which is the difference between the buy and sell price.

Brokers

Direct dealing, without a broker, is 'out of fashion', dealer feedback suggests. As in the money markets, dealers may use a voice broker, who operates as a go-between for dealers, but this method of broking foreign exchange has been increasingly giving way to electronic inter-bank broking platforms.

The trend towards electronic trading has led to a situation where supply and demand no longer entirely dictate exchange rates, according to analysts. As one put it, there is a new 'liquidity mirage' by which some large banks promise at any time to trade a given amount of currency at a given price. Analysts fear that the commitment could put banks in the position of holding what they cannot sell.

Investors

Investment funds do most of the foreign exchange business, and they invest real money. The fund manager may manage foreign exchange risk through a currency overlay programme, which hedges currency exposure from overseas investments, or seeks to generate return for assuming extra risk, known as Alpha.

On anecdotal evidence, the hedge funds do up to half of all foreign exchange trading. They do high frequency trading and include foreign exchange in a basket of asset classes for synthetic arbitrage purposes, making money out of a statistical likelihood.

Hedge funds operate as the buy side in posting their own prices and, in some cases, are effectively making a market, which is contributing to a blurring of the dividing line between the buy and sell side. They can drive a currency further up or down than it would otherwise go, and this sometimes sends the foreign exchange market into chaos. On 22 September 1992, George Soros initiated his most famous transaction. His hedge fund vehicle, the Quantum Fund, took a US $10 billion short position in sterling on a bet that it was overvalued. The British government raised interest rates to prop up the currency but Soros only increased his position. The Bank of England eventually withdrew the pound from the European Exchange Rate Mechanism (ERM), and sterling plummeted in value. Soros made an estimated US $1 billion from his bet.

The central banks are major customers in the foreign exchange market, trading their reserves in a process known as 'reserves adjustment'. They may sell their reserves in a foreign currency to support their own. They regularly adjust their massive US dollar reserves, and so become significant buyers and sellers of sterling, the yen and euro, as well as dollars. They can trade anonymously through the Bank for International Settlements (BIS), which serves as a bank for central banks.

Sometimes, central banks work together internationally to keep exchange rates at an agreed level, as for example under the Louvre Accord in 1987. But this practice is less common nowadays. Open intervention by central banks can fail, as when the pound was withdrawn by the ERM (discussed above).

Companies are heavily involved in foreign exchange, although their participation has dwindled compared with the capital flows of speculators and they are not yet often using those portals that enable them to post their own prices. If, for example, a UK firm is selling into another country, sterling could become stronger, and make its goods more expensive. The firm can hedge against the risk of such currency fluctuations and it can also speculate on foreign currencies.

Another scenario is when a company knows that it will receive a large US treasury coupon payment in November and takes the view that the dollar will go lower before then. It may then, for instance, take a short position in dollars using the options market.

Companies have not always traded foreign exchange wisely or prudently. In the 1980s, Japanese companies were involved in a scandal where they traded more in currencies than was justified by their business. Disgraced US energy company Enron had also done a lot of foreign exchange business.

Retail traders deal through retail foreign exchange platforms, and have sometimes been abused.

Exchange rates

Traders focus on the exchange rate, which is how much a foreign currency costs outside its country of origin. Currencies may be expressed against the dollar, but sterling is the exception and it is normal to talk of dollars to the pound. The most traded currency combination is the US dollar/euro, according to the BIS.

In recent years, cross rates, where the US dollar is not included as one of the currencies, have gained in significance. Cross trades in liquid currencies take place without reference to the US dollar exchange rate.

Supply and demand

When a currency is not fixed against another, the demand is driven by supply and demand. The demand can be related to transactions.

To exercise some control, central banks can adjust the money supply. The higher the interest rate of a country, the more its currency is in demand from speculators but, as George Soros showed (see above), selling on a large enough scale can counteract interest rate rises.

At the time of writing, China, Japan and some other Asian countries have an exchange rate that is formally or otherwise fixed against the US dollar, which gives them an international trading advantage over countries with floating rates such as the UK.

Transaction types

When a company trades overseas, it must agree with its trading partner not only which currency should be used, but also whether delivery should be immediate or subsequent. Depending on delivery needs, the currency transaction may be spot, or use derivatives. Let us take a look.

Spot market

The spot transaction is the most common type of currency transaction. Two currencies are exchanged at once, using an exchange rate agreed on the day. Dealers quote spot rates as a single unit of the base currency against some units of the variable currency.

There is a different rate for buying the currency than for selling it, and the difference is the spread. The spread is the market maker's gross profit, and varies depending on the customer's or counterparty's status as well as on the currency's liquidity. The transaction, with some exceptions, takes two working days for cash settlement (T+2).

The spot market is not always liquid, although liquidity is boosted by automated trading where it might otherwise be lacking. When there is high volatility but few trades, market makers have been known to remove their quotes because they cannot hedge their exposure.

Derivatives

There are a variety of currency derivatives, and they are traded on the over-the-counter (OTC) market. We discuss some below.

Forwards

Forward contracts in currencies provide for the sale of a stated amount of currency at a specified exchange rate and on a specified future date or within a given time period. If you will need dollars in six months, you can buy them now in the forward market.

Let us consider a UK exporter to the United States that does not know in which direction the exchange rate between the two countries' currencies will move over the next three months, or how far. To avoid the currency exposure, the exporter can, after completing its business transaction, sell its dollars forward and, after three months, receive a fixed sterling price for them.

The bank's role will be to take the dollars from the exporter at the three-month forward rate. Because it is due to repay these dollars after three months, the price that it charges now, the spot rate, will have to cover its own risk.

General interest rate parity means that the difference between the spot rate and the forward rate equals the interest rate differential between the two countries over the period. The bank will usually cover its risk by a foreign exchange swap.

Futures

Currency futures are traded in multiples of fixed size lots, and delivery dates are standardised. The Exchange is the counterparty to transactions, which effectively removes the counterparty credit risk, and traders must put up margins that, if necessary to keep their position covered, they will maintain.

Options

We have seen how options work in Chapters 8 and 9, and these can be in currencies. Besides straightforward (or 'vanilla') currency options, there are exotic options. They may be used, among other things, to trade against the volatility of volatility.

Among the exotica are barrier options, where banks 'knock' deals in and out at various levels to make them more marketable to clients. Let us take a hypothetical example. If there were €1.20 to the US dollar, and a client of a bank was to buy the right to buy euros at €1.25 to the dollar in six months' time, the cost could be 2 per cent of an underlying €1 billion, which the client could say was too expensive. The bank may instead sell a €1.25 call option for three months, but to make it cheap, knock it out at €1.28, which would mean that the client would lose everything if the currency reached this level. Let us say that the client only made real money at €1.25. The return would increase up to €1.28, at which point the client would lose all to the bank. Barrier options eventually started being traded in their own right, and volatility arising from such trading often surpassed movements in the underlying currency, although affecting it.

Channel trading demonstrates how, for example, the euro/US dollar variations, influenced by options trading, move within a narrow range, then jump out of it into another. Instead of a zig-zag on the graph, there is a zig, a straight line, and then a zag.

Each of the barrier trade positions will be hedged or dealt against by both sides of the transaction, which multiplies the turnover of the options markets.

Swaps

In a currency swap, a company may raise an amount in the currency that it can borrow most cheaply, and swap the proceeds with the equivalent amount in a target currency. After interest rate swaps, this is the most common type of swap.

Electronic trading

Electronic trading has increased the efficiency and transparency of the market, reducing arbitrage, and it is rapidly growing. Prices can now be obtained from one portal without the need to check other sources. Retail traders have access to the same prices as wholesale ones.

Today, 56 per cent of global foreign exchange trading takes place electronically, but by 2010 the proportion will have risen to 75 per cent, according to a 2007 report by consultants Aite Group.

An analyst's perspective

Chris Furness, head of currency strategy at 4CAST, a market analysis company, has information feeding into him from three sources: fundamental, technical and market analysis. Fundamental analysis covers how exchange rates reflect interest rates, inflation, speculative capital flows and economic factors.

Figures from the United States are the most important, followed by those from the eurozone, including those from individual countries within it, according to Furness. Japanese and Swiss currency data are sometimes important because of interest rate movements within those countries, which affect interest rate differentials.

The most important figure about 20 years ago was the US money supply, but it is now the monthly non-farm payroll numbers, which show US employment, according to Furness. Price data is currently significant and he also looks at the US trade figures. If there is a record trade deficit, the dollar will come under pressure, and if it falls other currencies will rise, with bigger reactions seen when expectations are exceeded in either direction.

Expectations about inflation influence interest rate expectations rather than the other way round. 'If there is talk of raising US interest rates, the minutes of a previous Federal Reserve Bank meeting could become important,' Furness says. He believes that technical analysis (see Chapter 20) can become a self-fulfilling prophecy in foreign exchange because of huge numbers of users in the marketplace. In his view, such analysis has become indispensable in timing transactions.

Market analysis covers activity in each market, and indicates the greatest position of liquidity. In early 2006, for example, there was major dollar repatriation related to a tax window by the United States government allowing US companies to repatriate profits made abroad at a very low tax rate. 'This is partly why the dollar started to lose ground,' says Furness. 'When there is movement in one direction, the hedge funds and momentum players get involved, and the movement becomes exaggerated.'

Purchasing power parity (PPP) says that exchange rates will converge to a level at which purchasing power is the same internationally, so countering inflation. It is the oldest theory of how exchange rates are formed but, according to Furness, it rarely works in the short term.

Economists say that an imbalance between exchange rates and inflation is driven by speculative capital flows seeking to make money from currency differentials and can last a while, but PPP works better over the long term. Governments take PPP seriously in the quest to keep their currencies stable.

Default risk

Default risk arises in foreign exchange and any party to a transaction needs to exercise due diligence in checking out the counterparty. There are settlement and pre-settlement risks.

In the past, the settlement risk has been greater because settlement was manual, using paper transactions, which was expensive and left scope for errors. The settlement risk arose because one party paid out before the other.

One solution has been netting, by which two parties offset trades, making it necessary to pay out only net amounts. The risk is that if one of the parties defaults, a liquidator could challenge the netting agreement, leaving the non-defaulting party having to join a queue of creditors in claiming for losses.

Larger trades in particular may be required to put up collateral, otherwise known as margin, for trades, adding to it where necessary to cover their open position.

Straight-through processing has gone a long way towards a solution that cuts costs and errors. It has replaced manual and paper based processing, and the journey from trade inception to settlement is electronic, which is appropriate for the automated trading in this market.

The Society for Worldwide Interbank Financial Telecommunication (SWIFT) has provided the foreign exchange market with connectivity and standards through its electronic network. Continuous Linked Settlement (CLS) provides a payment versus payment model, enabling both sides of a foreign exchange trade to settle simultaneously.

Some credit risk remains, particularly pre-settlement, and participants in foreign exchange markets must have reciprocal credit agreements in place, with limits based on the counterparty's credit risk.

Further research

To find out more, I recommend visiting the website of inter-dealer broker ICAP (www.icap.com), and registering online with the ICAP Knowledge Centre, where you will have access to some excellent free courses on foreign exchange.

15

The London Stock Exchange and its trading systems

Introduction

There are three tiers in the equity capital market infrastructure today: trading, clearing and settlement. They are integrated, but each performs a different function. In this chapter we will look at equities trading at the London Stock Exchange. Read this in conjunction with Chapters 16 and 17.

Overview

A stock exchange performs various functions, including the launching of new issues in securities and the dissemination of information. On the secondary market, its main role is to bring together buyers and sellers through a centralised trading system.

The London Stock Exchange (LSE) dominates UK equity trading, although on a pan-European perspective it has lost market leadership since Big Bang in 1987 (see Chapter 1). The Markets in Financial Instruments Directive (MiFID), implemented in November 2007, is intended to enhance competition, particularly across borders.

Until 1997, the LSE only offered one model of trading, known as quote driven, by which competing market makers quoted two-way prices in stocks on SEAQ (Stock Exchange Automated Quotation) screens. This facility remains essentially in place today, but mainly for smaller stocks. For larger stocks, the

LSE introduced the electronic order book, SETS (Stock Exchange Electronic Trading System), which has been a huge growth story with no system failure since it started.

Since November 2007 almost all Main Market stocks, as well as an increasing number of Alternative Investment Market (AIM) stocks, have been tradable on SETS or on a hybrid model that offers electronic execution alongside quotes displayed by market makers.

Trading facilities

Electronic order book

SETS is used for trading UK FTSE Euro top 300 securities, which include all the securities in the UK's FTSE 100 index, and the most liquid in the FTSE 250 (for an explanation of indices, see Chapter 4). The system matches *buy* with *sell* orders automatically where it can be done, as commentators have put it, like a game of snap.

In November 2003, the LSE introduced SETSmm, which provided an order-book trading facility for FTSE 250 stocks not already traded on SETS and some dual-listed Irish securities, and it has been gradually extended to cover the entire FTSE All Share index as well as a number of AIM securities.

SETSmm combines order-book trading with the liquidity backing of market makers. From November 2007, market maker support has been made available to SETS as well and the *mm* distinction has been dropped.

The growth has been impressive. In 1997, order-book trading averaged a few thousand trades per day. By June 2007, the total number of trades executed electronically through SETS and SETSmm averaged over 500,000 a day and in August 2007 totals regularly exceeded 1 million.

Price transparency

Prices on an order book are more transparent than those advertised on the quote-driven market maker system because they are firm and based on orders from the entire market and not solely on the decision of a small group of market makers, according to the LSE. Dealers can conduct large trades for clients on SETS that influence share prices immediately and are executed automatically when the buy and sell orders match. The order book also enables traders to point a machine at the market for arbitrage or to feed in large orders piecemeal to reduce market impact, so that overall liquidity is improved.

Some argue that SETS is not immune from manipulative tactics because of its transparency. Some traders have placed orders with the sole aim of influencing the share price and so paving the way for a larger trade on better terms. Orders may be removed at the last minute.

Traders may put their money where the high volume seems directed only to discover they have followed a red herring. It is reminiscent of Flipper, the legendary trader in the Schatz, a two-year government bond future, who placed large bogus buy orders that attracted copycat buying before he unexpectedly turned seller.

Iceberg facility

The iceberg functionality, introduced in November 2003, enables traders to enter a large limit order on the order book and reveal only part of it at any time. Once this 'peak' is fully executed, a new one will automatically replace it on the order book. This process of placing the large order in tranches will continue until the order has been exercised fully or a remaining amount has expired or been cancelled.

The procedure prevents intervening orders that make an impact on the price, which is a feature of tranche trading outside the iceberg system. The iceberg functionality is discreet and trades are not stamped 'iceberg' but they appear on the screen as an ordinary limit order. If the iceberg trade is in an actively traded stock like Vodafone it is less likely to be detected than in a smaller, less liquid stock.

Worked principal agreement

In a worked principal agreement (WPA) a market maker takes a position in a SETS or SETSmm stock of a minimum size, and is given time to trade it as principal to obtain better execution. Reflection of trade information is delayed until the end of the day and, if the order is given after 3.00 pm, the next day is considered to have started.

The minimum size of a position is based on the normal market size (NMS), which is a value assigned to a security by the LSE, and used to calculate the minimum quote size within which market makers are obliged to trade. For a WPA, the position must be at least 8 × NMS on SETS or 4 × NMS on SETSmm.

Trade information may be delayed further on some block trades, which are large trades completed in a single unit, usually of 10,000 shares or more. In this case, the trade size must be at least 75 × NMS in size, or 50 × NMS in AIM stocks.

Auctions

The LSE organises auctions for SETS and SETSmm. Auctions are also the sole means of electronic trading in SETSqx stocks, a hybrid quote-driven system discussed later in this chapter. They are open to anybody who trades the order book. Some might use the auctions to balance their books, and others to fulfil a trade that they want to execute.

Every trading day, a pre-market auction takes place for each stock between 7.50 and 8.00 am (London time), which sets the opening price for the day, and there is a post-market auction between 4.30 and 4.35 pm, which sets the closing price. SETSqx stocks have two additional auctions at 11 am and 3 pm. If there is sufficient volatility during the day in a particular stock, it can go into auction intra-day to establish a mid-price. If, for example, there is news of a hurricane hitting an oil refinery, market activity could move share prices a few percentage points and it could trigger an auction.

In the auction, market participants can enter limit buy and sell orders, and the LSE automatically calculates and displays the real-time 'uncrossing' price, at which the maximum volume can be executed provided a stock is crossed (ie, a buy order is equal to or higher than a sell order).

TradElect

The LSE has introduced a new trading system, TradElect, which went live in June 2007 in London after it had already been in use on the Johannesburg Stock Exchange. The system is among the fastest trading systems in the world, on a par with Nasdaq, the US over-the-counter (OTC) market in shares, and well ahead of NYSE Euronext.

'TradElect represents a significant advance on our previous technology,' says Robin Paine, chief technology officer at the LSE. TradElect, which was developed as part of a four-year Technology Roadmap Programme, utilises commodity hardware platforms that make it easier, cheaper and faster to expand capacity – the number of messages that can be handled – and to deliver new functionality.

On TradElect, the average time taken to process an order from receipt to execution to reporting back has reduced from 140 milliseconds on the old system to 10 milliseconds on the new one (one millisecond is one thousandth of a second).

'At the outset, TradElect provides more than four times the capacity of the system it replaced,' says Paine. 'As high-frequency algorithmic traders look globally for pools of liquidity in which to find alpha opportunities, TradElect sets new benchmarks in terms of system capacity and performance.'

Such advantages have helped cement the London Stock Exchange as the market where brokers can achieve the highest possible standards of execution for their clients. This is important under MiFID, which requires brokers to prove to their clients that they are trading their deals in a way that will give them the best execution possible.

Although TradElect went live in London only five months before MiFID was enacted, the technological prowess of an exchange's trading system has consistently been an important differentiator. TradElect was conceived in 2003 and was not specifically designed for the Directive. In other ways too the LSE was largely compliant with the Directive even before the new trading system was launched.

For example, the LSE already offered its domestic market the pre-trade transparency that MiFID has made compulsory through SETS. But there have been some tweaks to accommodate the display of limit orders, which are orders made to a broker to buy a specified quantity of a security at or below a given limit price, which led to the introduction of SETSqx.

From November 2007, market makers have been able to display quotes on SETS, which MiFID allows as an alternative to the rules that MiFID imposes for systematic internalisers.

Market makers

Market makers still take part in quote-driven trading that runs parallel to the order book. 'There has been a move towards electronic execution, but market makers are still there,' says Hugh Brown, head of product development strategy at the LSE. 'It's not a case of one or the other.'

Market makers provide liquidity and price formation in those shares in which they choose to make a market. They are wholesalers of shares and may specialise.

It is mainly in the area of small stocks that market makers are seen as useful. But in larger stocks people may go to a market maker rather than SETS to achieve immediacy in size, Brown says. 'London is famed for its capital commitment.' If, for example, a fund manager held a stock and then wanted to get out of it because of emerging bad news, the spread (difference between buying and selling price) on the order book for selling £10 million of the stock will be perhaps 500 basis points, which is 5 per cent, reflecting nervousness about the stock's prospects. A market maker instead may let the fund manager sell £10 million of the stock at a reduced spread of 400 basis points, which is 4 per cent. 'You get certainty of trading and a better price than if you had sold it all immediately through the order book,' Brown says. 'It is not necessarily better than if you had chopped the deal into small lumps and traded it patiently through our order book. That order might have been 200 basis points but, by using the market maker, you get certainty.'

In small retail trades in liquid stocks, to use a market maker may mean sacrificing 10 basis points on the spread for ease and simplicity, which may be worthwhile, Brown says. 'But for more sophisticated private investors, there is no reason not to use the order book.'

Every stock has a notional minimum of at least one market maker but in practice will have at least two, and mostly five or more. Competing market makers display continuous buy and sell prices on terminals globally.

The market maker has a responsibility towards the client companies in whose shares it has a market, but also to brokers and share dealers.

The large market makers such as Winterflood Securities can commit capital, but most market makers are part of an integrated house, and have a different business model. They may view market making as part of a corporate relationship and are responsible for very little dealing activity.

Until June 2007, market makers in the smallest stocks on the LSE still quoted their prices through the SEAQ system, a quote-driven market through which competing market makers display continuous buy and sell prices globally on screens. SEAQ does not support limit orders.

Since June 2007, SEAQ has operated only for stocks on the Alternative Investment Market. It has otherwise been replaced by SETSqx, which combines SEAQ-style quotes with periodic auctions to enable the display of unexecuted client limit orders, as required under MiFID,

The art of market making

Through the quote-driven system, market makers are committed to providing a price and to dealing in at least a certain minimum deal size throughout the trading day. They set their own prices based on their anonymous proprietary position and their knowledge of order flow as well as supply and demand.

The market maker makes its money on the spread, which is the difference between the bid and offer price. Bid is the price at which customers can sell, and offer the price at which they can buy. A bid-offer spread of 8–10 means that one can sell to the market maker at 8p or buy at 10p.

Market etiquette suggests that the broker should reveal to the market maker the whole size of any order for which it is seeking to transact only a part. If there were 10 market makers offering one NMS each at best price, a broker wishing to conduct business of 10 × NMS should reveal the full extent of its business to one market maker, which will price the business taking account of the size.

The market maker need only quote for one stock per telephone call, and if it is quoting the stock elsewhere or has not yet changed its price following an execution in it, it may declare 'Dealer in front' and not provide a quote. Market makers have occasionally misused this process.

Should the market maker be approached by a broker acting in a proprietary capacity, it is not obliged to deal. If the broker is large or has a strong relationship with the firm, it may be able to negotiate a price better than the spread on screen. One of the criticisms about market making is that it does not promote a level playing field.

The order book requires settlement in three working days, and trading with paper certificates is not allowed. Market makers are more flexible about when settlement is required, and paper certificates may be used.

If one market maker has dealt with another anonymously, or privately through inter-dealer brokers (IDBs), the screen price is altered. Market makers may use IDBs to balance their books. If one has bought a lot of shares, it may unload some, perhaps through an IDB, onto other market makers. But most market makers now use SETS to balance their books because it offers greater liquidity, according to the LSE.

Users

Users of the LSE trading systems include retail service providers (see below), hedge fund managers, market makers and sell-side brokers, including retail to a small degree, and member firms trading on their own account. Let us take a more detailed look.

Retail service providers

The Retail Service Provider (RSP) network was developed by Merrill Lynch and other financial institutions, and is mutually supportive with market makers. The RSP is the interface between retail brokers and the equity markets. Brokers use RSPs for the vast majority of the 10 million plus retail trades a year. The RSP appears opaque in how it operates.

When asked by a customer for a price, the stockbroker relays the request electronically to the RSP, which will send back the best price it will have determined, with reference to both the order book and quote-driven market makers.

The broker may keep his client holding on the phone (or internet) while he gets the price from the RSP, and if it is satisfactory, he can execute the trade immediately. But if the client wants to trade on the order book, the broker will place it and say, 'I'll call you back when it's hit.'

A few retail stockbrokers offer their clients the ability to put the order directly onto the order book, and a Level 2 data feed will enable the investor to watch the order's progress.

The RSP is itself a market maker in some stocks to a size limit, beyond which it will refer the trade to its own market makers, which provide a service in both quote-driven and order-book securities. Brokers choose how many RSPs they poll; it could be three or a dozen.

Brokers may use different ways to allocate the prices quoted by RSPs, and not all are equally to the trader's advantage. A large internet broker is likely to have an RSP relationship with at least five or six market makers, and it will contact all of these for quotes, the most competitive of which it will relay to the client. The price achieved on dealing may be better than quoted. Other brokers rotate RSPs in turn on the basis of one per deal, communicating the price received to the customer. Some claim that retail brokers are not always interested in getting the best price for customers and that they are focused solely on offering the easiest and cheapest services.

Before MiFID was implemented, the LSE advised that retail clients should ask their broker how it dealt with limit orders (whether published to the order book for all to access, or warehoused for only RSPs to access) because this could affect the prices they could get. In the post-MiFID world, the greater transparency of limit orders will put pressure on the RSPs, according to Brown. 'We'll make as many limit orders visible on SETS as possible, and these limit orders will be able to be executed with each other or any other order coming into the market from any participant.' The result could ultimately be more and cheaper execution, which is good news for brokers, Brown says. 'RSPs will continue as before but the big question for them is one of margins, though they should benefit from increasing volumes.' With rising liquidity, spreads will tighten and trading costs will go down, Brown says.

Hubs such as Proquote and Royal Blue provide a central facility for routing quote and execution messages between private client providers and RSPs. In reaction to competitive pressure, they have reduced entry costs for RSPs and brokers alike.

Hedge funds and others

Hedge funds often prefer DMA (direct market access) to the traditional model whereby they pay a broker to execute trades on their behalf. The trades still go through the broker's system, but the fund itself controls the trading, and pays much lower commission as a result. The LSE takes the view that the price improvement so obtained offsets the cost of setting up the appropriate technology, and that private investors could benefit from trading in a similar way, although some day traders are not convinced.

If hedge funds cannot spare the cash outlay for the positions in shares that they would like, or they want to keep their holdings more opaque, they will use contracts for difference (CFDs), says Brown. This will affect the share price because the shares are held as security against the CFD trades, he says. For more about how CFDs work, see Chapter 9.

Hedge funds in particular, but also investment banks and pension funds use algorithmic trading, which is computer-based trading applying mathematical models known as algorithms. It requires fewer staff to administer than traditional trading. The models used will generate both the size and timing of the trade based on a volume-weighted or time-weighted average price. Algorithmic trading can split a large trade into smaller ones to reduce market impact and cut trading costs.

Concerns are sometimes raised that algorithmic trading can power a market rise or fall as programmed traders follow momentum triggered by buyers or sellers. Some firms run programmes known as sniffers that discover momentum in stocks, giving them a cue to jump onto the bandwagon. Algorithms follow many different trading strategies, which can even serve to counteract each other, as fans of algorithmic trading point out.

16

Share trading venues and exchanges

Introduction

In this chapter, we will look at the exchange trading facilities for UK equities in the competitive environment encouraged by the Markets in Financial Instruments Directive. Read this chapter with Chapter 15, which covers the London Stock Exchange.

Overview

As the second edition of this book went to press, there are eight recognised investment exchanges (RIEs) in London, some concerned with derivatives. We will focus here on exchanges that trade UK equities, where only the London Stock Exchange (LSE) (covered in Chapter 15) and PLUS Markets Group (see below) are currently authorised to operate primary as well as secondary markets. virt-x, a cross-border exchange for pan-European blue chip stocks, is authorised only to operate secondary markets. Equiduct plans to operate a secondary market model. We will also look at the multilateral trading facilities, which provide an alternative to exchanges, and at systematic internalisers. Anonymous trading takes place in the dark liquidity pools, which we will also examine.

The choice of trading venue could impact on execution, and firms under the Markets in Financial Instrument Directive (MiFID) are required to have a *best execution* policy. As we will see in Chapter 22, best execution relates to price and execution expenses for retail investors, but is a broader concept for others, including factors such as speed and likelihood of execution.

To achieve best execution, it is perfectly reasonable for a firm to have only one trading venue, if it can demonstrate the best possible result. Occasionally, it may get a worse price here than elsewhere but this is acceptable if it would not be economical for the firm to move venues on that business.

It is not easy for newcomers to compete with the LSE in providing a trading venue because of the cost and complexity of building a system. But best execution is the most likely trigger for changing liquidity concentration in the established exchanges, Anthony Belchambers, chief executive at the Futures and Options Association and chairman at MiFID Connect, told the Securities & Investment Institute 2007 annual conference.

If best execution brings about sufficient liquidity, it will impact on the way the FTSE indices are compiled.

FTSE Group, compiler of the FTSE indices, will have a principal market for each security within the indices and, initially in the period after implementation of the MiFID, this will generally be the home exchange, which in London is the LSE, according to David Hobbs, director. In time, there will be a selection of the best markets for closing prices for compiling the indices, Hobbs says.

Let us now take a look at some of the main new players.

Exchanges

PLUS Markets Group

PLUS Markets Group has set itself up as a rival to the LSE, initially at the small-company end of trading through its provision of a quote-driven market maker facility. For details of its primary market, see Chapter 6. In 2006, over half a million trades, with a total of nearly £3 billion, representing 5.75 billion shares, took place on PLUS rather than on traditional exchanges.

The Group became an RIE in July 2007, which made it a full stock exchange with the same rights, privileges, immunities and status as the London Stock Exchange. PLUS is a market operator under MiFID, with a European passport for cross-border business.

Before it achieved RIE status, the PLUS-quoted primary market was only in competition with the Alternative Investment Market (AIM). As an RIE, PLUS Markets Group plans to extend its stock coverage to include a much broader range of primary products and offerings, including structured products.

'We will be offering trading in every security currently listed and traded on the LSE's main market and AIM, and also in every security listed in our own primary market,' says Nemone Wynn-Evans, the director of business development.

In January 2007, PLUS raised £25 million via a placing to strengthen its balance sheet, improve its trading platform, and develop and promote new company services and products as well as its existing product. In early 2007, it hired new senior staff. On 30 April 2007, PLUS signed a deal with OMX by which it would use OMX's trading technology to extend its coverage from 850 to 5,000 securities, including FTSE 100 shares.

PLUS is run by former LSE executives and every time it does a trade it takes business away from the Exchange, though currently only in the niche area of small companies. For the 260 companies in the FTSE Fledgling Index, PLUS claims to have around 45 per cent of the trading as a whole, on a regular basis.

Companies quoted on the AIM, unlike those on the Main Market, must give their consent to be traded on PLUS and, by mid-2007, not many had, although there had been an increase in market share of AIM and FTSE Fledgling stocks trading on its platform.

The Treasury has identified that it is a regulatory anomaly to have different treatments across the two markets and that furthermore it is inconsistent with the MiFID, which seeks to open up competition between trading venues. In a statement to the House of Commons on 20 February 2007, Ed Balls, Economic Secretary to the Treasury and Minister for the City, said that he was ordering the Financial Services Authority (FSA) to review the status quo, and, as the second edition of this book went to press, this review had started. Subject to the FSA's discretion, PLUS was expecting to be able to admit all AIM stocks to trading on its platform, without the need for consent, by the end of 2007.

The PLUS trading platform, based on a quote-driven system, claims to have substantial benefits in promoting liquidity in small and mid-cap stock trading, partly in terms of smoothing out price shifts caused by sudden volume surges and also in terms of the ability of market markers to price-improve in relation to specific orders.

There is feedback from market participants that there has been a 'drying up' of liquidity in small-caps when unsuitable stocks were moved to SETSmm, according to PLUS. The LSE has denied that liquidity is affected.

Order books such as SETS (provided by the LSE, and explained in Chapter 15) suit those market participants who prefer alternative methods of trading, such as algorithmic trades, and those who require direct market access to execute their business, according to Wynn-Evans. However, the PLUS platform suits those participants who prefer quote-driven trading, such as retail brokers and market makers, both of which play a valuable role in providing price formation and liquidity in those smaller stocks that trade less frequently.

Market makers often quote one price on PLUS and another on SETS. This is because on SETS, they are quoting prices for trading lots of much smaller size – usually a quarter of Normal Market Share (NMS) (the number of shares representing a minimum quote size) – whereas on PLUS they quote in multiples of NMS. The amount of risk capital that market makers commit to the PLUS Market is greater than on SETS and they advertise a wider spread to protect that capital. PLUS does not impose trade reporting fees and there is no central counterparty fee.

When asked whether brokers should access PLUS, the LSE quote-driven system, and SETS simultaneously for small stocks to ensure getting the best price, Wynn-Evans says 'Yes'. She maintains that PLUS frequently offers better prices, and brokers not accessing PLUS are missing out on the deepening pool of liquidity on its platform.

There was an independent study of the cost of trade execution on the PLUS service and SETSmm conducted by Ian Marsh, Professor of Finance at Cass Business School, and Panayotis Parpas of the Department of Computing at Imperial College, London. The study, commissioned by PLUS, analysed all trade execution data in February 2006 compared with SETSmm data for the same period. In total, 23,769 transactions in 348 different stocks were analysed.

The analysis did not give a complete picture and was not designed to do so. Under best execution assumptions, if a better price was available on SETSmm, the trade should have gone there, so it was perhaps unsurprising that PLUS shows some price advantages for trades executed on PLUS, according to Marsh. In the study, over 90 per cent of actual PLUS transactions took place at or better than the best offer price on SETSmm, but this was conditional on the trade happening on PLUS. There was no way of knowing the gains from trades on SETSmm because the hypothetical price offered by PLUS market makers after improvement, with which it would be compared, could not be determined.

Against this background, the average gain from the deals on PLUS over SETSmm was one-third of 1 per cent on deals up to 2 × NMS, rising to two-thirds of 1 per cent over 2 × NMS. The price comparison shows that best execution works and that the PLUS system gets better prices than SETS at least some of the time.

Equiduct

Equiduct is the trading name for EASDAQ; it plans to be an exchange with security market trading. In September 2007, the Börse Berlin said it had taken a majority stake in it with the idea of establishing a pan-European Exchange. It will trade, as far as the UK is concerned, the FTSE 250 shares (the top 250 shares by market capitalisation) and hopes to attract participants as they see results and comparison figures.

The Equiduct business model has both an order book/quote-driven hybrid market and also PartnerEx, which is a bilateral agreement between market maker and order-flow providers (either retail brokers or buy-side firms) that predetermines the parameters for executing trades such as maximum volume, price improvement and clearing and settlement location. Equiduct will electronically enforce PartnerEx relationships. The order-flow providers may be part of the same financial institution, enabling on-exchange internalisation.

Equiduct goes so far as to say that a regular order book and/or quote-driven market, including its own hybrid, cannot compete in all the key requirements for MiFID best execution, but PartnerEx can provide this solution.

The idea is that as fragmentation of liquidity across venues arises, PartnerEx can ensure that an order can be executed at the best price available in the marketplace against a single counterparty, inclusive of any predefined price improvement. Equiduct has a low flat fee structure.

Multilateral trading facilities

Multilateral trading facilities are competing in the same space as exchanges and are conceptually influenced by the model of the electronic communication networks (ECNs), which flourished in the United States in the late 1990s because the main US exchanges did not accept limit orders.

Chi-X

Chi-X, which is regulated by the FSA and is owned by Instinet, a subsidiary of Japanese broker Nomura, trades pan-European stocks with an initial emphasis on the London, German and Dutch markets and planned to offer coverage in approximately 80 per cent of European stocks by the end of October 2007.

'Our business is built on the US model,' says Peter Randall, director. 'Before we launched Chi-X we looked closely at models of the ECNs, and also the European models that struggled. We learned to provide a structure with easy connectivity, technology with robust capacity and scalability and an attractive rebate pricing model.'

The Chi-X technology is cheaper and more robust and provides faster trading than any of the exchanges, according to Randall. The claimed latency of the Chi-X system is two milliseconds, which is five times faster than the latency claimed by the LSE's new TradElect system (described in Chapter 15). The electronic pipes can bring into the exchange 30,000 instructions per second, which provides a capacity up to 10 times that of the LSE.

Such advanced technology is possible because it is recent, according to Randall. 'It's Moore's law in action, where every 18 months the functionality of technology doubles and the price halves,' he says.

Chi-X offers a low execution price, based on spreads that it says can be narrower than on the LSE, and uses a smart router that will find the best price, says Randall. 'If the price is better on the London Stock Exchange or Euronext, the deal will go there, and if it is better on Chi-X, it will go there. I hope in the future that stock exchanges may connect with Chi-X.'

The rebate model of Chi-X is, says Randall, not used elsewhere in Europe. It is based on the need for a maker and a taker to complete a trade. The maker buys or sells, initiating the trade, and the taker accepts it. 'If you're a maker, it's valuable for a market, and we will compensate you by giving a rebate,' he says. 'The difference between the fee taken from makers and the rebate is our revenue.'

For clearing, Chi-X has a non-exclusive agreement with Fortis, the provider of banking and insurance services, to use its European Multilateral Clearing Facility, which offers participants a 50 per cent reduction on the prevailing CCP (central counterparty) rates for Dutch, German and UK stocks.

With such features, Randall claims that Chi-X has better execution, but that he is not seeking to compete head-on with the LSE where there is an established pool of liquidity. Chi-X is seeking to attract statistical arbitrageurs, he says. 'People come to Chi-X if they want to do a trade. There is no guarantee of a two-way price.' This distinguishes Chi-X from the Equiduct offering (see above).

The statistical arbitrageurs may have been unable to get business done on the existing exchange infrastructure, says Randall. 'They may not be able to deal with the slower speed – even on the latest technology of established exchanges – or the electronic pipes may be small.'

Chi-X offers a larger number of types of order than those on the LSE. They include the pegged order, which tracks the side of the market for which it is entered. A buy order will track the bid price and a sell order will track the offer price.

More than 40 per cent of the LSE's revenues are derived from selling market data. At Chi-X, says Randall, zero per cent of revenues come via this route. 'To charge for selling market data is like going into a grocer, asking how much milk costs, and having to pay to look at a price list,' he says.

Staffing costs at Chi-X are minimal compared to those of established exchanges. The Chi-X business model aims to be profitable entirely from trading fees, which has, Randall points out, worked well for other Instinet trading technology. 'You don't need to make profits by hiring a lot of technology experts.'

Project Turquoise

Project Turquoise, a consortium of seven investment banks, is a pan-European share trading platform that was set up from frustration with the exchanges and their profits from trading tariffs, and was originally due to launch in November 2007. The concept of the new trading system was linked to Project Boat, a way for banks to comply with pre- and post-trade data requirements under MiFID.

The seven banks behind Turquoise are Citigroup, Credit Suisse, Deutsche Bank, Goldman Sachs, Merrill Lynch, Morgan Stanley and UBS. They are responsible for more than 50 per cent of Europe's share trading volumes.

The plan is to run the consortium on a not-for-profit basis, passing on savings to users. The system will aim to provide cheap dealing services, allowing trading on and off traditional exchanges. It will be based in London but will be pan-European in its reach.

The target launch date of November 2007 was delayed until the first quarter of 2008 amid reports that there had not been total agreement among the seven founding banks over plans to install a chief executive. Subsequent reports indicated a further delay until the summer of 2008.

As the second edition of this book went to press, there was no management team in place, and Turquoise had not yet said whose technology it would use for the trading platform, whether Sweden's OMX, which some considered the most likely, or another such as Chi-X or virt-x. The perceived lack of clear information about the Turquoise plan has led to uncertainty about its true intentions, as opposed to a mere protest.

In April 2007, it was announced that European Central Counterparty (EuroCCP), the European clearing subsidiary of the Depository Trust & Clearing Corporation (DTCC) of the United States, would provide all clearing and risk management services to Turquoise. Citigroup, one of the seven banks behind Turquoise, was selected as the agent for settlement, routing cleared orders to the preferred settlement venue.

How cheap Turquoise will make trading is another key issue. The trading volumes put through the founding banks are controlled by the hedge funds and other trading clients, who are obliged to seek best execution. If trading is not sufficiently lucrative, there are alternative avenues planned by Turquoise, including trading in dark liquidity pools (see below).

The London Stock Exchange perspective

At the 2007 convention of the Federation of European Securities Exchanges, Clara Furse, chief executive of the LSE, said it was worth examining Project Turquoise's claims that it would be able to significantly reduce exchange fees and that its mutual ownership structure was right and even superior.

On exchange fees, Furse noted that the average cost of buying a UK equity is around £6.50 per £1,000 traded, of which the exchange fee is 4 pence, or little more than half of 1 per cent of the total transaction cost. Clearing and settlement come to 2 pence, commissions an average of 85 pence, market impact approximately 60 pence and, unique to the UK, stamp duty is £5.

Even if investors avoided stamp duty by trading contracts for difference (rather than the cash equities), the fee charged by the LSE was likely to be less than 3 per cent of total transaction cost, Furse told the convention. 'So even if were to offer our services for free this would only reduce the cost of trading to the investor by 4 pence per thousand pounds traded.'

Furse told the convention delegates that it was only seven years ago that the LSE demutualised. 'Being mutual wasn't a great success in an ever more competitive environment for the London Stock Exchange, as the 1990s proved all too publicly!' she said. She noted conflicts of interest that are hard to resolve when only one part of the market controls the trading platform.

Systematic internalisers

A systematic internaliser (SI) is an investment firm that systematically deals on its own account by executing client orders outside a regulated market. The cost of building and maintaining a solution to monitor compliance for both pre- and post-trade transparency requirements is a requisite of being an SI and the costs are likely to be prohibitive for all but the largest firms.

The LSE and Equiduct are attempting to persuade firms to use their facilities instead of becoming SIs and so competing with themselves. The LSE has set a new, greatly reduced tariff for firms that match orders between their own clients.

If a bank uses the LSE's trading services and does pre-trade transparency on the system as well as post-trade transparency, it will not be subject to the SI requirements; this encourages it to avoid going down the route of being an SI.

Dark liquidity pools

The dark liquidity pools are electronic trading venues that match buyers and sellers anonymously, without quoting prices, and they give rise to OTC trading. This minimises the market impact of large block trades (the sale or purchase of a large number of shares in one transaction) or trades in stocks that have low liquidity and wide spreads.

Among the venues for such trading venues are private inter-bank platforms, and established pools in Europe such as the Portfolio System for Institutional Trading (POSIT), which allows broker crosses, where the buyer and seller trade at a keener price than the spread. The other main pool in Europe is Liquidnet.

Market feedback suggests that up to half of UK share trading by volume takes place off exchange in this way. There is some feeling that post-MiFID fragmentation of liquidity may send trading in the direction of the dark liquidity pools, and parties are developing ways to make them more accessible, such as through the LSE's FIX messaging gateway.

It is widely agreed that large stocks with narrow spreads are better traded transparently on exchange, so there is no risk of the market moving against the trader while the deal is waiting to be matched. But algorithmic trading in the dark liquidity pools may prove difficult for regulators to police, according to analysts.

Consolidation

Among exchanges across Europe and the United States, there has already been significant consolidation in the interest of creating efficiencies.

In April 2007, the New York Stock Exchange (NYSE) completed a merger with Euronext, which had itself been formed from the union of the Paris, Amsterdam, Brussels and Lisbon exchanges, through which it obtained the London-based LIFFE futures exchange.

In the same month, Deutsche Börse, the German stock exchange, announced it was buying International Securities Exchange, the US options exchange, for US $2.8 billion.

One month later, Nasdaq, the US high-tech exchange, said it would be buying OMX, the Nordic exchange group, for US $3.7 billion (£1.9 billion). The combined group expects to focus much of its efforts in London.

In June 2007, the LSE agreed a merger with Borsa Italiana, valuing the Italian exchange at £1.1 million. The LSE said that the combined group would operate the most advanced trading platform of any exchange and the most efficient post-trade services in Europe.

17

Post-trade services

Introduction

In this chapter, we will focus on post-trade services, mainly clearing and settlement, in the equity and government bond markets. We will see how professionals run these services in London and continental Europe, and what happens afterwards, involving, among others, the custodian and registrar.

Since the first edition of this book was published, there has been headway towards greater competition and efficiency in the clearing and settlement of transactions across European Union (EU) borders – a more expensive process than clearing and settling a domestic transaction using national systems. The driving force behind industry initiatives in this direction is the European Commission. We will look at these developments.

Overview

Let us define our terms. Clearing defines the settlement obligations of the parties to the securities transaction and assigns accountability. Settlement is when assets are actually exchanged: investors pay for and receive the securities bought, and are paid for and relinquish the securities sold.

London is a world leader in international equities trading, and most of the trading is through membership of the London Stock Exchange (LSE). Clearing and settlement generally takes place in the home country of the stocks. An exception is on the virt-x exchange, where trades are cleared through LCH. Clearnet in London or x-clear in Switzerland, and settled in one of various settlement locations around Europe. Additional exceptions may arise if alternative trading facilities for European equities, such as Project Turquoise and Chi-X (see Chapter 16), are successful.

Dealers in London sometimes use what is known as an agent bank to organise their foreign clearing and settlement abroad or, if volumes justify it, they open accounts with foreign central securities depositories (CSDs) and central counterparties. European equity, bond and repo transactions are settled through international central securities depositories (ICSDs) and CSDs. We will look at these in more detail in this chapter.

Clearing

Clearing is the link between trading and settlement; as the second edition of this book goes to press, the LSE has been phasing in what it calls 'competitive clearing' from the first half of 2007. Until this point, LCH.Clearnet was the only UK central counterparty. Its role was to become a buyer to every seller and seller to every buyer for eligible LSE trades, giving anonymity to trades pre- and post-trade.

Under competitive clearing, LCH.Clearnet undertakes the same tasks, but competes with at least one other central counterparty. LSE members may chose between LCH.Clearnet and SIS x-clear, part of the SIS group based in Switzerland. The LSE has said it will add Cassa di Compensazione e Garanzia, the central counterparty of Borsa Italiana, as a clearer that may be used for LSE trades.

In the first phase of competitive clearing, one or the other central counterparties provides risk management. Once a trade is done, LCH.Clearnet or SIS x-clear assumes any monetary and delivery risk, and so acts as guarantor to the transaction, collecting a margin from the trading parties that makes the transaction secure. In the years before competitive clearing, LCH.Clearnet, the only UK central counterparty at the time, had never been forced to tap its member default fund. This was valued recently at £582 million, together with a £200 million insurance policy.

The central counterparty has a second role in clearing transactions, which LCH.Clearnet says is to establish 'who owes what to whom'. In the second phase of competitive clearing, the central counterparty would assume responsibility for netting, but until competitive clearing is introduced, netting will continue to be outsourced to the CREST system, the UK settlement system (discussed in the next section).

Netting reduces the number of trades that settle by as much as 98 per cent because all the buy and sell trades in the same security from the same firm are added or subtracted from its account and a single netted transaction is settled. Although netting is optional, most investors prefer to use it where available, which is for UK equity trades on the LSE's SETS (Stock Exchange Electronic Trading System) platform and SEAQ (Stock Exchange Automated Quotations Systems) crosses.

Settlement

Settlement is the point in a transaction when the buyer and seller exchange securities for cash. The process has not always worked as well as it does now through CREST. Until August 1996, the LSE handled its own settlement of share trades, but not very efficiently. Following the 1986 market deregulation known as Big Bang, trading volumes exploded through the late 1980s, which put extra pressure on the LSE's Talisman settlement system.

The LSE decided to replace Talisman with Taurus, which was designed to bring about compulsory dematerialisation of all UK corporate securities. Critics said it tried to satisfy too many conflicting market interests. On the advice of two management consultants, the LSE abandoned Taurus in March 1993 and decommissioned Talisman in April 1997.

At the LSE's request, the Bank of England established a securities settlement task force chaired by its director Pen Kent, which recommended a phased introduction of more cost-effective settlement for UK equities, including the introduction of rolling settlement. CREST was proposed as a new settlement system for UK equities and bonds.

Euroclear UK & Ireland Limited, previously known as CRESTCo, is the UK's only CSD. It was capitalised in October 1994 and owns the CREST system. CREST settles money market instruments, bonds and equities, but not futures or other derivatives trades, which are settled between counterparties directly. By August 1996, CREST had settled its first transaction.

In those early days, all trades settled on a gross basis, that is, transaction by transaction. Netting, as we discussed under 'Clearing' in the previous section, was launched in July 2002. From this point until competitive clearing is fully introduced, CREST receives gross LSE trades, assesses them for stamp duty, nets and dispatches the relevant trade information to LCH.Clearnet as central counterparty, and provides a transaction report for the Financial Services Authority. In early 2007, it was proposed that CREST will discontinue some of these roles, as LSE members will determine to which central counterparty the gross trades will be routed for netting and clearing.

Euroclear UK & Ireland charges for each transaction cleared by the CREST system and it charges for settlement on a gross or net basis, depending on the client's instruction. This is likely to continue.

The real-time process

Settlement takes place through CREST on Settlement Day, no matter how long the agreed settlement period, which is the time between the trade date and settlement date. Settlement is a real-time electronic process conducted on a delivery versus payment basis, which entails the simultaneous and irrevocable transfer of cash and securities. Full legal title of the securities is transferred at the point of settlement.

Settlement in CREST is in 'central bank money'. Cash movements are ultimately reflected in accounts held at the Bank of England, which are facilitated by appointed commercial banks serving as CREST settlement banks. Each settlement bank maintains a pool of cash resources with the Bank, part of which is reserved strictly for CREST-related payments.

Clients of Euroclear UK & Ireland, including stockbrokers, custodians, fund managers, market makers and all forms of intermediaries, each have an account with a settlement bank of their choice. Each settlement bank transfers cash payments on behalf of Euroclear UK & Ireland clients to and from the other settlement banks during each day. These cash transfers are made using CHAPS (Clearing House Automated Payments System) for payments in euros and the Bank of England's RTGS (Real Time Gross Settlement) system for sterling.

At the end of each settlement cycle, CREST will notify the Bank of England's RTGS system of the inter-bank payments that took place. RTGS will release earmarked funds that were not used and it will allow the settlement banks to rebalance their liquidity before they restart the process.

Crest's settlement rate is around 98–99 per cent by value, but 91–92 per cent by volume, with failure usually arising because a broker has not received stock from its client.

CREST runs a 'settlement discipline regime' consisting of matching and settlement standards, and if a broker breaches these standards, Euroclear UK & Ireland may impose a fine or take other disciplinary action.

Safekeeping and custody

Euroclear UK & Ireland does not provide safekeeping facilities, but it offers corporate action and other custody-related services.

Some foreign banks and insurance companies deal with CREST through a local or global custodian. The custodian safeguards the financial assets of its customers and processes trades and corporate actions such as dividends and interest collections, rights offerings, scrip issues and takeovers. In addition, the custodian typically offers value-added services such as performance measurement, securities lending desks, fund administration, tax services and a range of banking services.

Registrar services

After settlement, Euroclear UK & Ireland notifies the registrar appointed by the security's issuer of the change in the security's ownership. Examples of UK registrars are Lloyds TSB Registrars, Computershare and Capita Registrars.

The balance of assets held in CREST must be reconciled with the register four times a year.

London's advantages

LCH.Clearnet is based in London. Euroclear UK & Ireland is also based in London although it is ultimately owned by Euroclear, a Brussels-based entity. In the case of market failure, the London location provides comfort to participants and adds to the perception of London as a major financial centre.

Let us see how this can work. When Barings collapsed in 1995, the London Clearing House (as it was before combining in 2003 with Clearnet, a French counterpart) identified Barings' open positions with other banks, so they could be closed out with minimum market disruption. It worked closely with the Bank of England and exchanges to resolve the issue.

Cross-border activity

The Markets in Financial Instruments Directive

By the time the second edition of this book is in your hands, the November 2007 deadline for implementing the Markets in Financial Instruments Directive (MiFID) (see Chapter 22) will have passed. Under Article 34 of the Directive, investment firms from one member state have right of access to central counterparty clearing and settlement systems in another member state, which should reduce costs. MiFID gives regulated members the right to designate the clearing and settlement systems of their choice in order to achieve best execution for trades in any EU-regulated market.

In the post-MiFID environment, the monopolies enjoyed by stock exchanges will have gone, and the fortunes of stock exchanges and alternative trading facilities will more closely be linked to the choice of clearing and settlement venue they can offer to clients. Settlement systems are cooperating more, as, for example, between DTCC and the Euroclear group to support the recently formed NYSE/Euronext exchange, particularly in settlement of dual-listed securities.

Given the increasing integration of European securities markets, the European Union wants seamless, competitive and safe EU clearing and settlement services. At present, there is a variety of clearing and settlement service providers. When securities are trading across borders, transaction settlement is relatively expensive and complex and can involve multiple intermediaries, all of which take a fee.

Competing settlement

Investors usually choose to settle multi-market, cross-border trades in domestic securities through one, or a combination of, either agent banks, which sell a wide range of services, or international CSDs, which provide more commoditised wholesale services. Let us look at each in turn.

- The agent banks may use CSDs and ICSDs to settle trades for their clients, or instead complete the settlement of client trades on their own books. They offer value-added services such as portfolio valuation and fund administration services. The agent banks may offer their services across multiple markets, as do Citigroup and BNP Paribas, for example, while other agent banks, such as KAS Bank in the Netherlands, specialise in offering value-added transaction services to foreign investors in their home market. The agent banks do not report any market share figures.
- International CSDs (ICSDs). Europe has two ICSDs. One is Euroclear Bank, which is wholly user owned and part of the Euroclear group, which owns several CSDs, including Euroclear UK & Ireland in the UK. The other ICSD is Clearstream Banking Luxembourg, wholly owned by Deutsche Börse. They each provide settlement and custody services for domestic and international securities and are interconnected by an electronic bridge, enabling a customer of one ICSD to settle a trade with a customer of the other. The ICSD has a higher cost base than a CSD, due to the multi-currency, multi-market complexities of its service offering.

Some of the main agent banks, who have organised themselves into a group named Fair & Clear, had objected to the banking status of the ICSDs that own CSDs. A banking status enables the ICSDs to offer credit and securities borrowing services to customers and help them avoid failed transactions; without this service, many transactions would fail.

The agent banks contended that the CSDs, which are part of the local-market infrastructure, faced potential new risks when owned by entities offering credit services: namely, a potential bankruptcy risk. They also held the opinion that the two ICSDs could receive preferential treatment and tariffs from the CSDs they own, potentially creating an unlevel playing field.

Fair & Clear aimed its criticisms mainly at Euroclear Bank, which owned several CSDs including Euroclear UK & Ireland, then known as CRESTCo. In January 2005, the Euroclear Board restructured the company so that Euroclear Bank no longer owned CRESTCo and the other CSDs in the Euroclear group. Instead, Euroclear Bank became a separate, sister company to the CSDs, thereby addressing Fair & Clear's concerns.

All of the Euroclear group national and international CSDs are now owned by a holding company – Euroclear SA/NV – which also owns the technology and offers shared services (human resources, legal, etc) that are purchased by each Euroclear operating entity under audited, OECD inter-company transfer-pricing principles. Euroclear and the Fair & Clear agent banks do not have entirely separate interests. Euroclear Bank supplies services to agent banks and buys services from them. Among the 24 users on the Euroclear Board, two are Fair & Clear agent banks.

Giovannini Group barriers

The Giovannini Group reports have spurred moves towards a more competitive and coherent pan-European approach to clearing and settlement. The Giovannini Group, a team of market experts led by Alberto Giovannini, chief executive of Unifortune Asset Management, was appointed by the European Commission to focus on market practice, legal and regulatory inconsistencies within clearing and settlement in Europe.

In its two reports of 2001 and 2003, the Givoannini Group identified 15 barriers preventing efficient clearing and settlement arrangements in the EU. Charlie McCreevy, European Commissioner for Internal Markets, said that a relaxation of national requirements for legal and tax issues would make a huge contribution to finding solutions to the unresolved Giovannini Group barriers. But there has been less progress on removing the nine public-sector barriers than for the six barriers tackled by the private sector. By 2007, many private-sector recommendations were at an advanced stage towards implementation, including harmonisation of opening hours of settlement systems and the provision of intra-day finality. Industry agreement has also been reached on eliminating national differences in corporate-action rules and procedures, and in IT communication protocols.

EU Code of Conduct

Earlier, the European Commission had been considering a directive on clearing and settlement, but the fear was that it could have unwanted consequences, including a slowing down of moves towards settlement-infrastructure consolidation and market-practice harmonisation.

The European Commission abandoned the idea and instead proposed an industry-led solution with an EU Code of Conduct to improve competition in the sector. The Code, signed in November 2006 by the LSE, LCH.Clearnet, CRESTCo and Euroclear, among others, is designed to improve investors' ability to trade, clear and settle securities transactions in a consistent, coherent and cost-efficient framework across Europe. Signatories must meet standards set in price transparency, access, interoperability and service unbundling, among other areas. The Code has set a deadline for each of the standards, with the final one on 1 January 2008.

Through the Code, Commissioner McCreevy has given the market an opportunity to find its own solution, which is very much in the style of the UK Financial Services Authority, as when, for example, it investigated short selling and, without being more prescriptive, called for more transparency, a move that led to Euroclear & Ireland, then known as CRESTCo, making stock lending data available on its website.

In January 2007, Euroclear chief executive Pierre Francotte said the success of the Code would depend on whether the parties involved implement it, and whether it was extended from only equities to bonds. He said that the Commission would have to stay actively involved to ensure immediate progress.

TARGET2-Securities

In summer 2006, the European Central Bank (ECB) announced a plan to build its own eurozone securities settlement infrastructure, TARGET2-Securities, which the European Commission has supported. The Bank of England is not actively involved in the debate on TARGET2-Securities although it has taken a non-interventionist interest. But the matter has been of interest to the City, given that between 40 and 50 per cent of all EU financial services business originates from London. The ECB has not yet committed itself to seeing through the project, which is provisionally scheduled for a 2013 implementation.

Under the TARGET2-Securities plan, the ECB would replace private-sector CSDs in the eurozone as the single provider of settlement processing activities. The CSDs would, however, continue to provide all other related processing services, such as custody, collateral management and issuer services.

The idea is to achieve lower costs and lower settlement risk. Euroclear, which is trying to achieve the same objectives (discussed later in this chapter), is not against the idea in principle, provided the ECB's approach can deliver better market benefits. But the ECB has not yet provided a convincing business case that settlement will be cheaper with TARGET2-Securities.

In a January 2007 article, Karel Lannoo, chief executive at the Centre for European Policy Studies, said that the EU is bringing more competition into securities markets with the MiFID and the EU Code of Conduct, but the ECB is going in the opposite direction with its proposed creation of an EU securities settlement monopoly.

At a conference in Brussels in January 2007, Sir Nigel Wicks, chairman of Euroclear, suggested that if TARGET2-Securities went ahead, it was unclear whether national securities regulators would be able to continue supervising securities settlement, and the ECB would enjoy for its TARGET2-Securities business the same independence and lack of accountability that it had enjoyed for its monetary policy function. He questioned whether EU competition law would apply to TARGET2-Securities and, if so, what it would mean in practice.

Wicks is an interested party as Euroclear had already embarked on its plan to create its own single settlement system covering multiple markets (see below).

Euroclear

In January 2007, Euroclear completed the first phase of its own programme of moving to a single platform, and aims to have consolidated all of its five existing settlement platforms into one by 2010. With a wider scope than Target2-Securities, Euroclear's single platform will not only converge securities settlement activity onto one platform, but will include all processing requirements for custody, issuer services and other types of transactions in more than 35 currencies.

Taking into account the Giovannini Group recommendations, Euroclear also included in its programme the objective of achieving full harmonisation of market practices within the five domestic markets for which the Euroclear group acts as CSD, which are Belgium, France, Ireland and the Netherlands as well as the UK. There has been strong market buy-in. Most, if not all, of the market rules practised within the five markets will become identical and in line with the rest of Europe, so removing many of the barriers to cross-border settlement identified in the Giovannini Group reports.

The pan-European market for Euroclear will be achieved in phases (see box below), the first of which was to provide a single settlement engine by 2007, leading ultimately by 2010 to a single processing platform.

Euroclear's plan for a 'domestic market for Europe' for securities settlement

Roll-out	Initiative	Benefit
2006/07	Single Settlement Engine	■ Based on a single settlement algorithm. ■ Real-time positioning and booking of all cash and securities movements at Euroclear. ■ Provides a foundation for more platform consolidation.
2007/08	Euroclear Settlement of Euronext-zone Securities (ESES)	■ One processing solution for the Belgian, Dutch and French markets. ■ Harmonised market practices for these markets covering all securities transactions. ■ An interim measure until the future single platform is ready.
2008/10	Common Communications Interface	■ Single access point to all Euroclear entities and services, and standardised messages.
2008/10	Single Platform	■ One processing platform covering domestic and cross-border transactions for the Belgian, Dutch, French, Irish and UK markets, and a wide range of foreign securities. ■ Harmonised market rules across markets. ■ Delivers €300 million per year in market savings.

The future

Commissioner McCreevy has given the clearing and settlement industry its own chance to create a more competitive and efficient pan-European environment through MiFID and the EU Code of Conduct but, should this fail, he has said there will be mandatory measures. There is talk of improving the supervision of clearing and settlement on the basis of standards jointly provided by the European System of Central Banks and the Committee of European Securities Regulators, which have some overlap with the Code of Conduct, but are much more prescriptive.

The ECB has not yet clearly specified the cost benefits of the TARGET2-Securities plan but the discussions continue and the plan, as at September 2007, seems to have moved, as one industry source put it, from 'if' to 'when'. Ultimately, it will be up to Euroclear and the other eurozone CSDs to decide if they want to join, and they are waiting for a convincing business case. The agent banks such as BNP Paribas and Citigroup are more supportive, not least because TARGET2-Securities would prolong their roles in bridging EU capital market inefficiencies until 2013 and might enable them to have direct access to the TARGET2-Securities platform and bypass CSDs to settle euro-denominated trades.

Euroclear's plan for a single platform is underway and, once it has been completed, will remove the inefficiencies of having to access multiple systems through chains of intermediaries in order to settle cross-border transactions. Euroclear CSD customers will be able to more easily expand trading opportunities by diversifying across markets.

With a harmonised Europe, there will be no difference in market practices between one market and another. A rights offering in the UK, for example, will be processed the same way in any other EU market. The agent banks make their money from managing market differences and inefficiencies for clients; they will find that some of the value-added services they offer today will no longer be in demand once these differences and inefficiencies disappear. If they are to survive, they will be forced to adjust their business model, which may well involve moving into new services and to more markets outside Europe, such as Asia and South America, which are not undergoing such a transformation.

18

Investors

Introduction

In this chapter, we will take an overview of the types of investor operating in the City. We will look first at retail investors, and then turn to institutional investors. Read this with Chapter 19, which covers pooled investments.

Retail investors

The retail investor market in the UK is large, and many smaller stockbrokers specialise in serving retail investors' needs. By number of trades, private clients have a significant share of the market. In 2004, 40.8 million agency bargains were traded on the London Stock Exchange (LSE) on all markets, according to Compeer. Private clients trading through members of the LSE accounted for 10.5 million agency bargains, 26 per cent of the total, with institutions accounting for the remaining 74 per cent. But in terms of *sums invested*, private clients have only a small percentage of the total, although they also put cash into pooled investment schemes, which are used to invest across asset classes, including the stock market.

Some retail investors buy shares and hold them for the medium to the long term, while others trade over a short period. Traders can make money from stock markets when there is volatility. They can take short positions to gain from pricing downturns, as well as long positions to benefit from upturns. In bear markets, retail investors often make the mistake of hanging on to loss-making positions too long.

Market gurus encourage retail investors and traders to make their own investment decisions. There is much advice available from newspapers and magazines, financial websites and their message boards, some of which is poor or biased, and some more valuable.

Trading functionality – What facilities are available with your account? Can you set stop losses or tracking sell orders that can enable you to lock in your profits for a rising share? Can you set alerts so that you receive an email if a share price touches a certain level?

Phone service – Can you telephone the company to place a deal or ask for help, or are you restricted to the website?

Investment advice – can you get telephone advice or tips and research to help you?

Value for money – Find out how much it costs to deal. Is there a different commission structure for frequency and value of deals? What are the account fees and is there an "inactivity fee"? Can you pay in online using your debit card?

Monthly investing – Is this facility available? What are the terms? Can you also automatically reinvest your dividends should you wish to?

Investors are in the positive position that online competition has driven down the cost of dealing commission and there is a variety of different charging methods to be found. In broad terms, commission is split into two types: 'flat', a fixed cost per trade, often tied to doing a particular number of deals in any specified period or to a subscription fee and 'variable', a percentage of the value of the deal. Comparison websites let you input your typical trade and show you how prices compare. Once again, do make sure you've got the complete picture and remember that cheapest is not necessarily the best.

Some brokers' sites enable you to open an account online, others will require some paperwork, but don't jump at the first site you come to, have a look at what's on offer, call them for a chat, then decide. After all, your online broker's not just for your next trade but will be an important part of your investment life!

Some private investors have followed their own investment strategy and profited from it. But most do not have the same information resources as professionals, and they may have limited understanding of company accounts or how markets work. The Financial Services Authority constantly recommends that financial advice should be sought.

An investment club can be an enjoyable and interesting hobby, combining the chance to get together with friends and colleagues for learning about and investing in the stock market, and it has sometimes worked well for private investors.

The club structure enables like-minded individuals to meet on a regular basis, and everyone contributes an agreed regular sum, perhaps £30 a month, to an investment fund. This will finance the club's purchase of shares in companies researched and recommended by club members. Because investors have pooled their contribution, the club has bigger buying power. A broker will be more interested in a trade with £5,000 than one with £500.

Institutional investors

Institutional investors are financial institutions that manage savings collectively for small investors. They include investment companies, life insurance companies and pension funds. Fund management is the process by which assets collected by institutional investors are invested.

UK assets under management exceeded £3.4 trillion as at December 2006, according to the July 2007 *Asset Management Survey*, published by the Investment Management Association. Sometimes the institutional investor is also the fund manager and at other times the two functions are separated.

Let us see how fund managers work, followed by insurance companies and pension funds.

Fund managers

The fund manager decides how to invest money held in a fund, whether it is a pension fund, an insurance fund or an investment fund. The fund manager may be an independent investment firm, such as Fidelity, or part of a bank or an insurance company. Insurance companies and pension funds may use external fund managers to manage wholesale money because it enables them to diversify their risk, and to have managers specialising in particular markets.

Contrary to popular belief, conventional fund managers have far more trading power than the hedge fund managers (see below). They can move prices by their buy and sell decisions, and by accepting or rejecting a bid for a company in which they hold shares, may determine the success of the bid.

Fund managers cannot invest in anything they like, as they are subject to asset allocation and asset eligibility requirements. Some funds invest in large blue chips, others in small companies, some in the UK and others abroad. These boundaries are known as the fund manager's universe.

Some fund managers are top-down, which means that they start with the global macroeconomic view and, within this framework, select individual stocks. Other managers are bottom-up, which means that they focus initially on the stocks, and only then on the broader picture.

An independent trustee monitors the fund's compliance with its investment objectives, and managers have their own monitoring procedures and controls.

The IMA July 2007 *Asset Management Survey* suggests fund managers are partly responsible for diminishing international barriers, of which a key element has been the growing success of UCITS (Undertakings for Collective Investments in Transferable Securities). UCITS are European Union regulations that aim to create a single market for collective investment schemes across the EU.

In December 2001, UCITS III was adopted, which provides a European passport for investment managers throughout the EU, and broadens the activities they may undertake. Fund managers may use derivatives as an active investment vehicle, rather than only, as before, to hedge positions, and may compete with hedge fund managers (see below) in this area.

UCITS funds are now selling successfully beyond the European marketplace, particularly in parts of Asia and Latin America.

Hedge fund managers

Hedge fund managers aim at absolute returns, regardless of market conditions, and their funds tend to make more money than conventional funds. They are often run by ex-investment bankers and other specialist financiers who give up highly lucrative jobs to set up a fund, and who know enough about markets to exploit a sophisticated toolset of modern investment vehicles.

Hedge fund managers normally invest their own money alongside that of investors, and will usually reveal how much. They are attracting the capital of sophisticated investors, including, increasingly, pension managers who use hedge funds as a relatively new way to diversify their funds in a way uncorrelated to their equity positions.

Hedge fund managers use increasingly diversified strategies. The best known of these are derivatives-related arbitrage, which means making money by exploiting small available differences in price, and long–short equity funds, which involve, for instance, buying Shell because you think it will go up and shorting BP because you think it will go down, so you are sector-neutral.

A variation is fixed-income arbitrage. The strategy involves trading two bonds, both of which mature after a given time period, in the same currency, with the same credit and liquidity risks, but with different yields. The trader believes that the bonds should have *mean reversion* and that bond A will have a declining yield and so a rising price and, conversely, bond B will have a rising yield and falling price.

The trader will buy bond A, which is to go *long*, and use it as collateral to borrow bond B, on which he or she will go *short*. In this way, the trader seeks to make a profit on the yield and price differences between the two bonds in the belief that it will be temporary. The trader will not worry if rates rise or fall, but will simply want the gap between the yields, and so the prices, to narrow to neutral. The trade will make a loss only if the gap widens. In practice, a hedge fund may take 40 or 50 such pairs, of which some will go wrong but a majority should go right.

Hedge fund managers do very little pure short selling, which has unlimited down-side. They often move markets at sensitive times, including during the book build for a securities issue. For a more general look at hedge funds and how they work, see Chapter 19.

Insurance companies

Insurance-company-owned asset managers are the largest single UK group, with 31 per cent of assets under management in the UK in 2006 held by IMA members, according to the Association's *Asset Management Survey*.

Insurance companies invest premiums received from the insured to increase their reserves. There are two kinds of insurance business. The first is long-term insurance, which is mainly life insurance, and the second is general insurance, which provides, for example, motor or household insurance cover, and needs to be in short-term liquid assets to meet claims in short-term policies.

A number of insurance companies, notably at the smaller and medium-sized end of the market, may have in-house asset management firms, but are outsourcing some of their mandates related to the core insurance business, the IMA survey found. This is seen as contributing to the ability of third-party asset managers to win insurance mandates.

Other contributing factors include the advance of open architectures on insurance platforms, which is allowing the life and pension product offering to move beyond in-house managers, and the emergence of new insurance companies such as Paternoster to buy out pension funds.

Pension funds

Pension funds invest regular pension contributions from individuals and employers into funds. Small pension schemes are managed by fund managers but the larger ones may be self-administered.

The pension fund aims to make a high long-term return both to meet liabilities in the form of payouts to those receiving their pension and, if possible, to maintain a surplus. An actuary will advise the fund.

In the 1990s, pension funds were dogged by inadequate investment returns. Part of the reason was that companies had taken pension contribution holidays in the 1980s because stock markets were booming and the funds had been able to meet liabilities out of existing resources.

Under changes to accounting standards, pension funds have been required to account for future liabilities on a current basis, which means that they must have assets to meet them. As a result of the pressures, some companies have closed schemes or increased contributions, and there has been some shift in investment from equities into bonds.

Liability-driven investment (LDI) responds to the need to match the asset allocation of a pension scheme more closely with future liabilities, but it requires a more sophisticated approach than shifting from equities into fixed income, given the payment profiles of funds, coupled with inflation and interest rate risk, according to the IMA. So far, LDI accounts for only 6 per cent of total pension fund assets under management, and is seen by some as only a partial solution.

Pension deficits remain an issue. In mid-July 2007, UK pension schemes of FTSE 100 companies had a net surplus of £12 billion, which was after many years in the red, according to the 14th annual *Accounting for Pensions* report by consultants and actuaries Lane, Clark & Peacock. This was a snapshot figure at a particular time that could easily change. The firm noted that the surplus might not survive once companies reflected the latest mortality projections in their accounts, and that companies with pension schemes heavily invested in equities ran material investment risk.

19

Pooled investments

Introduction

This chapter is about pooled investments. We will focus on investment funds, including unit trusts and open-ended investment companies, and on investment companies. We will examine split capital investment companies and how venture capital trusts work, as well as real estate investment trusts. We will cover exchange-traded funds and hedge funds.

Investment funds

Investment funds are designed to maximise portfolio diversification. Investors may invest a lump sum or regular monthly payments. They will gain access to a professional managed fund with a variety of assets, so diversifying risks and reducing dealing costs.

Investment funds cover both unit trusts and open-ended investment companies (OEICs). The EU member states, including the UK, originally developed the OEICs to make cross-border investing easier. The concept was introduced to the UK in 1997.

The OEIC has some technical differences from the unit trust and, unlike the latter, is a legally constituted limited company. For practical purposes the two products are identical for the end-investor. Most funds are likely to become OEICs because this type of fund is more flexible than the unit trust, and can be marketed cross-border. Some OEICs are conversions from unit trusts.

Unit trusts and OEICs trade at prices derived from the net asset value and are open-ended, meaning that the fund may create or redeem as many further units (for a unit trust) or shares (for an OEIC) as are required to meet investor demand. You can view any fund's track record over recent years, but, as the regulator-driven mantra goes, past performance is no guarantee for the future.

Investment trusts – the City's "best kept secret"

The investment trust industry has been successfully providing cost efficient products offering strong long-term capital growth opportunities for more than a century. However, despite these attractions, investment trusts remain underused by investors, with many put off by perceived concerns over their complexity…now is the time to shed some light on the City's "best kept secret".

Investment trusts share many similarities with other pooled funds, but it is their differences which make them a great investment choice for a wide range of investors. However, as with all stock market based investments, it is important to appreciate that the value of investment trusts – and any income from them – can go down as well as up and investors may get back less than they invest.

Publicly listed companies

Like unit trusts and Open Ended Investment Companies (OEICs), investment trusts spread investment risk by pooling investors' assets across a diverse range of companies and markets. However, unlike unit trusts and OEICs, investment trusts are publicly listed companies, giving them investment flexibility, shareholder accountability and independent board oversight.

Investment trusts also only issue a limited number of shares and are therefore known as 'closed-ended' funds. These shares are freely tradable, which means that investment trust share prices, unlike 'open-ended' unit trusts and OEICs, are affected by supply and demand in the market.

Discounts and premiums

If demand is strong enough, investment trust share prices may rise above their net asset value, and the trust is said to be trading at a premium. However, if demand is low, then share prices will likely fall below their net asset value, at which point the trust is deemed to be trading at a discount.

This added dimension to performance means that investment trusts can outperform their underlying assets if demand is strong. If demand is weak, discounts can widen and performance can be constrained, although this does make the shares better value.

Supply and demand factors also mean that investment trust investors can face liquidity issues which other pooled fund investors do not have to deal with. However, these issues are addressed through discount control measures, such as share buybacks and the use of treasury shares, which help reduce discount volatility and maintain liquidity.

A longer term view

Another advantage of investment trusts due to their closed-ended structure is the absence of flows into or out of their underlying portfolios. As a result, investment trust fund managers can take a longer-term view than their open-ended counterparts throughout the market cycle, without being forced to sell holdings or invest large inflows as demand for their investment trust fluctuates.

Changing gear

The ability of investment trust managers to use gearing offers investors more exciting opportunities. In simple terms, gearing is the process by which an

In the case of unit trusts, there are two different prices for the units in existence. The price at which you buy is the offer price, and the other is at which you sell is the bid price. The buying price is generally more than the selling price, and the difference, known as the spread, incorporates any initial charges and dealing costs. The OEIC has a single price that is linked directly to the value of the fund's investments.

Income paid from an investment fund is net of income tax. Capital gains tax is payable on profits subject to the annual allowance (£9,200 for 2007–08). The trustee of a unit trust (the equivalent for an OEIC is a depositary) is usually a large bank and simply oversees the running of the fund. The trustee of a pension fund sets targets. In a unit trust, the manager appoints the trustee, but in a pension fund it is the trustee who appoints the manager.

Selection criteria

Risk profiles and management styles vary widely on investment funds and so does the five-year track record. You can find details of a fund's track record in the magazines *Money Management* or *Money Observer*, or on a website focused on funds such as Trustnet (www.trustnet.com). For other useful sites, see Appendix 1 under the heading 'Collective investments and similar'. Let us now look at charges and investment strategy, both factors to be considered in fund selection.

Charges

An investment fund is likely to have an initial charge, also known as a front-end charge, part of which is the commission paid to the adviser or broker who sold you the fund. The charge varies. For a few funds, it will be as high as 6 per cent of money invested. On a unit trust, most of the bid–offer spread consists of the initial charge. The OEIC has a more transparent presentation based on its single price, and it separately itemises the initial charge on the transaction statement.

In addition, there is an annual management charge, typically between 0.75 and 2 per cent of the value of the investor's holding each year. Other fees are between 0.75 and 2 per cent and are not part of the annual management charge. They cover administration, custody, audit and some legal expenses, including those for trustees and registrars, and are detailed in the annual report and accounts.

Total expense ratio

A useful figure to assess the charges of a unit trust, OEIC or investment company (see below) in comparison with those of others is the total expense ratio (TER). It is a single percentage figure showing fees as a proportion of a fund's average assets. The TER reflects internal charges in a way that many find more useful than the widely quoted management charge, although it excludes commissions paid to brokers by fund managers.

Under simplified prospectus rules introduced in September 2005, the TER comparisons are like for like because the calculation is standardised. This affects all UCITS (Undertakings for the Collective Investment of Transferable Securities) funds, which are those marketable across the EU and registered within each EU country. Other funds may calculate the TER by their own methods.

Investment strategy

The actively managed fund tries to beat the market. Value investing seeks to buy stocks that are cheap in relation to underlying assets. Growth investing seeks out stocks with good growth prospects.

The tracker fund aims not to beat the market but simply to track a popular market index such as the FTSE 100. Investors buy tracker funds because they are slightly lower risk than actively managed equity funds. Trackers may vary in their investment return, even when they are based on the same index, due to differences in both the fee structure and the tracking method.

Multi-manager funds have a strategy of maximising diversification. The two main types are a *fund of funds*, where a manager invests in a variety of other investment funds, and a *manager-of-managers* scheme, where a number of fund managers are each given part of the fund to invest in the stock market, and which costs less because it instructs managers rather than investing in an existing fund. In either case, the fund's performance depends on the skill of the stock selectors.

Investment companies

The investment company is a quoted company that invests in other companies' shares. It pools money from investors but, unlike an investment fund, it is not categorised as a collective investment scheme as defined by the Financial Services Authority (FSA). It may issue different types of shares and own subsidiaries.

Unlike an investment fund, which expands and contracts in size according to demand, the investment company is a closed-ended fund, which means that it has a fixed number of shares in issue at any one time. For every buyer of an investment company share, there must be a seller. The trust can issue new shares, subject to shareholder approval, and it can keep its assets in cash.

There are about 420 investment companies with assets of around £87 billion at 28 February 2007, made up of 270 conventional companies, with total assets of £79 billion, 110 venture capital trusts, with total assets of £2.5 billion and 40 split capital investment companies with total assets of £5.3 billion.

The share price of an investment company fluctuates with supply and demand and market movement, and according to the value of the net assets, which are total assets less total liabilities. On balance, investment companies are slightly riskier than investment funds because their discount or premium to net assets may vary and they are usually geared, although to varying levels. Unless the fund management is considered exceptional, the share price will tend to trade at a discount to net asset value.

Investment companies are less well known than their younger, open-ended cousins, but have a more adventurous image, and their unique characteristics and flexibility, including the closed structure and freedom to gear up (borrow), make them sometimes very attractive. They make up at least 10 per cent of the FTSE 250 index, and invest significantly in, among other areas, unquoted stocks, and so provide money for financing. They are owned half by institutions and half by private investors.

Investors in an investment company who want to make a complaint may not have the same access to the Financial Ombudsman Service as investors in an investment fund. But they do have access if the company was purchased through a manager-sponsored wrapper product such as a savings scheme, pension or individual savings account (ISA), or through a financial adviser, in which case there is also access to the Financial Services Compensation Scheme (see Chapter 30).

Investment companies can be self-managed, but in most cases the company employs a manager, who is answerable to the trust's board of directors. The companies vary by the type of stocks in which they invest. Some aim to generate high income while others go for capital gain, or a combination of both. Some invest in large blue chip companies and others in the riskier alternative of smaller companies. Also contributing to the risk profile is the geographical location; trusts that invest in emerging markets are more speculative than those that stick to Western Europe.

Any gains made by an investment company on shares are not subject to capital gains tax, but investors may be liable if they should sell the trust, subject to their annual personal allowance, unless it is sheltered within an ISA, personal equity plan or personal pension. This tax sheltering is the same as for OEICs and unit trusts, but not for closed ended investment companies that are not investment trusts, being registered overseas as in Jersey or Guernsey.

The trust distributes dividends after a 10 per cent income tax deduction but lower and basic rate taxpayers have no further tax liability. Higher rate taxpayers will suffer an effective tax rate of 22.5 per cent.

Investment companies, unlike investment funds, do not have trustees or depositaries. Instead, they have an independent board of directors to oversee the management of the investment company. In extreme cases, the board might choose to take the management contract elsewhere. Investment companies have the flexibility to do this because they are companies in their own right.

Most investment companies are accessible to investors through monthly savings schemes, for which the managers may reduce or waive dealing costs. They are sometimes promoted as a flexible way of investing, enabling investors to stop and restart contributions without penalty. Advertising of investment companies is allowed only in the case of wrapper products, and investors gain from the cost savings. But there will be a stockbroker's commission on trades, and buyers must pay stamp duty.

Many investment companies have no initial charge, unlike investment funds, and the annual management fee tends to be lower although this can depend on the sector. The spread is usually narrower than on investment funds, although it can be wider, depending on the number of market makers.

Inclusive of all fees to the investor, investment companies, in common with investment funds, often fail to beat the market average. Because of gearing, the trusts outperform in rising markets and underperform when markets decline.

Split capital investment trust

The split capital investment trust is a type of investment trust that has more than one class of share capital. Usually, one type of share is for income and receives all the income generated by the trust, and the other is for capital gain. The trust has a fixed lifespan, perhaps seven years, as compared with the unlimited life of other investment companies. At the end of its life, its remaining assets are distributed among shareholders.

In the bear market from March 2000, split capital investment trusts saw their share prices plunge. When one fund collapsed in value, others followed because a number were linked by cross-share holdings and the funds had high levels of debt. By December 2003, 26 of about 95 split capital investment trusts were either in liquidation or had suspended dealing. The FSA conducted its largest ever investigation into the split capital trust sector.

On 24 December 2004, the FSA agreed a final £194 million negotiated settlement with 18 out of 22 firms under investigation, with no admission on their part. It was perceived as a climbdown from the £350 million that the FSA had originally demanded, although two firms had declined to participate.

Lawyers close to the fund managers involved said that the FSA had never had much of a case but had relied on its authority as a regulator to steamroller firms into a settlement. Public confidence in the split capital sector was damaged, although some conservatively run split cap funds have operated in an acceptable way, even throughout the crisis. The split cap sector declined from 123 splits with a total value of £14.1 billion in December 2001 to 45 splits valued at £5.7 billion by the end of November 2006.

In the aftermath of the scandal, the Treasury consulted on whether investment companies should be regulated as products by the FSA. It decided not to go down this route, much to the industry's relief. The Treasury took the view that the Listing Rules were an appropriate mechanism for split caps, and the FSA had already tightened them in response to the split caps fiasco. The Association of Investment Companies (AIC) introduced a code of corporate governance.

When in June 2007 the FSA decided to scrap a recently introduced relaxed regime for overseas investment companies listing in London (see Chapter 6), the AIC applauded the outcome, for which it had lobbied. The regime did not include such protection as cross-shareholding bans introduced after the split capital investment trust scandal, and an independent board of directors.

Venture capital trusts

Venture capital trusts (VCTs) are quoted companies that invest in small growth companies and aim to make capital gains for investors. They have been described as a form of investment trust. There is very little trading in the shares and market makers may offer a wide spread.

The VCT manager has three years to choose companies in which to invest and may meanwhile put money in cash, bonds or funds. The VCT must hold at least 70 per cent of its investments in qualifying unquoted companies trading in the UK. The balance can be invested elsewhere, including in gilts or large company shares.

From 6 April 2007, VCTs or enterprise investment schemes (EIS) have been given six months from the point of a sale of a holding to reinvest the cash. This is to help funds to comply with the VCT rule that at least 70 per cent of assets are invested in qualifying holdings at all times. But qualifying companies cannot raise more than £2 million from VCTs or EISs in any 12-month period.

The annual charges on a VCT tend to be higher than for conventional investment companies, partly because the funds are small and lack economies of scale but also because of the heavy research that some VCT managers carry out into sometimes small, not very transparent companies. The least risky VCTs are large, do not invest in too many start-ups, have relatively low charges, and have experienced management, according to industry sources. Investors may spread the risk by investing in more than one trust.

The TER (see the box earlier in this chapter) is sometimes capped for VCTs at 3.5 per cent but this is higher than the typical TER of 1.5 or 2 per cent for a conventional managed fund or investment company.

The annualised return over five years for VCTs launched in the 2001–02 tax year, without taking account of the upfront income tax relief, averages low single digits. In 2006, the Chancellor cut income tax relief to 30 per cent from 40 per cent, and investment into VCTs plummeted from £750 million in the 2005/06 tax year.

Tax relief is available on investment in new VCT ordinary shares to a maximum of £200,000. There is no longer capital gains tax deferral on investment. But if you have held your VCT shares for at least five years, your future gains (and losses) are exempt from capital gains tax and your future dividends received are exempt from income tax.

Under recently introduced rules, new VCTs can only invest in companies with gross assets of less than £7 million, down from the previous ceiling of £15 million. This reduces the range of investments open to managers of AIM funds.

The VCT plans an exit from its investments through a stock market listing or a takeover. If the company achieves a London Stock Exchange (LSE) listing, it may remain a VCT investment for five years. Should the VCT be taken over, its investors will be entitled to a cut of the payment.

VCTs may be bought directly, or though a stockbroker or financial adviser. The range of buyers has broadened beyond high net-worth investors, sophisticated investors and corporates. There are specialist VCTs and generalist VCTs, involving listed and unlisted companies.

Independent financial advisers may be keen to sell VCTs because of the high commission structure, typically 5 to 7 per cent, and have been known to highlight the tax break. The FSA has in the past expressed concerns that the risks are not being explained adequately.

Real estate investment trusts

A real estate investment trust (REIT) is a quoted company that conducts a property rental business. It does not pay corporation tax on rental income or capital gains tax from the rental business, and must distribute most of its earnings to shareholders.

The REIT was created in the United States in 1960. It has since been popular in Australia, Japan, Hong Kong, France and the Netherlands.

The UK regime for REITs started in January 2007. The attraction of the REIT for private investors is that it enables diversified property investment through a tradable investment asset.

Exchange-traded funds

An exchange-traded fund (ETF) combines structural elements of a unit trust and an investment trust. You can buy your ETF on margin, and settle using the underlying shares instead of cash. Unlike with a unit trust, there are no set-up charges, and anybody completing a trade will immediately know at what price. The first ETF in the UK was launched in April 2000, and was called the iFTSE 100. The product had already existed for seven years in the United States.

The ETF trades like an ordinary share on the LSE. Each unit tracks the movement of an entire index or sector, which provides the full benefits of diversification through a single instrument. There are ETFs based on both equity and fixed-income indices. An ETF usually pays a dividend, and its price tends to be at a small discount to net assets. The price can change at any time during stock market opening hours.

Like a unit trust, the ETF is open-ended, and can issue an unlimited number of units to meet demand. Because it is based offshore, there is no stamp duty on units purchased. You can technically sell it short, but there have sometimes been problems with borrowing stock to deliver.

There is a management charge on an ETF, typically paid out of the fund's income, which is often low, given that this is an index-tracking fund.

Between 1997 and 2007, global ETF assets under management grew from US $8.2 billion to over US $688.8 billion, according to June 2007 research by Deborah Fuhr, a managing director at Morgan Stanley Institutional Equity.

Hedge funds

A hedge fund is usually a specialist type of pooled investment that is free to invest in all financial instruments or markets, including high-risk instruments, and may employ a range of investment strategies involving the use of gearing (borrowings) and shorting (selling securities it does not have to profit from a falling market). It may be either an entrepreneurial start-up operation or part of a larger group. The hedge fund is often structured as a limited partnership, and it has unregulated status, but its investments will not be promoted to the general public.

Many hedge funds are registered in the Cayman Islands where there is lighter regulation, but some funds prefer registration in Dublin or Luxembourg for the European exposure. Some French banks, for instance, will register hedge funds in Dublin because they know that French investors want a regulated jurisdiction.

The fund may be managed elsewhere. In Europe, funds are typically managed from London because of the commercial clout that derives from being regulated by the FSA. London is the largest hedge fund management centre in Europe, and second in size only to the United States.

A hedge fund can fail as well as succeed, and it may be on a spectacular scale. Long Term Capital Management (LTCM) demonstrated the point with its high-profile failure in 1998. It was a hedge fund headed by John Meriwether, who had previously run the bond trading operations of Salomon Brothers. The fund was highly geared and used derivatives, taking positions in bonds. The mathematical model on which the fund manager relied failed to take into account the flight to liquidity in the debt markets after Russia defaulted on its sovereign debt in August and September 1998.

LTCM had theoretical liabilities because of its high gearing, on one estimate as high as US$1.25 trillion, and the Federal Reserve Bank intervened to persuade banks to provide extra support to the fund and so prevent a disruption in the financial markets. Since the LTCM collapse, the industry has become a lot more cautious. There has been less rigid following of mathematical models.

Hedge funds bring liquidity to the market, but the risks on individual funds remain. In September 2006, Amaranth Advisors, a US hedge fund, saw its losses reach about US$6 billion (£3.2 billion), which was 65 per cent of its assets at the start of the month. Amaranth had invested most of its funds on trades that bet natural gas prices would continue a rising trend, but they fell because of high reserves, coupled with a predicted mild winter and a respite from hurricanes.

Amaranth has paid back at least 65 pence in the pound to its investors and the funds that bought Amaranth's positions all made good profits, so although the newspaper headlines had looked bad, the reality is much more modest. The overall impact on the market was relatively insignificant, said Dan Waters, asset manager sector leader and director of retail policy at the FSA, speaking at an October 2006 Hong Kong conference.

The FSA does not seek to authorise or regulate the funds themselves, which are outside its jurisdiction. It aims to mitigate hedge fund risk through its authority over hedge fund managers and the prime brokers, which provide hedge funds with settlement, custody and reporting services.

In October 2005, the FSA set up a centre of hedge fund expertise, with supervisors in regular contact with 31 of the largest hedge fund managers, accounting for 50 per cent of the assets managed. There is baseline monitoring of lower impact firms and thematic supervision.

In mid-2007, 13 large hedge funds were looking at possibilities for a code of practice for the industry. This was a response to political pressure from Germany and elsewhere to impose greater disclosure requirements on the industry.

Hedge funds remain one of the City's greatest growth stories, providing liquidity and making the financial system more efficient. They have shown that they can preserve investors' capital and achieve a real return, which is more than conventional equities investment has achieved across a span of recent years.

About 6 per cent of UK pension funds now invest in hedge funds, compared with 9 per cent in continental Europe and Ireland, according to an April 2007 survey of over 650 European pension funds by Mercer Investment Consulting.

Funds of funds, which invest in a variety of hedge funds, provide diversification and possibly reduced risk, but not the same opportunities for out-performance. The FSA is keen on allowing them to be sold into the retail market. See Chapter 18 for details of hedge fund investment strategies.

20

Analysts and research

Introduction

Analysts have a highly paid and often influential job. In this chapter we will look at how they operate, and some of the conflicts they have faced, as well as briefly at strategists and economists.

The analyst

Fundamental analysis

The analyst focuses on the dynamics of particular markets and makes trading and investment recommendations. He or she builds up an eclectic mix of analytical tools combined with subconscious thinking. The underlying aim is to understand the discount rate curve, which represents the market's expectations for interest rates projected into the future. This curve determines the average annual return, or yield, on bonds and other financial instruments. The analyst attempts to make an informed guess as to how it will behave. The prices of all financial instruments are strongly influenced by this unseen curve and all financial instruments trade around it, like gravity.

Pure expectation theory has it that the discount curve at the front end is an expression of projected rates from the Bank of England. The theory of market segmentation explains the longer end of the curve as reflecting interest rates focused on particular maturities. Such theories are never the full truth.

The sell-side analysts who focus on the stock market are the ones most likely to come to public attention, through media exposure. They work for the stockbrokers and the investment banks, and issue research that is widely disseminated. The buy-side analysts work for large institutional investors and tend to have a broader role, with less focus on individual stocks or sectors. Their research will be internally disseminated.

In the 1970s, the sell-side analysts were backroom boys in the stockbroking community. They were better educated than their colleagues on the sales desk but less well remunerated. They were producing learned research and statistics and did not have to get their hands dirty selling shares to clients. Subsequently, with market deregulation, banks started acquiring stockbrokers, and analysts started playing a participating role in the marketing of new issues and sales of stocks while continuing their focus on research, which meant longer working hours. The work of analysts today is of value for various banking activities, including investment banking, trading and sales. An analyst typically follows six or seven large companies in a sector and backs up the salespeople with his or her specialist research.

Analysts often understand the specifics of the businesses covered, but less well than they should. Anecdotal evidence suggests that less than a quarter of them are qualified accountants. But they will have to consider company reports and try to forecast the future of a company. They indulge in informed guesswork that puts them, some would say, only a few steps ahead of tarot card readers. Even if they have worked in the industry they cover, their detailed knowledge soon becomes outdated, and may not be equally applicable to every company. Analysts are outsiders looking in.

The analyst channels efforts into forecasting the ratios valued most in the City such as earnings per share, the P/E ratio and discounted cash flow calculations (see Chapter 5). A company's basic figures may be culled from annual or half-year results. All listed companies in the EU have used International Financial Reporting Standards (IFRS) (see Chapter 26) in their accounts since 1 January 2005, and this harmonisation enables comparability across Europe.

Even in today's regulatory climate, which is sensitive to bias and conflicts of interests, the hidden agenda remains that sell-side analysts make *buy*, rather than *hold* or *sell*, recommendations on most stocks because they are scared of upsetting the underlying companies, some of which may be, or become, clients of their employer's lucrative investment banking division.

If listed companies give analysts a selective briefing or lead, they could be in breach of the part of the Listing Rules that deals with price-sensitive information and selective disclosure. The Listing Rules issued by the UK Listing Authority, part of the Financial Services Authority (FSA), require price-sensitive information to be announced to the market without delay. To stick to the rules, companies dole out the same bland information to analysts. Sell-side analysts who stumble on new information, which is what fund managers really want to hear, may have problems communicating it to their clients. Not all communication is official and analysts give big clients the best service they can.

Institutional investors know how to read between the lines, and perhaps glean from a telephone conversation with an analyst something extra. In keeping with this environment, fund managers rate analysts on quality of research as well as on forecasting record. But experience shows that an analyst who consistently makes ludicrous forecasts may not be taken seriously by salespeople within the analyst's bank.

The danger is that an analyst's report intended for the professionals may get into the hands of private investors, who may make the mistake of taking it too literally. Another danger is that, by this stage, it will probably be out of date. Research notes can need updating within hours or even minutes.

The Spitzer impact

The Spitzer settlement of April 2003 in the United States arose because of the conflict of interests between research recommendations and investment banking activity from within the same firm. New York Attorney General Elliot Spitzer found that Henry Blodget, a Merrill Lynch internet company analyst, had in private e-mails disparaged an internet stock that he was recommending to clients. Spitzer found other instances of biased recommendations across the industry.

Ten leading global investment banks settled the matter with the Securities & Exchange Commission, the New York Stock Exchange, the National Association of Securities Dealers and with Spitzer. As part of the redress, the banks agreed to amend their practices. They would physically separate research and investment banking departments to prevent the passing of information. Senior management would decide the research department's budget without input from investment banking. Research analysts could no longer be compensated in a way that reflected investment banking revenues. Investment banking was to have no part in decisions on company coverage, and analysts were prohibited from participating in new business pitches and roadshows.

The firms had to have firewalls that restricted interaction between research and investment banking. They would provide independent research to ensure that individual investors had access to objective investment advice. Each firm was to make its analysts' historical ratings and target forecasts publicly available. The firms entered into a voluntary agreement to restrict 'spinning' – the allocation of securities in hot initial public offerings (IPOs) to certain company executives and directors.

The scandal focused attention on a phenomenon that was hardly new. The cosy cooperation between research teams and corporate finance has worked in bull markets, but there is a tendency for it to be exposed when markets suffer a downturn. There is some feeling that the Spitzer settlement was politically motivated, and did not address the heart of the problem because it allowed banks to retain their business model. Understandably, ex-investment bankers, academics and independent commentators felt able to voice criticisms publicly more than those who held current positions in investment banking.

However it was criticised, the Spitzer settlement has set an international agenda. On both sides of the Atlantic, investment banks and brokers have been forced to reorganise their working arrangements to ensure greater segregation between analysts and corporate financiers. In early 2004, the FSA issued guidelines requiring those firms that held out investment research as objective to establish a policy for managing conflicts of interest. Significant in these are Chinese walls, which create a not always physical divide between analysts and investment banking. In mid-2004, the FSA introduced two new rules in which it narrowed the circumstances in which firms could knowingly deal ahead of published investment research, and required them to make it clear to clients whether the research was impartial.

Technical analysis

Technical analysts may work independently or for large financial institutions and are far fewer than their fundamental counterparts. They focus on price movements and make forecasts. Technical analysis has a greater serious following in foreign exchange and commodities than in equities.

The aim of technical analysis is to forecast future price and index movements based on past patterns in the charts. It may or may not be accompanied by fundamental analysis, which focuses on company fundamentals and the results.

The cornerstone of technical analysis is trend theory, which is rooted in the idea of crowd psychology. If the share price is rising, everyone tries to jump on the bandwagon, establishing an up trend. On the same principle, panic selling can start a down trend. Technical analysts believe that the trend will stay in force until it is unequivocally broken.

Trend theory originated with Dow Theory, which financial journalist Charles Dow started developing in the late 19th century after he noticed that stocks tended to rise or fall together. Dow Theory says that the share price reflects *everything* that is known about a stock and that there are three trends in the stock market – primary, secondary and tertiary – and they may all be operating simultaneously. Volume counts but is a secondary consideration, the theory says. Dow historians claim that the theory has an impressive track record. Critics say it is out of date and its signals come too late.

Chart patterns are based around trend theory and incorporate the concepts of support and resistance. Resistance is the high point on a chart where investors will not buy further and so the price has stopped rising and sellers have emerged. The *support* level is where investors have stopped selling. The more a support or resistance line is tested, the more effective it is considered.

The rectangle is a common continuation pattern. It is a pricing range where the price swings up to a resistance line, then down to a support line until breakout. The triangle is another continuation pattern. It consists of two lines that converge at an apex, one representing resistance and the other support. The more often the share price touches these lines, the more reliable the pattern.

The flag is another continuation pattern. It forms in a strong trend, typically in less than three weeks, and technicians consider it a reliable continuation pattern. It is a flag-like consolidation in the share price, formed on declining volume, followed by a sharp move like a flagpole.

The gap takes the form of a physical break in share price movement and is often a continuation pattern. The less frequently the gap arises, the more significant it is, particularly on a heavily traded stock. If trading volume rises with the gap, it also strengthens the message.

The head and shoulders is the best-known reversal pattern and is a bearish signal. The share price moves up and reverts to form the first shoulder, which is a peak in the trend. A sharp reaction will follow, and the share price dips to form a trough. It will then rise to a higher peak, which becomes the head, and will drop back again to form a second trough. The share price will rise once more, but can only form another shoulder before falling down and breaking the *support* level, which is known as the neckline.

The double top is another reversal pattern and it develops usually over some months. The share price rises and falls back, then returns to its old peak, or close to it, and reverts.

Every pattern shows how the dynamics of supply and demand play out. When either buyers or sellers get the upper hand, the line breaks out of the pattern. On an upside movement, trading volume tends to rise. If a breakout happens, technicians measure the full depth of the preceding pattern and project it as a minimum *from* the point of breakout. This is the target length of movement projected. Some technical analysts use the patterns to time trades and predict future price movements, while others are cynical.

After analysing price and volume and related trends, the analyst may use indicators that focus on, among other things, whether the market is overbought or oversold, its relative performance and its rate of change. Many indicators are based around the moving average, which shows changes in the average share price over a given period. Others are based around volume. Technicians use cycles, which are based on regularly recurring price patterns within a specified period, to measure time.

Every technical analyst has favoured techniques, and some believe the simplest work best. However, the variations are limited only by the imagination of traders and analysts and, a cynic would say, of software manufacturers. The types of charts in use vary. Short-term traders are increasingly drawn to Japanese candlesticks, which are an exotic alternative to conventional bar charts. For some, a line chart with its great detail may reassure, but others prefer to cut out the *noise* of intra-day share price movement and use a point and figure chart. Computer software enables the technical analyst to switch from one chart type to another.

Technical analysis caters also for those who shun simplicity. William D Gann was a technician with a unique, highly mathematical form of technical analysis linking price and time proportionately, with lashings of special numbers and astrological inferences. Courses in Gann theory tend not to come cheap.

Elliott Wave Theory is another tough nut to crack. It finds that the market always rises in five waves and falls in three, and so assumes a perpetual long-term bull market. The proportional relationship of the waves is linked to Fibonacci numbers, which have a mathematical relationship claimed to be deep-rooted in nature.

Many equities professionals in the City regard technical analysis as a somewhat fringe activity, but others take it more seriously. Some say it should be one tool for investors, but not the only one. Unusually for a fund manager, Anthony Bolton, who runs Fidelity's Special Situations fund, makes significant use of technical analysis.

Others

The economist has the job of generating value-added research on the functioning of the economy, and will seek to understand why the Central Bank behaves as it does. The strategist is a broadly based type of analyst who sits between the analyst and the economist, and who makes broad calls on a number of asset classes and markets.

All three will focus on statistics that throw light on, among other things, trends in inflation, interest rates and currency movements. They understand that statistics are approximate but require them to have been reliably sourced from a genuinely random sample, taking into account any unusual factors. Statistics from some countries may not be of the same kind (or quality) as from the UK.

The numbers may be presented in fractionalised detail but this does not mean precision. Statistics such as Gross Domestic Output, a measure of a country's economic output, are frequently revised, and are a guide. A one-off figure could be a temporary blip and figures should be compared over a period. What counts is the trend. A rising Gross Domestic Product (GDP) in a strong economy gives rise to inflation fears. If GDP rises by more than 3 per cent in each of four quarters in succession, the Bank of England will probably raise interest rates to restrain it.

Statistics, like financial ratios, may sometimes be calculated in more than one way. Unemployment is a good example. Economists consider more than one figure at once to get the broad picture.

How far you can use macroeconomic statistics and events for forecasting the future is open to question. A recent government project focused on neural networks posed the question: what happens when you shoot a US president? It has happened three times in the last century, including once fatally, and every time the reaction was different.

The professional forecasters sometimes wisecrack that their most recent forecast is their best one. Their forecasts may be revised *ad infinitum* and, even if they are often wrong, may provide a thought-provoking commentary on the market.

21

Financial communications

Introduction

Public relations and investor relations specialists, investors and journalists are linked into chain flows of corporate news and information. It is on this basis that shares are often traded. In this chapter, we will examine how the communications process works.

Public relations

Public relations (PR) agencies build the image of quoted companies to financial journalists and, in so far as they will listen, analysts. In choosing a PR agency, companies look for a track record, knowledge of the sector and proven delivery of results. In the event of a crisis, the company wants minimum impact on the share price. If it gets communication right, there could be a blip rather than a potential disaster.

Companies assess the impact of PR on the business, and not just the number of press cuttings. They use sophisticated measurement techniques. One insurance company, for example, knows it has its communication right when it delivers good results without provoking too many telephone calls from customers demanding a reduction in premiums on their policies.

Some companies will hire an agency on a retainer as a failsafe. For most of the year the agency will tick away at a maintenance level. But if a crisis arises, it will seek to protect the company's public image. At 5.00 pm in the evening, it will be ready to parachute a team in to help its client.

The agencies will represent companies during a takeover period, or for an IPO (see Chapters 6 and 7). The management of a company's communications during an IPO is best handled on a timetable, providing a drip of information in the market to colour perception, Matthew Hooper, managing partner of Shared Value, told a Moscow conference in March 2006. He said that investors looked for properly and accurately delivered news flow and that the press could eliminate speculation while remaining within legal reporting parameters.

Company results are normally published in March and September (based on a 31 December year end) and the PR agencies will have a major role to play in their distribution. The agencies have a billing structure that takes into account all time spent on client work and all expenses.

The skill of professional PR is to stay invisible, not to snatch the glory of the client, and to keep concealed how far the agency controls the agenda of the journalists. Signs of a PR agency's unseen hand are evident on a daily basis in the press. A handful of agencies are linked to all the main activity in the City, although there are rich pickings for other agencies in less high-profile businesses.

The large companies may have their own corporate affairs departments. These can be well informed and staffed by people who have the ear of the directors. But some in-house operations, not so well backed internally, 'just don't get it', according to industry sources.

Over time journalists have become more dependent on PR executives, finding them more accessible and more willing to explain basics than company executives. The relationship between journalists and PR could be described as symbiotic. Delve behind the headlines in the business or other financial press, and it is quite likely that the PR executive or PR agent had something to do with the placement of the story.

In the past, some PR agents have leaked price-sensitive information to the press with impunity. But regulations have tightened up and, under the market abuse regime, employees of PR agencies who do this may now be subject to civil or criminal action. From about mid-2005 industry fears put a kybosh on the 'Friday night drop', when PR agents would queue to give Sunday newspaper journalists exclusive stories of quoted companies. There is a feeling that the Sunday papers are now getting fewer scoops. In addition, the Takeover Panel has been known to censure PR agents for breaking the rules.

Black PR, where competing companies use the media to blacken each other's reputation, is a familiar tactic. On 13 June 2007, the *Financial Times* described how Kostyantyn Zhevago, owner of Ukrainian iron ore exporter Ferrexpo, which was to be listed on the London Stock Exchange two days later, had been wrongly accused in media reports of causing a local electricity company owner's death by shouting at him during a business meeting. Zhevago said that the media reports were black PR and that he had been cleared of any suspicion, the newspaper reported.

Investor relations

Investor relations (IR) covers the ways a quoted company liaises with present and prospective investors. Through IR, the company tries to gain a fair valuation for its shares to keep investors loyal and the shares liquid. Further important aspects of the role are to keep the market informed of price-sensitive information without selective disclosures and to provide capital market feedback to the board for its decision making.

In general, the in-house IR team sits close to the finance department and talks to analysts and investors. The corporate communications team on the other hand sits close to the chief executive, and deals mainly with the press. An in-house IR officer (IRO) will be talking to and having direct contact with both analysts and investors for much of the time, acting as a gateway between this audience group and the company. 'Day to day, the IRO will be updating analysts on their spreadsheets or helping investors to understand the company better, and will give strategic feedback to the company,' says Claire Fargeot, IR director at Buchanan Communications.

The IRO may have some contact with certain journalists too, who require a deeper understanding of certain aspects. For example, an IR officer will take many calls from investors and analysts in relation to a company's half-year results release, but also perhaps from some publications.

'Most journalists do not have the time or patience to battle through the finer points on a half year release – unless of course the company has been part of some media issue and the journalists want to get to the bottom of the story,' says Fargeot. 'The IR officer will be answering questions like "Why have you made such a provision for the pension deficit?"'

The IR business has as much to do with private as with institutional investors. 'The only decider is bang for buck and private investors tend to be smaller investors so they unfortunately also tend to get marginalised,' Fargeot says, noting, however, that the treatment of retail customers varies significantly between companies.

New requirements for all companies on the Alternative Investment Market to have a website with certain investor-dedicated information on it may help private investors, Fargeot says. 'But they will not reach Aunt Agatha in the country who does not have access to a computer.'

The real value of IR is downside limitation, as at a time of a hostile takeover bid, and corporate reputation protection, Fargeot says. If a company is performing well with a solid strategy, interesting investment proposition and appreciated management team, the share price should do well and reflect all these positive elements. IR adds value when all these positive things are in place but the share price does not perform as expected, according to Fargeot.

IR adds even more value when there is bad news to be disseminated or a capital markets crisis of confidence in the stock. The IR officer reinforces the company's relationships with a loyal base of investors or seeks out new investors to come on board and support the share price. IR can be useful in good times but it is much less visible, and the measurement metrics can be as unscientific as counting how many investors turned up for a given shareholder meeting.

Companies tend to outsource IR when they are either resource restrained or in trouble, according to Fargeot. Most financial directors do a large amount of IR work, and smaller companies in particular may have no extra resource to help in this area so they buy in the support they need, she notes.

Large companies buy in IR services when they want some independent feedback or to provide services that they are not currently receiving from their corporate broker. 'The company gets unbiased feedback from an IR agency, while the corporate broker will tend to tell the company only what it wants to hear,' Fargeot says.

Some companies spend nothing on IR except the management team's time and the publication of the annual report and accounts. Some spend £100,000 or more on the annual report alone. International companies may have teams of six to 12 IR people dotted around the globe but some companies have only a time-stretched financial director to handle all the IR.

As the legislative burden on companies is growing, so is the responsibility of the IR officers and their role as the interface between the company and the investing marketplace. Not all companies take IR as seriously as they should, and even some FTSE 100 companies fail to pay attention to areas that IR feedback suggests is important for investors and analysts.

'Most shareholders have no issue with voicing concerns if a company's IR activities are not hitting the mark, and IROs are now being sacked for poor performance just like CEOs that have been forced to resign when a company has severely underperformed,' Fargeot says. So far the IRO, like the public relations executive, is not regulated by the Financial Services Authority (FSA), but some believe that, in both cases, it is only a matter of time. Buchanan Communications makes more information about IR available on its website, with some interesting downloads, at www.buchanan.uk.com.

Corporate information flow

In April 2002, the FSA ended the monopoly of the London Stock Exchange Regulatory News Service (RNS) in disseminating UK company announcements and opened the market to others. The RNS is one of several primary information providers (PIPs) which the FSA has approved to disseminate regulatory information to the market. The PIP will send out company announcements through secondary information providers (SIPs) such as Reuters and Bloomberg.

If the news comes on a Saturday, it must still be disclosed, via press and news wires. At any meeting, however public, at which inside information is let out, there must be a prior or immediate announcement to ensure that the public has the information. The listed company must make a judgment on what information needs to be disclosed and when.

Companies must disclose related-party transactions, as by directors, and significant transactions, both of which require shareholder approval. To keep the market informed about the likely end-of-year results and to avoid a false market, companies may put out announcements on a more regular basis than is strictly required. The information disclosed should be complete.

Companies may delay disclosure of inside information if it is kept confidential and the non-disclosure does not mislead the market. This may be acceptable in negotiating mergers and acquisitions, where premature disclosure can scare away a party and prevent a deal from happening.

Companies send out releases providing news via a PIP, as a conventional way to inform the market. They may also send releases directly to investors, analysts and journalists, and perhaps publish them on their website simultaneously.

Journalists

A good story is said to be one that somebody does not want you to print. But financial journalists, particularly on daily newspapers, often have little time to investigate and probe. Journalists may rely heavily on PR input, including provision of news releases and, if they are lucky, free press trips to interesting places and events. The adage that you cannot bribe the British journalist may be true, but financial institutions know they can sometimes soften him or her up.

Journalists take the basic information in a news release and any information they can muster, often directly from PR people, to build their own piece. Some will use chunks of it verbatim. The news release may be slanted. If a company's sales are up but its profits are down, the press release may emphasise the first statistic. If net profits are down but pre-tax profits are up, the press release may focus on the latter.

Journalists tend to be suspicious of PR agencies but not all will see through the angle. Some are arts graduates without any specialist business education, and may be hampered by a lack of in-depth understanding of economics, finance and company accounting. Others, particularly on national newspapers, know their subject well and are highly respected for their professionalism.

Part of this professionalism may involve tapping sources who peddle only one side of the story and running with it in the newspaper, although later it may become clear that this is only half the story and that the source had an ulterior motive for providing the story. Andreas Whittam Smith, founder of the *Independent*, wrote in 1999: 'The iron law is that if information is to pass, both parties, not just the journalist, require a reward.'

The most superficial news but also the fastest is published by the news agencies, which are wholesalers of news. Such real-time financial news reporting is exciting work, but the demands on journalists are gruelling. They must obtain quotes quickly from experts, and rework source material to present their news reports. The agencies provide news on a collective basis. A journalist who is by-lined may have lifted whole paragraphs from stories of other journalists published earlier by the agency.

The journalists who work in some of these institutions are often young, bright and enthusiastic, but ignorant about markets. Many of them burn out after a few years and move on, sometimes into other trades and professions.

The other end of the spectrum is investigative journalism. The type of journalist who does this work is a rare breed, who probes rather than accepts, takes pride in uncovering scandals, and is not afraid to make enemies. Such journalists tend to be loners and may work as freelancers.

Even the best journalism has limitations. The press will highlight any perceived infringement or corporate failure and this will instil an 'apparent desire to place the blame on an individual or individuals', disguising the broader culpability of the organisation, according to risk management research by Dr Lynne Drennan at Glasgow Caledonian University.

Drennan has observed the process in the press treatment of Jeff Skilling as chief executive of Enron when the US energy company was hit by scandals in 2001, of Robert Maxwell, chairman and chief executive of Mirror Group Newspapers when his pension theft hit the press, and of Nick Leeson, the trader on the Singapore Monetary Exchange for Barings Bank.

A good story is everything. Martin Fridson, a managing director at Merrill Lynch, said in his book *Investment Illusions* that reporters had a tendency to approach not necessarily the best authorities but those who could provide colourful quotes.

But if the press is not perfect, it is for private investors the least slanted source of City information, former deputy City editor of the *Daily Mail* Michael Walters has said. The press has far more impartiality than the press in less developed countries. In some ex-Soviet block countries, it is a criminal offence to criticise the government in the media and, as the Moscow experience has all too often testified, retribution can kill.

How far the press reflects City opinion in a rising or falling market, and how far it dictates perceptions, is a matter of debate. The FSA has said that journalistic coverage of how it regulates the City can have significant impact.

Tipsters

The tip sheets and some financial websites often pride themselves as being contrarian, but that can translate into off the rails. At the height of the pre-March 2000 bull market, one financial website ran an online portfolio in which one of the main criteria for stock selection was that the conventional financial press had found the company valued too highly. The website kept saying overpriced but popular stocks would soar higher. This approach turned out to be a disaster.

Individual share tipsters also make such mistakes and they have an influence not always proportionate to their track record. They may lift their tips from secondary sources, rewriting them in their own words, combining material from several sources or modifying a conclusion to make the whole thing appear original. The writer who is not paid according to the number of recommendations will eventually turn out well. A track record can be glossed over, but the pages of the tip sheet must always be filled.

If the tipster wants to keep his or her reputation intact, it may pay not to be associated with one website or newsletter for too long. This way, his or her individual tipping record may never come properly under scrutiny. Many tipsters operate anonymously.

Others try to make their name. They may boast City experience but this does not in itself rubber-stamp their investment advice. The old adage applies, if they know so much about stock-picking, why are they not investing their own money for a living?

Showmanship is another tactic of the tipsters, and one of the all-time masters was US tipster Joseph Granville who, in his heyday, spoke to investors with his chimpanzee and a few bikini-clad models in tow. He would wear blinking bow ties and play the piano or dress up as a chicken. He once dropped his trousers to read stock quotes on his shorts. He has been known to dress like Moses and deliver the '10 commandments' of investing, and has purportedly walked on water.

When a small company tip is given prominence in a popular newspaper, the market makers increase the price. Other tipsters get wind of this and steal the idea. It is a spiral that can send up the share price all too briefly. Another big source of share tips is the internet bulletin boards. They are notoriously unreliable. Many who post on the internet have an ulterior motive. Their output, perhaps under several aliases, may slip untruths amidst a plethora of facts. Recently, the chief executive of a company criticised anonymously on the message boards tracked down the writer and sued him, and that led to a settlement. But writers who contribute to the bulletin boards from internet cafés have avoided identification.

Many tipsters have never invested directly in shares in their lives, and this tells its story. In today's regulatory environment, it is much harder for the tipster to hold shares in the company that he or she tips, but it happens. If the tipster buys through nominee holdings, or through a friend, in small amounts, it can be hard to detect.

In a landmark case, *Daily Mirror* journalists Anil Bhoyrul and James Hipwell in 1999 and 2000 made profits from buying shares before tipping them in the 'City Slickers' column of their newspaper and subsequently selling them into the price rise. In 2000, the Press Complaints Commission (PCC) ruled on the case. The two journalists were dismissed for gross misconduct, including breaches of the parts of the PCC's Code of Practice applicable to financial journalists. The PCC exonerated Piers Morgan, then editor, from any breach of the Code, but found fault with how journalists had been allowed to operate.

The PCC has since issued editors with guidelines to enhance the code of practice and has described the City Slickers case as a victory for self-regulation. In July 2005, the Treasury acknowledged that the PCC should be the competent authority for dealing with journalists making investment recommendations.

However, the Slickers were also to face a criminal prosecution from the Department of Trade and Industry (DTI). In January 2000, the London Stock Exchange (LSE) alerted the DTI's companies investigation branch to a very significant rise in the shares of Viglen Technology. Eventually, the DTI started a criminal investigation and a criminal prosecution was brought for market manipulation, in breach of the Financial Services Act 1986, applicable at the time.

In early 2006, one of the Slickers, James Hipwell, who denied misleading the market, was jailed for six months. The other, Anil Bhoyrul, who had pleaded guilty, had received a 180-hour community service order. Terry Shepherd, a private investor, was sentenced to three months after having helped the Slickers by publishing advance notice of their tips on the internet bulletin boards.

The national press covered the events in painstaking detail. If such a case were to arise now, the FSA itself could take enforcement action for market abuse. But criminal lawyers see this as unlikely because of the difficulty of proving the case.

Beyond tips

Discussion of the press would not be complete without reference to financial services advertising. The FSA focuses on financial services adverts likely to have a major risk impact on consumers, and it has fined some firms for misleading promotions.

22

Financial services regulation

Introduction

In this chapter, we will examine how financial services regulation has developed, and how the Financial Services Authority operates. We will cover some major developments in European Union legislation.

Overview

Given the financial services scandals over the years, and the increasingly global reach of ever more complex financial products, regulation of the City has had to become more sophisticated. It has evolved from the conflict-ridden adjunct it was in the late 1980s to the comparatively intelligent, well-resourced colossus that it is today.

To help firms cope with and understand the developing face of regulation, the compliance function within City firms has grown over this period from a back-office add-on burden to a valued stand-alone function, incorporating increasing specialisation, and with salaries that mean it is taken seriously. Let us see how it all came about.

History of regulation

The history of regulation is, as in most areas of the City, a tale of trial and error. The City had enjoyed informal regulation until Margaret Thatcher became prime minister in 1979. The 'iron lady' believed that if London was to remain

Europe's leading financial services centre, it had to lead by regulation. In 1986, Big Bang ushered in reforms, as discussed in Chapter 1, that were part of a move to reduce the role of the London Stock Exchange (LSE) as a private club controlling its members by its own rules.

There was a lot that was wild about the City in those days. Let us look at one area. In the mid to late 1980s onwards, share dealing firms licensed by the Department of Trade and Industry were using hard sell tactics to sell speculative shares to naïve investors, losing them substantial sums of money.

The licensed dealers picked up the private investor business that the stock exchange member firms, the perceived respectable end of the market, sometimes did not want to touch. When the Conservative Government launched its privatisations, which encouraged wider share ownership, the dealing firms made books in the stocks.

Small investors snatched a profit on new issues such as British Telecom and British Gas, as the government had intended, and millions were left with the impression that investment in shares was a way to make a quick buck. Many were tempted by cheap or commission-free dealing to sell their share holdings through licensed dealers. Once so hooked, many were persuaded to reinvest the proceeds into small speculative stocks that lacked liquidity, were perhaps traded only over the counter, and might not have properly existed. Such investors typically lost much or all of their money.

The licensed dealers either collapsed or were closed down or, occasionally, were taken over, and the inevitable scandals arose. The regulatory system rightly bore some of the blame, but it was under-resourced and no match for the masterminds behind the dubious firms.

The licensed dealer operations were small compared with the City as a whole and the victims were private investors, who accounted for, then as now, only a small proportion of share trades by value. But the fact that such scandals could happen showed that there were inadequate checks in place, and that consumers needed protection from commercial exploitation of their ignorance about investing.

The Financial Services Act 1986

The Thatcher Government itself was focused on consumer protection and it commissioned Jim Gower, a university professor, to prepare proposals for regulating the UK financial services industry. His recommendations led to the Financial Services Act 1986, implemented in full in February 1988.

The Act created self-regulation within a statutory framework for the financial services industry. Firms and their key staff were required to obtain approval from the regulators as a condition of running their business. The

Securities & Investment Board, known as the SIB, oversaw the self-regulatory organisations (SROs), which created rules for, policed and controlled authorised firms. Their authority was statutory in all but in name.

Among the SROs were The Securities Association (TSA), which authorised stockbrokers, and the Association of Futures Brokers and Dealers (AFBD). They later merged into the Securities & Futures Authority. The Financial Investment Managers and Brokers Regulatory Association (FIMBRA) authorised independent financial advisers and some share dealing firms. The other SROs were the Life Assurance and Unit Trust Regulatory Organisation (LAUTRO), which authorised life assurance firms, and the Investment Managers Regulatory Organisation (IMRO), which authorised fund managers; they later merged into the Personal Investment Authority (PIA).

Legislative changes extended across financial sectors. The Insurance Companies Act 1982 was introduced to regulate general insurance companies. The Building Societies Act 1986, was intended to make building societies more competitive.

Deficiencies in the new regime started to emerge. The spread of responsibilities among regulators for supervising financial conglomerates operating in more than one jurisdiction and across a variety of asset classes was not always clear and it could lead to a lack of action. Uncertainties and inaction arising from such a spread of regulatory responsibilities are arguably what led to the collapse of Barings. (See Chapter 2 for further details, and for a critical discussion of the Bank of England's previous supervisory role.)

The current regime

The Financial Services Authority

The powers and responsibilities of the Financial Services Authority (FSA) were established at midnight on 30 November 2001, when the Financial Services and Markets Act (FSMA) came into force. The new legislation incorporated 433 sections with 22 schedules, and was the first to have ever straddled two parliamentary sessions.

Unlike before, there was direct statutory regulation, which put much more emphasis on protecting consumers. The FSA became the single UK regulator for investment banking and insurance. The SROs and the SIB were abolished. The FSA has four statutory objectives: to maintain confidence in the UK financial system, to promote public understanding of it, to secure an appropriate degree of protection for consumers and to reduce the scope for financial crime.

The FSA authorises firms across the financial services industry, and approves individuals in key roles who work in it. Any firm undertaking regulated activity in the UK must be either FSA-authorised or exempt.

The FSA, like the SROs before it, has the power to withdraw approval from an individual that it considers not fit and proper to perform the controlled function to which the approval relates. It may impose a prohibition order that prevents any person from involvement in financial services activity and anybody who breached such an order would be committing a criminal offence. The FSA can apply for an injunction against any person or firm to prevent them from committing regulatory breaches.

More broadly, the FSA has the power to write rules and principles, codes and provisions. It is a private company, but it has statutory immunity from being sued from action taken in its official duties. The FSA is accountable both to a committee of non-executive members and to consumer and practitioner panels.

Once a year, the FSA must report to HM Treasury on how it has carried out its functions, and must hold a public meeting about it. The Treasury has the power to commission an inquiry into the regulator's operations, or a report on, for instance, a regulatory scandal. The Director General of Fair Trading may issue a report on any practice that it considers anti-competitive.

The FSA plans its rules in consultation with the industry and other parties. It publishes its consultation papers on its own website.

Over the years, the FSA has extended its reach over the financial services industry. It recognises exchanges and clearing houses. In 2002, it started to regulate credit unions (which are savings and loan societies based on a common interest) and, two years later, mortgage advisers. Since January 2005, its regulation of the insurance industry has included brokers in the wholesale market.

Like any regulator, the FSA is only as good as the people it employs and it has difficulty in attracting people with industry experience to work for a lower salary, albeit under less pressure, than in private firms. But a stint of working at the regulator has prestige, and there are secondments from the industry to the regulator and vice versa.

In recent years, the FSA has made some high-level appointments from the industry, including Hector Sants, managing director, wholesale and institutional markets, who joined the FSA in May 2004 from Credit Suisse First Boston where he was chief executive officer of Europe, Middle East and Africa. In April 2005, it appointed Margaret Cole, partner in the London office of the international law firm White & Case, as its new director of enforcement. She had experience of commercial litigation.

Let us now take a closer look at how the FSA operates and, in particular, what its principles-based regime means in practice.

The principles-based regime

The FSA regulates the financial services industry through broad principles, although it also has rules. There has been debate on how well the principles-based regime has worked, and whether it will survive in its present form. The US Securities and Exchange Commission (SEC) works in cooperation with the FSA and has a tough rules-based approach.

The principles are broad enough to enable the UK regulator to present a case more easily against firms than if it relied on rules, where lawyers could find loopholes. The FSA gives firms a steer on how to interpret the principles, but it is not always through official channels. It behoves the industry to attend to what FSA representatives say at conferences, or via press interviews, or in 'dear CEO' letters sent out to firms.

If the FSA finds a problem within a firm, it has made it clear that it will hold senior management responsible. This policy alone has helped to inculcate in firms a compliance culture from the top. The FSA takes a proportionate, risk-based approach to financial services regulation, which means in practice that it tends to focus on the problems that are the biggest threat to its statutory objectives. The FSA has found it harder to move against senior managers in corporates because they are not subject to financial services industry regulations.

The FSA does not work in isolation but it consults the industry before it introduces key regulatory initiatives or changes, and it sometimes invites the industry to find its own solutions. On this basis, in January 2006, the industry introduced its own requirements for unbundling, under which investment managers must disclose to clients how much they have paid for execution and research, and the regulator accepted them. The insurance industry has implemented its own solution for bringing about contract certainty (see Chapter 27).

If a firm is not satisfied with a disciplinary action of the FSA, it may refer the matter to the Financial Services and Markets Tribunal, run by the Lord Chancellor's department, which will rehear the case afresh, listening to evidence from both the FSA and the appellant. In appeal cases, the tribunal has shown itself to be independent.

The only large firm ever to have taken the FSA to a tribunal was the insurer Legal & General, and it was partly successful in its appeal against the regulator's £1.1 million fine. After an extensive hearing, the tribunal ruled in January 2005 that the FSA had failed to prove mis-selling at Legal & General, which it had alleged, although it had proved that the insurer had inadequate systems and controls for compliance purposes. It reduced the fine imposed.

In response, the FSA commissioned an independent review of its enforcement process, the Strachan review, which was published in July 2005. On the basis of this review, the FSA introduced a discount on the fines it imposed in cases of agreed early settlement, so making a prolonged and expensive investigation unnecessary. It introduced absolute transparency, previously missing, in all negotiations with the Regulatory Decisions Committee, an industry-led body that sits within the FSA and decides on penalties to be imposed.

The industry now routinely takes the early settlement discount in enforcement cases, which are based mainly on alleged breaches of principles. Some lawyers see a risk that the FSA's enforcement staff could become increasingly complacent and pursue cases based on an unrealistic interpretation of the principles, expecting that the defendant would be likely to opt for an early settlement and so the case need never be proved.

The FSA takes the view that the wholesale industry, which consists of financial institutions that deal with each other, needs less protection than consumers. A new training and competence regime came into force on 1 November 2007, under which examination and competence requirements are imposed only on firms conducting regulated activities for retail investors. These requirements for the wholesale sector will have been abolished, which should have increased flexibility without raising or lowering standards.

Some large firms in the industry have welcomed the move because it gives them a chance to develop their own training programmes, but there may have been an adverse impact on the transferability of individuals between firms, particularly across jurisdictions. The United States has an examination culture entrenched in its financial services industry, and is unlikely to change it.

European legislation

The Financial Services Action Plan (FSAP) is the EU initiative to improve the single market in financial services. At its heart is the Lamfalussy process. This is a four-level approach to resolving shortcomings in the regulatory and legislative system for financial services in Europe.

The FSAP is responsible for imposing an EU-wide regime that is bureaucratic and prescriptive in many ways. Lawyers say that the EU directives imposed under the plan are a halfway house between principles-based and rules-based regulation.

The pan-European Directives, of which there are more than 40, have mostly now been implemented, including by the FSA. The UK regulator has criticised some of the legislation and, in most but not all of the Directives, there is not much wriggle room for individual country interpretation.

The challenges in implementing the legislation can, however, be different for individual countries, depending on their previous regulatory regime and their culture. Let us now take a look at a few of the most important EU Directives.

Market Abuse Directive

The Market Abuse Directive (MAD), implemented in the UK on 1 July 2005, allows the FSA to choose between pursuing market abuse, including insider dealing, as a civil case, requiring proof *on the balance of the probabilities*, or as a criminal case, with the much higher standard of *beyond reasonable doubt*. Previously, the only option was a criminal case.

Even with this flexibility, the FSA has found it difficult to bring many successful actions for market abuse. In March 2007, the FSA said it had found possible 'informed' trading ahead of 23.7 per cent of takeover deals in 2005. Although this was a reduction from the 2004 figure of 32.4 per cent, the level of potential informed trading had hardly moved from 24 per cent in 2000.

In mid-2007, the FSA set out the results of a thematic review of firms' control of inside information about takeovers in its *Market Watch* newsletter, part of its soft guidance for firms. It said that feedback to the review had helped it to identify factors that could contribute to leaks that might arise around public takeovers. These include accidental leaks, intentional leaks to the media for strategic positioning and intentional leaks for market misconduct purposes.

In the newsletter, the FSA said that, even if it could not find evidence of insider dealing, it could fine banks without proper controls. Lawyers have said that the controls, while important, cannot prevent wilful criminal conduct. Industry feedback notes that unusual trading activity before a takeover was announced could have arisen from speculation and rumours, and ensuing momentum trading, and not necessarily from a leak.

On Monday 2 July 2007, in a farewell speech to the City, John Tiner, then chief executive of the FSA, urged the government to give the regulator power to offer immunity to those providing evidence of market abuse.

Prospectus Directive

The Prospectus Directive, implemented in July 2005, aims to give common disclosure standards across the EU member states when securities are made available to European investors through a public offer or trading on a regulated market. The Directive has introduced a single passport for issuers, which means that once a prospectus is approved in one market state, it must be accepted by the others. An obstacle has been that many EU states still have extra requirements, and some provisions of the Directive are open to different interpretations.

Transparency Directive

The Transparency Directive was implemented in January 2007. It covers continuing obligations of issuers whose securities are admitted to trading on an EU-regulated market, including the publication of financial reports, which should be prepared according to International Accounting Standards or equivalent, or reconciled to these.

The Directive also includes disclosure requirements for major shareholdings in all companies admitted to trading on an EU-regulated market. The requirements for content and timing are more demanding than before in most EU member states.

Unlike the Prospectus Directive, the Transparency Directive requires minimum harmonisation, which means home member states are able to impose additional requirements, potentially making it difficult for international participants.

Markets in Financial Instruments Directive

The Markets in Financial Instruments Directive (MiFID) was implemented by the deadline of 1 November 2007 in the UK, but there were laggards elsewhere, most notably Spain. MiFID replaces the Investment Services Directive (ISD), which had emphasised mutual recognition between member states. The Directive, as often elsewhere in EU legislation, requires maximum harmonisation, meaning that member states are not supposed to gold plate EU requirements by adding to them.

EU-wide standards in some main areas of investment business will be established. The main changes are in pre-trade and post-trade transparency, best execution, client classification, transaction reporting and data consolidation. Let us look at each.

MiFID imposes pre-trade transparency obligations on the large banks that are systematic internalisers in liquid shares. The internalisers must publish buy and sell prices up to standard market size and honour them, even at retail size. A teething problem has been how to define *systematic internaliser* and *liquid*.

Under post-trade transparency requirements, details of all trades executed in a security admitted to a regulated market must be published.

MiFID imposes a best execution requirement from which only eligible counterparties acting as principals (ie, trading on their own book) are excluded. The criteria that a bank or broker is to apply in achieving best execution depend on the type of client with which it deals. For retail investors, best execution is the total consideration, including expenses related to the order's execution through to trade settlement, although other factors may be given priority if they deliver the best result. For professional investors, best execution must take into account speed, cost (including commissions, fees and costs such as clearing and settlement), likelihood and price.

How far best execution should apply to international bonds and OTC derivatives has been a subject of controversy. In bonds, trades tend to be of a large size, and transparency for individual orders could have a significant impact on market price, industry feedback suggests.

MiFID has changed client classifications. The previous client categories of private, intermediate and market counterparty are dropped. The new categories are retail, professional and eligible counterparty, and the criteria are slightly different, based on such issues as type of investment, amount invested and investor knowledge. A teething issue has been the time and expense envisaged in transferring clients from the old categorisations to the new.

There is a new pan-European transaction reporting obligation for most asset classes. There is a greater choice in trading venues, with the result that quotes and trades in the same security are published through various channels, giving rise to the risk of data fragmentation (see Chapter 16).

MiFID enables companies to compete outside their home market on more of a level playing field. Under the ISD, if a firm entered transactions in another member state, it needed to be registered in that state, known as the host state. Under MiFID, such cross-border transactions are regulated by the country where the firm is located, in other words, the home state.

This makes it cheaper for small companies in particular to conduct business across borders because the legal costs of compliance with local laws will have been removed. Firms may relocate to a member state with favoured regulations, or may seek to expand by offering products abroad but without establishing branches in those locations.

Generally, MiFID has ushered in a much greater administration burden. Firms must maintain and update more extensive records than before for any regulated activities involving conflicts of interest, and must take a more pro-active approach towards finding conflicts.

In November 2006, the FSA estimated an initial overall cost of implementing MiFID in the UK of between £870 million and £1 billion with ongoing costs of around an extra £100 million a year. The regulator said that the Directive could generate some £200 million per year in quantifiable ongoing benefits, attributable mainly to reductions in compliance and transaction costs.

Capital Requirements Directive

The Capital Requirements Directive (CRD) was approved by the European Parliament in September 2005, and applies to all credit institutions and certain investment firms. It is the common framework for the implementation of Basel II rules on capital measurement and capital standards (see Chapter 3).

23

Financial fraud

Introduction

The City attracts fraudsters because of its substantial movements of money through various asset classes and its global connections. In this chapter, we will look at some scams linked to the City, the resources available for dealing with them, and the success achieved. We shall examine the roles of regulators, police, the government and various organisations, as well as legislative developments. Read this with Chapter 24, which covers money laundering.

Overview

The financial services industry suffers £1 billion a year in losses from fraud, according to a report published in early 2007 for the Association of Chief Police Officers based on research by Professor Michael Levi, a criminologist and fraud expert at Cardiff University. Financial fraud increasingly crosses asset classes and jurisdictions, and at a more sophisticated level is organised by gangs of professional criminals who can shift easily from one fraud to another. The proceeds are often laundered into the banking system (see Chapter 24) and used to fund further fraud.

The government is taking action to combat fraud. The Fraud Act 2006 came into force in January 2007, replacing the complicated array of over-specific and overlapping deception offences. It has established a new general offence of fraud by false representation (which includes 'phishing', discussed later in the chapter), by failing to disclose information and by abuse of position.

There is more change to come. The Fraud Review, commissioned by the government and published in July 2006, was followed by a public consultation and, in March 2007, the government launched its response, *Fighting Fraud*

Together. It proposes steps such as setting up a National Fraud Strategic Authority to lead and coordinate fraud prevention activities, and a National Fraud Reporting Centre to gather intelligence and measure fraud.

The idea is to provide a one-stop shop for fraud victims and to prevent duplication in fraud reporting, providing a more sophisticated sharing of data between different areas of financial services, government and non-government agencies. The proposals are under discussion by working groups and costings were to be submitted in October 2007, with the start of the new framework in April 2008 at the earliest.

The government's proposals include a review of how courts should address issues arising from fraud, and discussion about implementing a financial courts jurisdiction with specialist judges so that all aspects of fraud proceedings can be dealt with in one place. Another idea is to explore a way of encouraging early guilty pleas through a safe legal framework, which protects defendants' rights but also improves the experience of victims. The use of plea bargaining to put pressure on criminals to give information about their colleagues has worked well in the United States.

Financial fraud is borderless. A 2003 extradition treaty between the UK and United States ratified by both countries in April 2007 modernises and extends the extradition arrangements, aiming to make it easier to bring offenders from either state to justice.

The extradition arrangements came under criticism when three former employees of NatWest Bank were extradited to Texas in 2006 to stand trial on seven federal counts of wire fraud in relation to the Enron case. The UK originally ratified the treaty to show solidarity with the United States in the fight against terrorism. Critics said the *NatWest three* extradition showed that US prosecutors were using the treaty to pursue alleged white collar fraud cases and that the British government should never have ratified it.

In the UK, attitudes towards bankers and insurers have conspired to make certain types of fraud more acceptable, including exaggerated insurance claims, according to financial crime stakeholder research published in March 2007 by the Financial Services Authority (FSA), the City regulator.

Boiler rooms

Let us look at an area of the City where the combined efforts of the FSA and the City of London Police have not been able to crack a problem. This is the fraud committed by boiler rooms selling worthless shares from Spain or Germany or elsewhere abroad to UK residents.

The FSA runs a campaign against boiler rooms, and names some of the offenders on its website in a list that is unavoidably outdated. If the firm is operating from abroad, the Authority will not in practice be able to take action against it, except if UK-based individuals are linked to the scam, which is sometimes the case. The City of London Police coordinates Operation Archway, the national intelligence reporting system for boiler room fraud.

The boiler rooms were once only a telephone sales scam but now they use the internet as well. Until the early 1990s and beyond, these firms operated freely in the City as well as abroad. With a tightening up of financial services regulation over the past couple of decades, they are less likely now to be based in the City but will target UK investors from jurisdictions such as Spain, Gibraltar, Hong Kong, Croatia and elsewhere.

Let us look at how these bucket shops operate. The dubious brokers are expert at hard-selling shares in unknown companies, which, if they exist at all, are probably not generating revenue. They represent the stock they are pushing as a hot investment opportunity. Anyone who sends in money to this outfit will lose every penny.

The salespeople prefer to call targeted investors, whom they sometimes call 'punters'. If the investor rings them, the call is likely to be diverted from a UK line to the hideout abroad where they work. The salesperson will be using a false name. Such tactics make it hard to trace the fraudsters. The jurisdiction where the operation is physically based will have been chosen because local police are not much concerned what businesses are doing if they are not targeting nationals. If the police start investigating, the telesales team simply moves to another jurisdiction.

The outfit will refer investors to a website representing the company whose shares it promotes. The site paints a glowing picture of the company, which is often represented as high tech. The fraudsters provide glib descriptions. The company promoted as an investment opportunity may not exist or, if it does, may be small, generating no revenues, and desperate to raise capital.

Regulation S allows US companies to sell stock oversees without registration under the Securities Act, which means non-US citizens are not given the same level of protection as their US counterparts. The boiler rooms often push 'Reg S' companies, perhaps quoted on the US Pink Sheets, the centralised quotation service which has in the past included some fraudulent companies. To qualify for a Reg S exemption, shares must be sold offshore to a non-US resident and not resold into the United States for a year. There can be an international market in the meantime for the shares, but in practice they can be very hard to sell.

The telesales people in boiler rooms are often paid a commission on sales of between 10 and 60 per cent of the money paid by investors for shares, which is exceptionally high compared with the usual remuneration in advisory stock broking. Once a salesperson has opened up a client account, the lead is passed onto a 'loader', who proceeds to load the individual with as much stock as he or she is willing to buy, within as short a time as possible.

The stock offering from the fraudsters may be a pump-and-dump. This is a planned sales campaign that sends the share price artificially spiralling. The promoters will have bought shares earlier through a nominee account and made a huge profit from selling out high, at which point the share price collapses, leaving most investors holding overpriced stock that they cannot easily sell.

The crooks may represent their share selling campaign as an initial public offering (IPO) or a private placing and invite you to subscribe early at a special price. The dealer may send out a prospectus. This will have some unrealistic profits and cash-flow projections, and will be full of warnings.

'You will be in and out within a month,' the broker may say, and promises clients a small profit – big enough to entice them, but not enough to make them suspicious. After buying the new stock, investors may never be able to sell out, but this will not be immediately apparent. The broker will say clients should stay invested because of market conditions or the exchange rate. If the firm allows investors to sell, it will be only if they reinvest in an equally dubious stock. Whichever way, the clients will never see their money again. Sometimes, the approach is not as subtle as this, but the fraudsters simply pocket the proceeds of any cheque sent in. If so, they may claim to offer shares in respectable blue chip companies.

The victims are often older and experienced investors and they tend not to learn from their mistakes. In June 2006, the FSA published a survey of 100 investors hit by boiler room fraud, and found that 64 per cent were over 50, 41 per cent had been investing for more than 11 years and 13 per cent were conned by more than one boiler room. Of those surveyed, 20 victims, the largest number, were from London and the South East, where the average investment was £21,823.

One may ask how such a situation could be allowed to arise in the first place. Every boiler room has a limited life but, on its collapse, it often re-emerges under another name, and an outfit may approach the victims and offer to recover the money they lost for an upfront fee. It is a scam linked to the first one.

An unscrupulous firm occasionally takes over a struggling company whose good name it exploits. The new owner will stave off suspicious regulators and others, often hiding behind lawyers, as the firm rips off clients. The merged company, like other boiler rooms, can operate only for a limited time.

Clients are the lifeblood of the boiler rooms and there are always more of them. The boiler rooms can pay a fee and obtain share registers where shareholders who hold paper certificates are named, with their address, and their details can be used to obtain a telephone number. Fortunately, the vast majority of shareholders keep their shares in a nominee account, rather than in a certificated form, and they do not have their details on the share register.

The Companies Bill introduces a new offence, 'abuse of the register', which should make it harder for boiler rooms to access the share registers. The Bill received Royal Assent on 8 November 2006, and all provisions should be in force by October 2008. The FSA has said that the legislation will help to protect certificated shareholders but will do little to protect the investors whose names and contact details are already in circulation amongst boiler room operators.

Advanced fee frauds

Away from investments, the boiler rooms specialise in the advance fee fraud, a spurious loan offer presented as conditional on payment of an upfront fee. There are variations on the theme but the outcome is always the same: the promoters take the fee but do not pay the loan.

The 419 fraud is the best known type of this; it is named after the section of Nigeria's penal code that addresses fraud schemes, although this scam is not exclusively from Nigeria. The fraudsters will send the potential victims everywhere an e-mail, sometimes purporting to be from a Nigerian government or bank official, which contains an ungrammatically worded plea for help. The impression is given of an uneducated but sincere correspondent.

The approach deploys various types of request, of which the most common is to make temporary use of your bank account for depositing what are claimed to be large government or other funds in exchange for a commission of up to 30 per cent. Anybody who responds is asked to pay an upfront fee to release the cash subject to the transfer – and, if he or she pays up, further related fees. The fraudsters are only interested in receiving the upfront fees and will not subsequently proceed, or even pretend to proceed, with the promised transaction. They are often operating from home using telephone lines registered to an unrelated party so the call will be almost impossible to trace. Any individual fraud can continue for months or years.

If the mark should hesitate to pay advance fees, he or she may be invited to complete the transaction in Nigeria or a neutral country. If the mark makes the trip, he or she will be fleeced by the crooks, and accomplices claiming to be local police may demand a further fee to retrieve the funds. Parties enticed to Laos who resist paying money may be threatened by the fraudsters, and cases of kidnap and murder have been documented.

A variation is when a supposed bank offers loans for a fee. The non-existent entity, represented through a website, claims an address, which in the past has been in Guernsey, Jersey or the Isle of Man, perhaps in a street that does not exist. The concept of a bank may instil confidence in the mark, particularly if, as is often the case in these scams, its name sounds similar to that of a big recognised financial institution. Once the operation has stolen some money through receipt of advance fees on the promise of substantial loans, its internet presence will disappear. A few months later, another website may pop up, run by the same fraudsters under a different name, but with a giveaway similar logo. The stopping and starting process may continue indefinitely, raking in fees en route. It is hard to prove who the perpetrators are since anybody may go to an internet provider, get a name, and start a website online with no identification checks.

Another variation is the lottery scam where a letter or e-mail tells the mark that he or she has won a large sum. To claim the lottery money, the mark needs to pay a large arrangement fee but, if he or she pays it, no windfall follows. Alternatively, an e-mail may arrive from a purported legal firm saying that the mark is the only known beneficiary of the will of a person who has just died, and it may be backed by an e-mail providing further false information and some contact numbers. Again, an advance fee will be demanded.

The City has had some limited success in catching advanced fee fraudsters, and there has arisen an enjoyable culture of baiting them by pretending to be about to go through a transaction. The scam has claimed all too many victims in the UK as well as in the United States and elsewhere, and the victims are reluctant to complain because the proposition on which they willingly entered negotiations was dubious. On a worst case, the fraud victims try to recoup their losses by entering further related transactions with the conmen.

Identity theft

Identity theft or concealment is a theme that runs through a lot of fraud, as well as money laundering. Individuals have often used an invented name, or a real name that is not their own, to open accounts with the idea of perpetrating fraud. Many bank accounts opened in the distant past are not properly verified, according to money laundering reporting officers.

The crooks rely on firms not doing extra due diligence. They are adept at falsifying identification such as passports and gas bills. Some of the best efforts are, in simulation terms, works of art.

There is no difficulty in buying on the internet either a false passport or a passport in countries whose names have changed, or even a valid new passport in, for example, African countries. In one case, the equipment used to make false passports was more modern than the Home Office's.

There are known geographical black spots, including some within London, from which many false applications from a few crooks emanate. An offshore international business company can be set up with no reporting requirements, whose ownership is anonymously defined through bearer shares.

The crooks open accounts at one financial institution then another. Sometimes, members of staff who have moved from one firm to another recognise the names of account applicants and holders from a past job. Financial services employees have been known to cooperate in fraud, and cynical compliance officers take the view that everyone has a price.

The UK attracts the largest amount of credit card fraud in Europe. One of the growing frauds is phishing, where crooks disseminate an e-mail to large groups of people falsely representing that it has been sent by a legitimate financial institution, with the aim of persuading the reader to release credit card or bank details. Another technique is to telephone the mark, pretending to be from the credit card company, and to ask for card details to 'check suspicious activity' on your card.

At the automated teller machines (ATM), criminals can now read and record card details and PIN numbers remotely by attaching a card reader to the front of the card slot and a pinhole camera above the keypad. As a simpler alternative, they can operate a grab-it-and-run. At one point in 2007, gangs of young Romanians, both male and female, were posing as distributors of free newspapers near cashpoints in the West End, particularly around Oxford Circus, Mayfair and Goodge Street, and the City of London. They waited until their victim, typically a woman, had keyed in her pin number and hit the 'get cash' option before they approached her on both sides, jostling her and thrusting newspapers in her face. Under cover of the newspapers, one of the team on the left hit the £200 button and another on the right grabbed the cash. They worked so fast that typically nobody in the queue to the ATM even saw it but assumed they were simply harassing her to take a paper.

An ATM fraudster can make between three and four million pounds a month, which is why some perpetrators will go so far as to kill people to gain turf, according to one money laundering reporting officer.

Insurance and reinsurance fraud

Insurance fraud can be broadly split into either claims fraud, which is against the insurance or reinsurance companies (see also Chapters 27–30), or fraud within the company itself. Informal feedback from regulators suggests that fraudulent claims amount to 5–10 per cent of premium, of which only 10 per cent is discovered and averted, but much of this is guesswork. The latest regulatory thinking is that throwing further resources at claims fraud prevention does not work but that consumer education is needed to stop the widespread misapprehension that to cheat an insurance company is a victimless crime.

Reinsurance companies can receive dubious claims from insurers, and their own underwriters or claims people have been known to put pressure on the company not to investigate favoured clients. In some reinsurers, the board pays lip service to fighting fraud but the work gets dumped on overworked claims departments. Many firms cut back on hiring investigators to save costs.

Eastern Europe has proved a hotbed of large and dubious reinsurance claims. Munich Re has had substantial and sometimes unjustified reinsurance claims from warehouse fires in Eastern Europe. To deal in such countries as Russia can be problematic, and local representation is important, Munich Re says. It has found that courts in Russia base their decisions on contractual documentation and there is some sentiment that to win a case, one needs to know the right people.

Respectable insurers sometimes find their name is hijacked by fraudsters. Allianz, the German insurer, is fighting an ongoing battle, involving liaison with the Federal Bureau of Investigation (FBI) to stop fraudsters who hijack its good name and website images, including in e-mails, in an attempt to lend credibility to their enterprises.

Lloyd's has found its name used by fraudsters, although individual syndicates are named only rarely in the bogus documentation. The frauds against Lloyd's have tended to be in the United States, which demonstrates the international nature of insurance fraud. Lloyd's has been involved in many prosecutions, not all of which reach court.

Fraud may arise from within insurance and reinsurance companies and it may involve theft of premiums or company assets, or fee churning, where intermediaries take commissions through reinsurance agreements and the initial premium is reduced to nothing by repeated commission. Some fraudulent operations have been based in London, and others elsewhere, for example in the United States, sometimes with a domicile in an obscure offshore or non-existent named jurisdiction, and perhaps with a London contact office.

The fundamental nature of insurance company frauds has arguably not much changed in the last 17 years. At the September 2007 annual meeting of the International Association of Insurance Fraud Agencies (see later in this chapter) in Lisbon, Andy Wragg, senior manager for international regulatory risk at Lloyd's International Market Access, pointed out that insurance insolvencies in recent years had shown some of the same characteristics as those highlighted in *Failed Promises: Insurance Company Insolvencies*, a report published in February 1990 by Congressman John Dingell's subcommittee in the United States.

In some recent insurance company insolvencies, problems flagged by Dingell such as inadequate reserves, misleading financial statements and general falsehoods have still been emerging, Wragg noted. But the insolvencies are far fewer than in the five years before the Dingell report and coordination between regulators has improved, he said.

Fraud busters

Financial Services Authority

The reduction of financial crime is a statutory objective of the FSA although, unlike its other three objectives, that is one component of the broader government intervention in this area. The objective is considered to be mainly linked with prevention of money laundering, and only 10 per cent of the regulator's annual resources are applied to it.

At the FSA's Annual Crime Conference in January 2007, John Tiner, then chief executive, said that in the previous two years, the regulator had delivered a new training programme to equip its supervisors to identify financial crime risks in firms, and had extended its links with industry and law enforcement to exchange information.

In early 2007, the FSA created a new Financial Crime and Intelligence Division, which should enable it to tackle financial crime more rapidly and in more depth. The FSA aimed to address the rising information security and hi-tech crime risks, which would involve close collaboration with other regulators.

The FSA has pointed to a close relationship between threats and opportunity in today's regulatory regime, citing increasing evidence of cross-border attempts by firms and individuals of dubious backgrounds to enter the UK market via authorisation, change of control or passporting under the Single Market Directives. There are listings, both on the Main Market and on the AIM, for which it is difficult to undertake really effective due diligence, it has said.

In the FSA's March 2007 financial crime stakeholder research, a view was expressed that the UK is too soft on fraud and money laundering, and it was noted that jail sentences are significantly shorter than in the United States. Most stakeholders welcomed the FSA's recent move to a risk-based approach to fraud prevention within regulated firms, but there was a view that it might leave room for abuse.

City of London Police

The City of London Police force has 158 officers dedicated to preventing and investigating fraud, and is well resourced for this purpose in comparison with other police forces. In 2006, 75 per cent of crime investigated by the unit was cleared up. The fraud squad makes good use of fraud data. It has a good database on plastic cards, and another on boiler room frauds.

If government proposals following consultation on the Fraud Review come about (see early in this chapter), the City of London Police will be elevated from south-east lead to national lead force. The force has agreed to take on between four and six cases of serious fraud a year that fall just below the Serious Fraud Office's (see below) acceptance criteria.

Insurance Fraud Bureau

The Insurance Fraud Bureau (IFB) was launched in July 2006, eight months from conception, after the Association of British Insurers approved the use of current industry shared data to tackle fraud. The IFB levies from its members its running costs, which are £8.6 million over five years. Bogus and inflated insurance claims cost the insurance industry over £1.5 billion a year and add 5 per cent to the premiums of honest policyholders, according to the IFB. The Bureau focuses less on the opportunistic insurance frauds such as a false claim for a burn on a carpet, which the insurance industry can deal with itself, and more on sophisticated cross-industry frauds such as staged motor accidents.

The IFB works closely with business partners in using analytics to focus on and identify networks of fraudsters. It can then take pre-emptive action at an early stage, and where there is the option, it prefers to prosecute. Based on the Bureau's work, the police by May 2007 had seized £5 million of assets and arrested nearly 40 key individuals. The police response across the UK has been patchy, although strong in London and in a few other locations; this is partly a resource issue, according to John Beadle, chairman of the Bureau.

Insurance Fraud Investigators Group

The Insurance Fraud Investigators Group is a UK-based not-for-profit organisation focused on detecting and preventing insurance fraud, mainly in UK claims. It has more than 100 members, including insurers, police authorities, investigators, lawyers and loss adjustors. The group aims to allow its members to share intelligence via a secure web-based system. The organisation has strong links with law enforcement and regulatory and trade bodies, and other anti-fraud organisations.

International Association of Insurance Fraud Agencies

The International Association of Insurance Fraud Agencies (IAIFA) was formed in 1986 and is focused on insurance fraud. The association coordinates the efforts of law enforcement agencies, government bodies and the insurance industry in the fight against fraud. Lloyd's (see Chapter 28) is a member of the IAIFA and was a sponsor of its 2007 annual meeting.

In 2007, under the presidency of Dr Bassel Hindawi, director general of the Insurance Commission of the Hashemite Kingdom of Jordan, there were plans to strengthen the IAIFA, including through the establishment of a new office in Geneva, with a permanent secretariat. The association aims to give the insurance industry a larger role in the organisation, to obtain further financial support through membership fees, and to establish links with organisations such as the International Association of Insurance Supervisors. A database and training programmes are in the process of being created.

Serious Organised Crime Agency

The Serious Organised Crime Agency (SOCA) came into being at the start of April 2006. It replaced the National Criminal Intelligence Service (NCIS), which closed down at that point, bringing together its responsibilities with those of the National Crime Squad. The SOCA took control of the organised crime investigations previously conducted by Customs and Excise and the immigration service. The agency has a policy of intervention to reduce 'harm' to the UK, and initially refers investigations in which it intends to participate to the Serious Fraud Office (see below). Its skill lies in covert active, rather than reactive, investigation.

Unlike the NCIS previously, the SOCA can give any information to anybody if this would be consistent with its aims of targeting organised crime. The SOCA has started to share data in a way that had previously not been possible, according to Ian Cruxton, deputy director, Midlands SOCA. In an industry presentation in May 2007, he said the first year of SOCA had been 'clunky', but that SOCA enjoyed a strong relationship with the City of London Police.

In its 2006/2007 annual report, SOCA said that its operational work in its first year included, among other things, the consolidation of the existing intelligence picture resulting in the identification of harmful criminals who had not previously been operational priorities; more than 1,700 arrests in the UK and globally flowing from SOCA work; high quality domestic criminal justice casework; the seizure of more than 74 tonnes of Class A drugs; the exclusion of potentially dangerous criminals from the UK; activity against international aspects of crime on a new scale for the UK, particularly against money laundering; £29m recovered from criminals; continued specialist support to police forces; fraud prevention and issues of warnings.

Assets Recovery Agency

The Assets Recovery Agency (ARA) is an independent government department that became operational in 2003 under the Proceeds of Crime Act 2003 (POCA) (see Chapter 24 for more about this legislation) to perform civil recovery and criminal confiscation roles in England, Wales and Northern Ireland, and tax investigation in the UK. The Criminal Asset Bureau (CAB) in the Republic of Ireland helped to create the ARA, and prompted thinking in the UK on the POCA before it was enacted.

The ARA has a statutory purpose of reducing crime by confiscating the profits of, among other things, people trafficking, drug dealing, deception, theft, extortion and theft of intellectual property. It does some criminal confiscation where other bodies cannot, but focuses more on civil recovery and on tax.

'We operate the Agency within a hierarchy,' says Alan McQuillan, interim director of the ARA, who has a police background. 'The best way to reduce crime is to prosecute criminals, send them to prison, and take the money. If we can't do that, we will use civil powers to sue and take money from the criminals, and, if not that, tax them.'

In civil recovery actions, the Agency steps in where people cannot, for a variety of reasons, be prosecuted, or where they are acquitted. The action is against the assets, not the individual, and is on the basis that the assets are 'dirty'.

'Defendants will often provide the defence – "I'm innocent, and didn't have the *mens rea* [guilty mind] to commit the offence, but I accept the assets are the proceeds of crime." Trials may collapse for evidential problems, because for example, witnesses do not turn up or the defendant falls ill or dies.' says McQuillan.

In a 2006 case, Dylan Creaven was trading microchips between the Republic of Ireland and the UK, and was involved in a fraud network that stole around £200 million from HM Revenue and Customs. Creaven was prosecuted but his defence was that while some of his partners were corrupt, he was an innocent party. The jury acquitted him. In a joint action by the ARA and the CAB, his assets were frozen, and £18.5 million was recovered in a settlement.

The ARA only takes cases referred by law enforcement and other departments and agencies, selecting those most likely to reduce crime. The ARA needs reasonable grounds to suspect dirty money, and it needs a court order from the High Court to freeze money, which means convincing the court on the balance of probability that the money is dirty and will disappear if the ARA does not freeze it.

Human rights activists have failed in attempts to stop the ARA from making civil recovery actions but, from 1 January 2006, legislation has allowed people to get at their own money to defend themselves.

The ARA has been criticised for limited recoveries in relation to set-up costs, which were around £60 million over the first four years. In 2006, it recovered £16.5 million, which, for the first time, was slightly more than the base budget for the year. At the end of 2006, the Agency was working on 143 cases with gross value, based on money frozen, of over £145 million, which is a pipeline of work going forward.

'Our experience is that the average civil case takes four years, which is twice as long as we had expected,' said McQuillan. The ARA makes huge use of settlements, but demands high settlement figures – usually 80–90 per cent of the assets – and not the 50 per cent more common in commercial settlements.

'Our aim is not to get in as much money as we can, but to reduce crime. It's a different psychology,' McQuillan says. 'Companies involved in litigation will settle on a commercial basis. But I will take a case to court costing more than the money brought in if it disrupts the criminal network, and this is part of our statutory remit.'

In pursuing a case, the ARA 'follows the money trail', and takes huge investigation leads from suspicious activity reports (SARs) (see Chapter 24), McQuillan says. 'If Jo Bloggs is referred, we look first at his activities, and then the investigation spreads in ripples. We look at SARs, tax records, where people bank, basic records, and we look at the money flows alongside the alleged criminal activity.'

Cases extend to countries outside the UK, including Sweden, France, Spain and Ireland, as well as the United States and South Africa, where the ARA has a sister agency. The ARA talks to foreign law enforcement agencies.

Assets recovery could be the core part of any action against fraud, and the Agency has worked closely with the Serious Fraud Office (see below) in recovering assets in the case of Izodia, a company from which cash had been stolen. In September 2006, Gerald Smith was sentenced at the Cambridge Crown Court to eight years' imprisonment for misappropriating over £34 million belonging to Izodia and for false accounting.

In its May 2007 Asset Recovery Action Plan, under consultation until November 2007, the government set targets for asset recovery of £250 million a year after two years, which McQuillan describes as 'challenging' and, in the unspecified future, £1 billion a year. As part of the consultation, it was proposed to extend the 12-year limit under the POCA, under which the ARA can only take civil recovery action for property gained in the last 12 years. Another proposal under consultation was to reward whistle-blowers with a percentage of assets recovered, which has worked effectively in the United States.

The ARA is an accreditation body for the training of financial investigators, including police officers. POCA professionalised this training, and investigators now have to go through a professional training course and meet regular competence requirements. Every three years, investigators go through a review – and, if they fail to meet requirements, could lose their licence. Training is no longer free of charge, which means there is more focus on making sure that investigators who have it will not retire soon afterwards, as has happened in the past.

The ARA is a small organisation, with a £15.5 million budget for 2007, which covers both investigation and training. It has 50–60 investigators, 30–40 lawyers and paralegal staff, and some tax experts and accountants, all part of an integrated team. A third of its capacity operates from a Belfast office, where costs are 20 per cent lower than in the mainland UK, and the rest from London. Staff are often seconded from other agencies, including the entire tax and forensic accountancy teams, and some investigators, according to McQuillan.

Under the Serious Crime Bill, introduced in January 2007, the ARA's investigative functions will merge with the SOCA (see above), and its training and accreditation functions into the National Policing Improvement Agency. This is part of a government strategy to distribute the ARA's powers to other agencies and prosecutors.

'In the long term, mainstreaming powers will increase the volume of assets recovered and hurt criminals. At the very least it should also be cost neutral but, in the short term, there will be significant additional costs until the money recovered from cases starts to come in,' says McQuillan.

Serious Fraud Office

The Serious Fraud Office (SFO) is an independent government department with 310 permanent staff, and is part of the UK criminal justice system. It started operating in April 1988 and has jurisdiction only over England, Wales and Northern Ireland.

The department investigates and prosecutes serious or complex fraud cases exceeding around £1 million in value. It selects cases on such criteria as whether they have a significant international dimension, give rise to widespread public concern, or are complex and require specialist input.

The SFO's cases tend to have a gestation period of four to five years, and the cumulative conviction rate stands at about 70 per cent. About 65 per cent of the cases have an international dimension, and the SFO liaises with authorities in many jurisdictions. The SFO has had some high-profile successes, including the BCCI investigation, which led to six convictions, the latest in April 1997, and the Barlow Clowes case, where the principal defendant, Peter Clowes, was sentenced to 10 years in February 1992. In the Guinness case, following an SFO investigation, the four principal defendants were convicted in September 1990.

The SFO's failures have been no less publicised. One was the Blue Arrow trial, which cost taxpayers an estimated £40 million. Another was the 1996 indictment of Ian and Kevin Maxwell, sons of Robert Maxwell. They were found not guilty of fraud charges after a trial that had lasted eight months and cost taxpayers £25 million. This is one of the cases that led to government proposals to scrap jury trials in complex fraud cases on the basis that juries do not understand complex fraud. The House of Lords has so far rejected them.

In recent years, the SFO has become better resourced, although critics say that it still does not attract the best investigative staff because it cannot afford to pay private-sector rates. The SFO has a budget of around £40 million a year, funded by the Treasury, to cover the normal run of operations and has the ability to make applications for more. It has recently taken on further office space.

Structurally, the SFO had five operating divisions, one of which was created to look at what it termed a blockbuster case in relation to generic drugs price fixing. In 2007, it created a sixth division to look at another blockbuster case, the UN sanctions busting case in relation to Iraq. The SFO has developed some new responsibility for investigating overseas corruption where, for example, British companies offer bribes to overseas government officials to win commodity contracts. The SFO now keeps a register of all British companies against whom allegations of this practice have been made.

In 2007, Lord Goldsmith, the Attorney General, announced that former New York prosecutor Jessica de Grazia would be leading a review of the SFO to consider how it might most effectively investigate and prosecute cases. The six-month review, ongoing as the second edition of this book goes to press, aimed to compare investigation and prosecution methods of the SFO with those used in the United States and other countries and see if it can learn anything from them.

The SFO does work closely with other City bodies fighting fraud, and has been forging closer ties with the City of London Police. It shares with the police a special vehicle that it parks outside the house in raids, and that has facilities to make copies of computer disks and other evidence, so that the originals can be handed back on the spot. The SFO needs to be accompanied by police officers if warrants are to be served.

The FSA sometimes refers cases to the SFO, as it did with Torex Retail, a software company listed on the Alternative Investment Market, following a shock profit warning. The SFO started its investigation of the company in

January 2007, and has since conducted a number of searches but made no arrests.

The future

In recent years, simpler legislation and a greater commitment of regulatory and police resources have helped to combat fraud. But no matter how much emphasis the authorities put on catching the villains, it is often only the small fry who are caught. This is partly because the big fraudsters, who are also money launderers (see Chapter 24), are sophisticated and operate across international borders. Cross-jurisdictional communication between regulators, although vastly improved, remains uneven.

Fraud can be very complex, and the standard of proof – beyond reasonable doubt – required in a criminal case makes it often time-consuming and expensive to bring a successful action. Juries have problems understanding fraud, which has long been a grievance of the SFO. Prison sentences in this country are too short, critics say, to act as a deterrent to the fraudsters. There are never enough resources to fight financial fraud, and there is also a more sinister theory that the government does not really have the will to address it.

In the United States, law enforcement is better resourced (again see Chapter 24), with access to more advanced crime detection techniques, and the sentences are far harsher. The US influence is likely to spread more in the UK, particularly if we adapt plea bargaining, which, given the current support of the Treasury, seems likely.

24

Money laundering

Introduction

In this chapter, we will see how money laundering works, some regulatory measures to combat it, and some problems arising. We will also consider the scale of the problem. Read this chapter with Chapter 23.

Overview

Money laundering is the washing of dirty money through the financial system to make it clean. Cocaine production in South America, oil production in Africa and terrorism in the Middle East are all fertile sources of dirty money that ends up getting washed. Money laundering is multi-jurisdictional, taking place in London and other big financial centres but also offshore and via the internet. Differences in regulation and legislation among jurisdictions remain, making the money launderer's job easier, and it can be hard to pinpoint the geographical jurisdiction of some transactions. There is often a political focus on being seen to take anti-money-laundering action.

The textbook approach to money laundering is to break it down into three stages. The first is placement, in which the launderer introduces dirty money, the proceeds of crime, into the legitimate financial system; the second phase is layering, by which he or she attempts to separate the proceeds in time and space from the original acquisitive crime by moving them through a series of financial transactions; the third stage is integration, at the end of which the launderer has created a legitimate explanation for the source of these funds, allowing them to be used openly as an individual would use honestly acquired assets.

Know your client

Financial services regulation and legislation, including in London, focus on account-opening procedures and it is hoped to detect placement at this stage. Banks and other financial firms must verify the customer's identity, using 'Know Your Customer' (KYC) procedures, and should recognise and report suspicious transactions. The procedures are far from foolproof and there is a case to be made that, in the long run, the shift towards electronic banking and electronic money will debilitate them further.

Money launderers are sometimes helped by individuals within financial services firms, or the firms themselves. It helps that there are corrupt officials, politicians, lawyers and other advisers across continents, and whole jurisdictions that will turn a blind eye.

As a further protective measure, launderers can easily conceal their identities. As we saw in Chapter 23 under the subheading 'Identity theft', false passports are in circulation. Money laundering reporting officers are appointed by financial services firms and have many duties but they are not trained to detect the fakes.

If the conventional banking system seems too risky, launderers may use the *hawala* system, which works by allowing cheap and unrecorded money transfers. Through this system, which is widely used today, a person pays dollars in the United States to a broker, who informs his partner in another country, who makes an equivalent payment in the local currency. No physical transfer of funds will have taken place, and the broker and his or her partner settle amounts owed through fake invoices of, for example, the firm's ostensible import–export business.

Action against money launderers

Global

The Financial Action Task Force on Money Laundering (FATF) was established by the G-7 Summit held in Paris in 1989. It was given the task of examining money laundering, reviewing action taken and setting out what needed to be done. The FATF started with 16 members and now has 34, with China as the latest recruit in mid-2007. It is hoped that Korea and India, currently FATF observers, will soon be additional members.

In April 1990, the FATF published its 40 Recommendations on money laundering, which it has since revised. There has been a lack of uniformity in implementation of the Recommendations, which are now incorporated into EU legislation (see below under 'European Union').

The Financial Services Authority (FSA) in the UK is helping the FATF in developing a risk-based approach to its policy development and, in April 2007, Gordon Brown, then Chancellor of the Exchequer, announced he had appointed James Sassoon, the Treasury's representative for promotion of the City, to act as president of the FATF for the 12-month period starting July 2007.

Since the 11 September 2001 attacks on the United States, constraints on cooperation between law enforcement offices globally have been lifted and information flows have improved, although a perceived mistrust between investigators across countries remains.

The Egmont Group is an unlimited network of financial intelligence units, established at a 1995 meeting in Brussels. It has 105 member jurisdictions after Bolivia was struck off. The group has its own secure website and enables cross-pollination of intelligence on financial investigations around the world. 'It is quick and precise but it is only intelligence and, in criminal matters, letters of request are also needed,' Stephen Annis, a detective constable in the economic crime department of the City of London Police, told the September 2007 annual meeting of the International Association of Insurance Fraud Agencies in Lisbon.

The United States

Under the Bank Secrecy Act (BSA) of 1970, which was the first legislation to combat money laundering in the United States, banks must report cash transactions of US$10,000 or more. To deposit amounts too small to trigger reports, 'smurfers' have been known to make small payments to accounts in many banks simultaneously. The Money Laundering Control Act of 1986 amended the BSA to make it more effective, and defined money laundering as a federal crime. It made structuring transactions to avoid BSA reporting a criminal offence.

Shortly after 9/11, the US government launched the PATRIOT Act, an acronym for Providing Appropriate Tools Required to Intercept and Obstruct Terrorism, to combat international terrorism. The Act said that financial institutions should make specified KYC checks and it significantly expanded the powers of US law enforcement for the announced purpose of fighting terrorism. It introduced 'reverse' money laundering, which refers to the criminal purposes to which money is put after it leaves the bank.

The PATRIOT Act aimed to control foreign banks dealing with US institutions and has led to substantial anti-money-laundering activity, some of which, industry feedback suggests, has seemed to be for form's sake. Non-US financial institutions that fail to comply with the Act may be denied access to all financial markets dealing in US dollars.

European Union

Across the European Union, the first EU Money Laundering Directive was introduced in 1991, in response to the FATF's 40 Recommendations on money laundering (see under 'Global' above), and became legislation in member states. Its only predicate offence was money laundering from the proceeds of drug trafficking.

The second Money Laundering Directive, in 2001, widened the predicate offences to include organised crime, corruption and other serious crimes, and it brought new gatekeepers such as accountants into the regulated sector.

The Third Money Laundering Directive was to have been implemented by the end of 2007, with the support of the FSA and the Treasury. The Directive incorporated FATF's 40 Recommendations into law and has added terrorist financing to the predicate offences. There are some new definitions, including one for politically exposed persons, and more detail, including a distinction between enhanced and simplified due diligence.

The Directive has an explicit risk-based approach written into it, which means that firms must apply a proportionate approach, focusing more on areas of greater risk. The UK Treasury has acknowledged industry complaints that some jurisdictions might take advantage of this flexibility, but takes the view that good regulation rather than more EU legislation is the answer.

The UK

In implementing the first Money Laundering Directive, the UK extended the single predicate offence (see above) to include money laundering from the proceeds of all indictable crimes.

The UK implemented the second Money Laundering Directive through the Proceeds of Crime Act 2002 (POCA). The Money Laundering Regulations 2003 were secondary legislation to support adherence to the Directive requirements.

Suspicious activity reports

Suspicious activity reports (SARs) are a disclosure of money laundering or that another person is engaged in money laundering and are made to the Serious Organised Crime Agency (SOCA) (see Chapter 23). SARs can also be made under the Terrorism Act 2000. SOCA adds value to SARs by investigating, and then it farms the reports out to investigation agencies such as the police (see also box below).

In the first few years after 9/11, firms made far too many SARs to SOCA's predecessor body, the National Criminal Intelligence Service (NCIS) to cover themselves, although there has since been more of an attempt at keeping the reporting relevant.

Analysis funded by the assets recovery community and internal work within the SOCA have suggested that SARs are a highly valuable resource, according to the government's May 2007 Asset Recovery Action Plan. Even relatively simple preliminary checks suggest that financial institutions had good grounds for their suspicion in a significant proportion of cases and the SARs are probably the most underused source of intelligence, it found.

The City of London Police claims, unlike some police forces, to check all the SARs that are passed on to it. Resources to catch money launderers are not so advanced as in the United States, and the big money launderers almost always get away with it. Sometimes the police have some luck, connecting names on separate SARs and matching fingerprints of suspects with those held on a police computer as a result of, for example, drink-drive convictions. The Egmont Group, discussed earlier in this chapter, provides intelligence that can help to clinch an investigation's success.

The Proceeds of Crime Act 2002

The Proceeds of Crime Act 2002 (POCA) provided new financial investigation tools and is very broad ranging. The new money laundering offences in POCA are easily understood by juries, and many of the anomalies and complications in earlier offences are swept aside, according to the Asset Recovery Action Plan, a May 2007 consultation from the Home Office.

Under POCA, an employee of a financial institution may go to jail for having failed to follow the correct anti-money-laundering procedures, which includes filing SARs, now to the SOCA (see above). Firms must wait seven days to receive consent to continue with suspicious transactions and, in the meantime, must stall, but not tip off, the client. If consent is refused, a firm will be constrained from continuing for 31 days, which allows time for the police to investigate.

If a financial services firm is required not to release client funds, it can put itself in an awkward position if the account holder wants access to them. It may be in breach of POCA either if it pays the customer, or if it withholds the funds and so tips off the client without giving them a sensible explanation.

In 2005, Stephen Judge was faced with a dilemma of this kind while working at a spread betting firm and he subsequently became the first British money laundering reporting officer to be prosecuted for authorising a payment without receiving consent. The Crown Prosecution Service later dropped the case, giving as the main reason that it could not establish that the funds repaid to the client were criminal property.

Systems and controls

So far, the FSA has not announced the discovery of any money laundering but it penalises firms that it has discovered have inadequate systems and controls. In December 2002, it fined the Royal Bank of Scotland (RBS) £750,000, the first penalty against a financial institution for failure of money laundering controls since the FSA assumed regulatory control in this sphere in December 2001. The fine had been low because the bank's management addressed the shortcoming promptly and took an open and constructive approach to the regulatory investigation, according to the FSA.

The cases have continued and, in February 2007, Nationwide Building Society was fined £980,000 for systems and controls failings in a case based around theft of a company laptop. In May of the same year, BNP Paribas was fined £350,000 for systems and controls failures that enabled an employee to steal £1.4 million.

Regulatory developments

The FSA's money laundering rules, known as the Money Laundering Sourcebook, were replaced on 31 August 2006 with high-level provisions. Firms are required to have systems and controls enabling them to identify and manage money laundering risks and adopt the same risk-based approach as in the 2006 Guidance Notes of the Joint Money Laundering Steering Group (JMLSG), which are an example of industry self-regulation.

In August 2007, consultation was underway to amend the JMLSG Guidance to bring it into line with the Money Laundering Regulations 2007, which will implement the provisions of the Third Money Laundering Directive (see under 'European Union' above).

The size of the problem

The Treasury has said that £25 billion of criminal money passes every year through the economy. If this figure is right, which nobody can verify, it is uncertain whether it represents fresh money, or simply £5 billion circulating through the system five times. Recoveries are miniscule in comparison with any sum of this kind. In the 10 years to 2002, only £44 million was recovered, although recovery targets are now rising.

Nowadays, law enforcers, including customs, aim to recover more than this amount in a single year but, on one money laundering reporting officer's estimates, at best fewer than 1 per cent of money launderers in the UK are caught, and it is hard to achieve even this.

25

Overview of corporate governance

Introduction

This chapter explains how corporate governance works. We will look at, among other things, the Cadbury Code, the Combined Code and the Myners Report, and the Listing Rules. Read this with Chapter 26, which focuses on governance in relation to accounting.

The concept

Corporate governance is about how a company conducts its corporate affairs and responds to stakeholders, employees and society. It covers ethical, legislative and other rules specifying how a company should act.

The issues are not new. In 1776, Adam Smith said in his book *Inquiry into the Nature and Cause of the Wealth of Nations* that managers could not be expected to manage other people's money with 'the same anxious vigilance with which the partners in a private copartnery frequently watch over their own', and that 'negligence and profusion, therefore, must always prevail'.

The corporate governance framework in the UK and elsewhere has, at least since the early 1990s, been a mixture of regulation and best practice. There has been more regulation introduced into the UK's corporate governance framework recently. Much of it has been through the EU, including the Business Review (see Chapter 26) and mandatory audit committees, but some has arrived in the new Companies Act, including codification of directors' duties.

Most independent studies on different corporate governance regimes place the UK at or near the top in standards. The UK approach combines high standards of corporate governance with relatively low costs, is proportionate, and is relatively prescriptive about how the company's board organises itself, according to a November 2006 publication, *The UK Approach to Corporate Governance*, by the Financial Reporting Council (FRC), which is responsible for corporate governance in the UK.

Clearly corporate governance has made enormous progress since the business excesses of the late 1980s, including collapses such as that of Polly Peck, and frauds such as the plundering by Robert Maxwell, chairman of Mirror Group Newspapers, of his companies' pension funds (see Chapter 31).

The Cadbury Code

To combat such abuses, the Committee on the Financial Aspects of Corporate Governance was set up in 1991. It was also known as the Cadbury Committee, after its chairman Sir Adrian Cadbury, and was backed by the FRC, the London Stock Exchange (LSE) and the accounting profession.

In 1992, the Committee produced the Cadbury Report, with codes of best practice applicable to UK listed companies. The Cadbury Code, as these codes became known, set a direction and standards for corporate governance.

The Code proposed that a company should be run by its board, which should be held accountable, that the role of chairperson and chief executive should be separated, and that at least three independent non-executive directors should be on the board. Audit remuneration and nomination committees should comprise mainly non-executive directors, and there should be independent communication between non-executive directors and the auditors through an audit committee.

The reforms were mostly for listed companies, but were considered good governance guidance for any organisation. The Cadbury Code was not legally binding, but companies listed on the LSE were expected to 'comply or explain': that is, either to follow the provisions of the Code or to explain why they had not done so (see under 'Listing Rules' later in this chapter).

Since 1992, there have been regular additions to the Cadbury Report recommendations.

The Greenbury Committee

The next focus was on the high earnings of company directors in companies with a mediocre performance, an anomaly often highlighted in the press. In July 2005, the Greenbury Committee, led by Sir Richard Greenbury, produced a code on directors' pay, which focused on lack of transparency, including in share options. The committee set out to link pay with performance, recognising that high-calibre directors needed to be paid properly.

The Combined Code

In 1998, the Hampel Committee, under the chairmanship of Sir Ronnie Hampel, reviewed Cadbury and Greenbury. It put the case for continued self-regulation in corporate governance. This gave rise to the Combined Code, which has set out the main guidelines for UK corporate governance. The Code requires boardroom practice to be clearer and more formal and it has taken corporate governance to investors (for more details, see under 'Revised Combined Code' later in this chapter).

The LSE issued the Combined Code in 1998 as an appendage to the UK Listing Rules. On 1 May 2000, the Financial Services Authority (FSA) took over the LSE's role as UK listing authority, and administers the rules.

Unlike Cadbury and Greenbury, the Code concentrates on a principles-based approach but, like them, it operates on the basis of 'comply or explain'. If a company takes a different approach from the Combined Code, it must explain this to shareholders, who must decide whether they are content with it, which means they must have the right information, and the right to influence the board.

Companies are required under the Listing Rules to include a statement in their annual reports on how they have applied the Code. Under UK company law, shareholders have significant voting rights, and can under some circumstances call an Extraordinary General Meeting.

The Turnbull Report

Internal controls were next on the agenda, and the Turnbull Report of 1999 provided guidance in this area to listed companies, superseding the Rutterman Report of 1994. Turnbull said that internal controls should be both embedded in an organisation's operations, and responsive to changing risk inside and outside the company. In October 2005, minor revisions to Turnbull were announced.

OECD Principles of Corporate Governance

In 1999 the Organisation for Economic Cooperation and Development (OECD), a Paris-based organisation of industrialised countries, created the OECD Principles of Corporate Governance, which were loosely based on the Cadbury Report and others, and represented the lowest common standard acceptable to OECD members.

The Principles were widely accepted as a benchmark. In 2002, they were revised for the purpose of providing further guidance only, after consultation between representatives of OECD and non-OECD governments, businesses and other bodies.

The revised Principles, approved in April 2004, aimed to rebuild and maintain public trust in companies and stock markets and advocated greater transparency. They asked governments to ensure effective regulatory frameworks, companies to be accountable, institutional investors to become more aware, and shareholders to have an effective role in determining executive compensation.

In December 2006, the OECD announced it had released a methodology to facilitate the use of the Principles, which could be used by independent assessors and for self-assessment. Unlike some existing schemes, it is focused on outcomes.

Directors' Remuneration Report Regulations

In August 2002 the Directors' Remuneration Report Regulations came into force. They aimed to improve disclosure and accountability to shareholders, and to enhance the competitiveness of listed companies by clarifying the link between pay and performance.

Under the Regulations, listed companies are required to publish a report on directors' remuneration with their annual report and accounts. The report must contain details of individual directors' remuneration packages, the company's remuneration policy and comparative company performance graphs.

Directors have a personal obligation to provide relevant information, and must prepare, circulate and file the remuneration report correctly, failure of either being a criminal offence, punishable with a fine. Auditors must confirm that auditable information has been properly prepared. The company must put an annual resolution to shareholders on the remuneration report, but the result of the shareholder vote is advisory.

Higgs and Smith

The UK government asked Derek Higgs to report on the role of non-executive directors, whose role had come under renewed scrutiny after the Enron fraud. Higgs liaised with the Smith Committee, established by the FRC under Sir Robert Smith, which focused on the audit committee's role and the relationship between external auditors and the company that they audited. The Higgs and Smith reports were published together in January 2003.

Higgs said that non-executive directors should support shareholder interests, and have stronger communication lines with the company's main shareholders; at least half the board members, excluding the chairperson, should be non-executive directors; and non-executive directors should meet at least once a year without the chairperson or executive directors.

The Higgs report was controversial. Some non-executive directors have complained that it did not encourage investors to be sufficiently flexible towards corporate governance, and that it required non-executive directors to be assessed regularly but did not impose the same rule on executive directors.

Higgs suggested an expanded Combined Code, incorporating amendments on audit committees suggested by Smith, and the FRC started consultation.

The Revised Combined Code

The Revised Combined Code on corporate governance was published in July 2003, and applies to reporting years starting from November 2003. It made the Combined Code still more principles-based, and encouraged more transparency and greater shareholder accountability.

Under the Revised Code, all listed companies should have a nomination committee, whose members are mostly independent non-executive directors; before a chairperson is appointed, his or her time commitment should be assessed, and no individual should chair more than one FTSE 100 company; the chairperson must ensure that directors receive timely information; and disclosure in the annual report is compulsory.

Executive directors should not have more than one non-executive directorship in a FTSE 100 company and should not chair one, according to the Code. The chairperson and chief executive should have separate roles, non-executive directors should be independent, and appointments to the board are made on merit. Directors' pay should be linked to corporate and individual performance, based on a formal and transparent procedure, and directors must not help to decide their own pay.

In financial reporting, the board is required by the Code to present a balanced and understandable assessment of the company's position and prospects. A system of internal controls should be maintained and reviewed annually. The audit committee should consist only of independent directors, and should make recommendations on the appointment and removal of external auditors.

Most of the revisions to the Code were in the detail. Probably the most significant new element was a requirement that the board should formally evaluate its own performance following which the chairperson should take any action necessary. But some directors believe that evidence is lacking of the link between evaluation and greater effectiveness, and that too much attention is given to simplistic aspects of board performance such as attendance at meetings, and not enough to less easily assessable aspects such as the commercial ability and ethics of directors.

In October 2005, Edis-Bates Associates published a survey of company secretaries' views on the Combined Code, intended to help the FRC in a review on its implementation. As many as 71 per cent of company secretaries who responded believed that the rules on evaluation were working, although in smaller companies they were less inclined to agree.

Not everybody takes such a positive view. In late 2005, researchers for a survey by Hanson Green interviewed 20 chief executives and chairs about corporate governance. Most of them said that the Revised Combined Code had led to very little return in relation to time and money spent. A survey by Russell Reynolds interviewed nearly 60 company chairs about the Revised Code and 65 per cent of them thought it had had little impact on performance.

In January 2006, the FRC published the results of its own review. It found that, since the introduction of the Revised Code, there had overall been an improvement in the quality of corporate governance among listed companies, and a more constructive dialogue between boards and their main shareholders. This showed a lot more support for board evaluation than might have been expected in 2003, according to an FRC spokesman.

In June 2006, the FRC published an updated version of the Combined Code, incorporating some minor changes.

Listing Rules

Under the Listing Rules, new applicants for listing must ensure that directors are free from conflicts of interest between corporate and personal interests, unless the company has arrangements in place to manage these conflicts. The FSA dropped a proposal made in October 2003 for an equivalent continuing obligation because the Combined Code and company law adequately covered these requirements.

The extract in the Listing Rules requiring companies to 'comply or explain' in relation to the Combined Code is shorter than the Code itself. 'But it is as important because it gives the Code its force,' says Chris Hodge, head of corporate governance at the FRC.

The Model Code, an appendix to the Listing Rules, is a code of conduct imposing restrictions beyond the law. It aims to stop directors or employees of listed companies, and linked parties, from abusing, or placing themselves under suspicion of abusing, unpublished price-sensitive information. It applies especially in periods shortly before results are reported. In July 2005, the FSA simplified the Model Code as part of its revisions to the Listing Rules, extending it to persons discharging 'managerial responsibility'.

The Myners Report

Pension funds came under individual scrutiny after the Maxwell pension theft and subsequent legislative changes. The Myners Report, commissioned from Paul Myners by the Chancellor of the Exchequer, together with a set of voluntary principles for occupational pension schemes, was published in 2001.

Myners highlighted the need for greater transparency in how pension funds were used. It found that many pension fund trustees lacked the investment expertise to assess services sold to them by investment consultants and fund managers, and relied on a small number of investment consultants supplying bundled actuarial and investment advice.

Myners found that pension funds devoted insufficient resources to asset allocation, and that unclear contractual structures created unnecessary incentives for short termism in investment. He said there was insufficient focus on adding value through shareholder engagement, and that pension fund trustees should voluntarily adopt best-practice principles for investment decision making on a 'comply or explain' basis. Only individuals with the right skill and experience should take decisions, he said.

The performance of all advisers and managers should be measured, and trustees should assess their own performance, according to Myners. Trustees should engage with investee companies when it was in the interest of their fund members, and investment strategies and returns should be reported annually. An anti-fraud compensation provision should be extended.

The government agreed that the principles would benefit pension funds, consumers, industry and itself. The Myners recommendations went ahead. In

December 2004, the government reported that implementation had achieved only partial success.

The National Association of Pension Funds (NAPF) has been undertaking a further review of trustee compliance with the Myners Principles, which should have been completed by October 2007. The NAPF says that in the new world of pensions, some of the Myners Principles appear less relevant. Among other things, the shift from equities to bonds has reduced the potential impact of shareholder engagement, and the spread of financial innovations has obliged trustees to delegate more to advisers, which runs counter to the Principles, according to the association.

Developments across Europe

Most countries in Europe have a 'comply or explain' code. The concept of 'comply or explain' is now recognised in EU law in the 4th Company Law Directive. This is a positive development if it means less demand for detailed regulation at the EU level, according to Chris Hodge at the FRC.

In many European markets, many companies have a majority shareholder, Hodge notes. 'There is arguably more justification for a regulator to take action to protect minority shareholders than over here where ownership tends to be more dispersed.'

In October 2007, Charlie McCreevy, Commissioner for European Internal Markets, retreated from a campaign to give all EU shareholders an equal voice in running EU companies. He may have found it difficult to muster enough backing from EU member states and the European Parliament for the original 'one-share, one-vote' proposal. A study that McCreevy had commissioned in June found no evidence that a lack of shareholder democracy was a cause of a company's poor performance.

The future

The FSA's principles-based regime, with its emphasis on management responsibility, as discussed in Chapter 22, makes corporate governance a major issue. Regulators, senior management, listing authorities, analysts and investor-related trade bodies have an interest. Rating agencies take account of corporate governance when they give companies a credit rating. In 2007, corporate governance was a frequent theme on FSA supervisory visits to financial services companies. It is a key focus for compliance and risk management functions within the firm.

Over time, there will be pressure from the stock market, environmental and other groups, and league tables to promote good standards, according to consultants. How far companies see corporate governance as red tape, and how far they apply it in spirit, remains an issue, particularly, industry sources believe, for some foreign companies trading their shares in London.

There is disagreement on the profitability of best practice in corporate governance. McKinsey's Global Opinion Survey (2000, updated in 2002), a widely quoted piece of opinion-based research, found that 80 per cent of respondents would pay a premium for well-governed companies. Other studies have supported this finding but scepticism lingers, not least because of the subjective nature of data in opinion-based research.

26

Accounting and governance issues

Introduction

In this chapter, we will focus on accounting and governance. We will consider the widespread impact of the Sarbanes–Oxley Act. We will consider developments in European auditing and disclosure rules, and the business review required by the Accounts Modernisation Directive. We will see how International Financial Reporting Standards have made accounting more transparent. Read this with Chapter 25, which provides an overview of corporate governance.

Accounting scandals

Corporate governance has gained a higher profile after major accounting scandals. In June 2002, WorldCom, a US telecoms group, revealed a US $11 billion accounting fraud and, a month later, it made a Chapter 11 bankruptcy-protection filing.

Enron, a US energy company, went bankrupt in December 2001 and, in May 2006, former Enron bosses Ken Lay and Jeffrey Skilling were found guilty of fraud, conspiracy and other charges. They had both pleaded not guilty and had denied knowledge of fraud schemes, putting the blame on junior managers.

In December 2003, Parmalat, the Italian food and milk products company, almost defaulted on a small bond issue. Shortly afterwards, it was discovered that the group had falsified its accounts to conceal losses and that substantial sums had been embezzled, mainly by Calisto Tanzi, the group's former chairman and chief executive.

The Sarbanes–Oxley Act

The US Congress phased in the Sarbanes–Oxley Act 2002 shortly after the Enron fraud as an emergency piece of legislation, based on reforms agreed with the New York Stock Exchange. The Act, named after its authors, Democrat senator Paul Sarbanes and Republican congressman Michael Oxley, mainly affects a company's external auditors, internal accounting professionals and IT providers.

The Act met the recognised need for stricter auditing controls. At Enron, the Arthur Andersen team in charge of the company audit was found to have destroyed documents to conceal the truth, which showed a need for greater controls.

Sarbanes–Oxley aims to reinforce the independent status of external auditors and requires procedures that stamp out creative accounting. Financial reports should be auditable and supported by data, as well as proof against alteration, with systems in place to detect this.

Under Sarbanes–Oxley, accountants cannot mix auditing with certain activities, including actuarial or legal services, and bookkeeping. Auditors are supervised by a Public Company Accounting Oversight Board that is answerable to the Securities and Exchange Commission (SEC), the US regulator of financial markets. They are required to maintain audit records for five years. Failure to comply may be punished with a fine and up to 10 years' imprisonment. The company's audit committee must pre-certify all other non-audit work.

Under the Act, significant extra disclosure is required in the report and accounts, as well as ethical guidelines for senior financial officers. Guidelines are required on analysts' conflicts of interest. There is a ban on personal loans to executive officers and directors. Accelerated reporting of trades by insiders is required, with no such trades allowed during pension fund blackout periods. The Act increases corporate responsibility for any fraudulent actions taken, and there are criminal and civil penalties for securities violations.

The chief executive and chief financial officer must sign off financial statements to confirm compliance with the provisions of the Securities Exchange Act 1934. If the statements turn out to be incorrect, the signatories could be held criminally liable under Sarbanes–Oxley, even if they had not intended deceit. They could receive a fine of up to US$1 million and up to 10 years' imprisonment. If they certified the inaccurate statements wilfully, the fine could be US$5 million, and the prison sentence 20 years.

Sarbanes–Oxley requires organisations to introduce adequate IT systems and assess their adequacy annually. To assist the process of justice, whistle-blowers are protected. Civil penalties are added to disgorgement funds to relieve victims.

US listings have become less attractive to foreign companies as a result of Sarbanes–Oxley, and the London Stock Exchange has attracted listings from companies that might have previously chosen New York. Sarbanes–Oxley applies to those companies that issue securities in the United States, which includes about half those included on the UK's FTSE 100 Index. It also applies to companies that own a US subsidiary or are required to file reports with the SEC. The company's physical location is not significant, although the national rules of a non-US country will prevail should they conflict with the Act.

By early 2007, the United States started to soften some of the Sarbanes–Oxley requirements. In March, the SEC published new rules for deregistration by foreign companies, adopted that month, which eliminated conditions that had been considered a barrier to entry. Until this point, a foreign issuer could only have exited the registration and reporting regime required if it had fewer than 300 resident shareholders, which was a difficult requirement for a foreign issuer to meet given the increasing globalisation of financial markets.

From March 2007, the criteria for exiting this regime changed, and the main condition for allowing the exit is now that the US average daily trading volume of the securities has been no greater than 5 per cent of the average worldwide trading volume for a recent 12-month period. The SEC said that the amended rules would encourage participation in US markets and increase investor choice. In April 2007, SEC commissioners endorsed measures to improve Sarbanes–Oxley implementation to ease small company burdens.

There is some transatlantic crossover, and many of the non-contentious parts of Sarbanes–Oxley have for a long time been part of UK law. 'In some respects UK legislation is tougher than the US,' says Chris Hodge, head of corporate governance at the Financial Reporting Council (FRC). 'US shareholders would love to have the same rights as their UK counterparts.'

In the United States the enforcement powers rest with the SEC so things tend to be more rule-based as regulators have to be seen to be consistent, Hodge says. 'In the UK we can build in more flexibility because the power rests with the shareholders and the market.'

European auditing and disclosure rules

On 16 March 2004, the European Commission (EC) published a draft proposal on auditing rules with the aim of enabling investors to be more confident that company accounts were accurate. This was part of the update of the 8th

Company Law Directive on statutory audit, which the Commission tabled in 2003 to prevent auditing scandals such as Enron and Parmalat.

In September 2005, the European Parliament in Strasbourg backed the EC proposal, which would guarantee the independence of auditors in relation to the management of major listed companies. It requires listed companies to have an audit committee or a body with equivalent functions to oversee the auditor's work, and to rotate audit partners regularly.

The EC has said it sees no need for a single corporate governance code across the European Union (EU) and that, in most cases, rules should be left to each member state. But it has introduced some common requirements to be implemented.

Revisions to the 4th Company Law Directive will require all EU-registered companies listed on an EU market to include in their annual reports a statement on how they have complied with the relevant national code, and to describe their internal controls related to financial reporting, according to the FRC. The revised 8th Directive will require the same companies to create an audit committee with at least one independent member. As this second edition was being prepared, the Department of Trade and Industry was consulting publicly on the revisions. It has said that the new requirements will come into force on 1 April 2008.

Business review

Financial statements do not meet all the information needs of users and there is an acknowledged need for other information. In 1992, the Cadbury Committee concluded that shareholders needed a coherent narrative of a company's performance and prospects, which could be provided by a forward-looking operating and financial review (OFR).

The OFR became a statutory requirement for all UK-listed companies to publish for financial years starting on or after 1 April 2005. It was an implementation of the EU Accounts Modernisation Directive, which requires large and medium-sized companies to include a business review in the directors' report, which is part of the annual report and accounts.

On 28 November 2005, Gordon Brown, then Chancellor, announced a surprise intention to remove the requirement to publish the OFR because the business review had largely identical main requirements, and government policy was not to impose regulation on UK businesses above the relevant EU directive requirements.

Many felt that the OFR had been a sensible move towards corporate transparency, and listed companies had invested a lot of time and money into meeting the publication requirement. But nearly all listed companies will still have to adhere to the Accounts Modernisation Directive. The business review required by the Directive puts less of an onus on firms than the OFR to give information about the future and there is less clarity on how far it requires owners to understand the strategy of the business, but many of the requirements remain the same.

The Financial Reporting Review Panel, part of the FRC, has legal authority to review directors' reports and, if it finds they are not compliant with the Companies Act 1985, may compel the companies to revise them. The Reporting Standard on the OFR has given way to a Reporting Statement of best practice, which is voluntary. The guidance in this statement is more specific than required in legislation, particularly on forward-looking information.

Under the Companies Act 2006, which received Royal Assent on 9 November 2006, there are further provisions in relation to the business review. It is to be given a statutory purpose, which is to inform the members of the company and help them to assess how the directors have performed their duty under the Act, and to promote the success of the company.

The Act will require quoted companies to provide additional disclosures, as far as the directors judge necessary to understand the business, including the main trends and factors likely to affect its future development, and information about environmental and social issues, and the company's employees. Directors will have some protection from liability for statements or omissions in, among other things, the directors' report.

On 15 January 2007, the Accounting Standards Board, an operating board of the FRC, published a review of narrative reporting by UK companies, based on best practice, and of compliance with business review requirements. It found that companies were complying with legal requirements, and were good at providing descriptions of their business and board meeting minutes, and the current development and performance of the market. The greatest area of difficulty was the disclosure of forward-looking information.

In January 2007, the International Accounting Standards Board asked an international team that had focused on the benefits of adding a 'management commentary' to financial reports to prepare a proposal to add this project to the Board's formal agenda, which was to be considered in summer 2007.

International Financial Reporting Standards

For financial years beginning on or after 1 January 2005, International Financial Reporting Standards (IFRS) came into force for the consolidated accounts of all listed companies in the European Union.

Under IFRS, the cost of stock options estimated at the date of grant has been included as an expense on the income statement for the first time. Many companies have restructured their remuneration schemes to avoid calculating the expense, which requires option valuation models.

Goodwill must be recognised and tested annually for impairment, and there must be significant disclosure of key assumptions and sensitivities. Valuing of intangible assets such as brands has proved more complex than anticipated, according to accountants.

Dividends are no longer accrued, unless they are declared before the year end. Deferred taxes are calculated on revaluations as well as on timing differences and feedback suggests that this broad area of accounting has been challenging, as predicted. There are many methods to apply in accounting for actuarial gains and losses.

The classification of leases into operating or finance accounts has had to be reassessed. Hybrid securities such as preference shares are classified as debt rather than, like before, as equity because there is a focus on the substance of the transaction, which in this case may resemble a debt instrument. Derivatives must be put on the balance sheet at fair value and marked to market through the income statement.

The 'fair value' reporting requirement can lead to much more volatility on the income statement because some transactions related to hedging derivatives must now be recorded for the first time. Changes in value to investment property must now be in the income statement.

Pension deficits under IFRS appear on the balance sheet and must be valued, with key assumptions disclosed. So far, most companies have not yet converted the accounts of subsidiary and parent companies to IFRS, but have preferred to remain with UK Generally Accepted Accounting Principles (GAAP), where disclosure and some other requirements are fewer.

The transition to IFRS has been successful. In 2006, most groups published their IFRS accounts on schedule, with no share price crashes. The financial statements under IFRS have become longer, but resources committed to producing them have not proportionately increased. Industry feedback suggests that companies have used boilerplate descriptions for disclosures.

Companies quoted on the Alternative Investment Market have had to prepare their accounts in accordance with IFRS for periods beginning on or after 1 January 2007.

By 2009, the requirement for foreign companies listed in the United States to publish a reconciliation of IFRS to US GAAP is seen as likely to be removed. This would be a huge cost saving, but raises the issue of reciprocation. In May 2007, the SEC started a consultation on whether companies can use IFRS instead of US GAAP.

27

Insurance: the London companies market

Introduction

In this chapter, we will focus on insurance and how the London companies market is made up. We will see how underwriting works, and will examine the impact on insurance of world events such as terrorism, as well as regulatory developments. Read this with Chapters 28, 29 and 30.

Overview

Insurance is a service that offers financial compensation in return for a premium payment should an adverse event occur. In an insurance transaction, one party, the insurer, undertakes to pay another party, the insured, money if a specified form of financial risk should arise. For this service, the insured pays the insurer a fee, known as a premium. The insurer insures its own risk by placing reinsurance with a reinsurance company (see Chapter 29).

The UK has the largest insurance market in Europe, and third largest in the world behind the United States and Japan, according to a November 2006 report by International Financial Services, London (IFSL). Net worldwide premiums of the UK insurance market totalled £166.7 billion in 2005, up 9.9 per cent on the previous year, but 3.2 per cent below record premiums generated in 2000, the IFSL reported. The figures do not take into account overseas premium revenue generated by foreign branches and subsidiaries in the UK.

Insurance may be categorised under three broad headings: general insurance, life and pensions, and health and protection. Of the 772 insurance companies authorised to carry on insurance business in the UK, 568 do only general business, which is insurance of non-life risks where the policy offers cover for a limited period, usually a year. A further 159 insurers are authorised specifically for long-term business (life insurance and pensions), and the remaining 45 insurers are composites, which do both.

Today the Financial Services Authority (FSA) regulates and supervises the UK insurance and reinsurance industry, including brokers, along with the rest of the financial services industry. The UK insurance regulatory model is considered more coherent than the US model, where individual states are involved.

As a broad generalisation, the FSA is more willing to stand back from wholesale than retail insurance. For consumers, it sees motor insurance or household insurance sales as less of a problem than sales of protection products.

London

The London market covers general insurance and reinsurance business, and is the only place in the world where all 20 of the world's largest insurers and reinsurers have offices. London is a 'leading' market, setting the rates and providing the intellectual capital for risks written elsewhere. It is one of the leading providers of insurance and reinsurance to the United States, the world's largest insurance market.

The London market is split between the company market, which consists of insurance companies, and Lloyd's, which consists of syndicates (see Chapter 28). Most of the companies are members of the International Underwriting Association (IUA). The insurance company market grew in the 1970s as foreign insurers opened City offices. The London market now employs about 40,000 people in London and another 10,000 employees in the UK.

London has both non-Lloyd's brokers, and Lloyd's brokers. Most of the larger brokers are in both categories and London is a broker-led market. Acquisition costs, consisting of brokerage and commissions, are by far the biggest part of the expenses in the Lloyd's profit and loss account.

Types of business

The London market covers a high proportion of very large or complex risks. There are three main types of business: marine, aviation and transport, known as MAT; home–foreign; and non-MAT treaty reinsurance.

The London market's MAT business developed from Lloyd's marine underwriting, and Lloyd's does more than half of this business. Home–foreign business covers writing risks from London that are outside the UK. This type of business is roughly split two-thirds from Lloyd's and the rest from insurance companies. Non-MAT treaty reinsurance is for general risks – that is, non-transport – of which insurance companies do around two-thirds, and Lloyd's the remainder. For an explanation of treaty reinsurance, see Chapter 29.

Let us focus more on marine insurance, where London has the largest share of net premiums in the world, 20.2 per cent in 2005, down from 21.5 per cent in 1995, according to the IFSL.

Insurance companies and Lloyd's are both involved as marine underwriters, covering such classes of business as: cargo insurance, indemnifying the policyholder against loss of goods; hull insurance, which covers the ship's structure; war risks; building risks; specie (valuable risks); rigs (exploration rigs and oil production platforms); yachts; docks; incidental non marine; and inland marine.

For marine liability coverage, there is some mutual pooling of risks by ship owners. Protection and indemnity associations, known as P&I clubs, are mutual insurance cooperatives that were created to serve the marine industry. They mainly insure their members against risks not covered by the Lloyd's or marine companies' policies, including collision damage and liabilities for loss or damage to cargo, pollution, loss of life or personal injury on ships, and collision liability.

P&I clubs are wholly owned by the ship owners, which makes them both insurers and insureds. Unlike companies, they actively help the ship owners manage their risk. They advise on contracts and provide legal help in claims.

The International Group (IG) of P&I Clubs is a legalised, non-competitive cartel based in London, which consists of 13 not-for-profit insurance organisations providing coverage for over 90 per cent of the world's ocean-going tonnage. Clubs are individually liable for claims up to US $6 million, above which claims are shared between the 13 group members. There are some other P&I insurers, both mutual and commercial, outside the IG, which tend to cover smaller vessels.

The underwriting process

The London market, whether the insurers are companies or Lloyd's syndicates, works as follows. A broker seeks insurers for specific risks, and must find a 'lead' underwriter who will accept the first share, perhaps 25 per cent of the risk, and so establish the policy terms, and then find 'following' underwriters who will subscribe on this basis. This risk syndication can be spread across anything from one or two to 10 or more companies or syndicates on each risk, with great variations across different classes of business.

Underwriting itself remains dependent on human judgment. The pressure on underwriters is not that different to what it always has been, according to Robert Hiscox, chairman at Hiscox, in an interview in World@Risk in 2006, published on behalf of the IUA. He said that when he started as an underwriter in the 1960s, underwriters relied on their gut instincts and had no aggregates or models. He added that reliance on models when they were first introduced resulted in large losses and, even today, models do not exist for all risks.

Some underwriters will take more risk than others, but their approach should be consistent with the risk appetite of the firm for which they work. The quality of underwriting may vary according to information received, advice taken and risk modelling, as well as the type and amount of business taken on, premiums payable and reinsurance terms. Market conditions play a part.

There is an insurance cycle and to manage it is a major part of the underwriter's job. In the part of the cycle called a hard market, insurance rates rise because demand exceeds supply and profits tend to accrue, attracting extra capital into the market.

As the supply increases again, it creates a soft market, where insurance rates fall, and lead insurers focus on market share rather than profit. Underwriters may look to write business that is loss making in the short term. The FSA says it understands this approach but a disciplined and well-managed environment is needed to achieve such an outcome.

A major disaster leads to a hard market, where insurance rates rise, particularly in the classes of business that are most affected by the disaster, which may be welcomed by the industry. After the 11 September 2001 terrorist attacks on the United States, aviation rates in particular hardened, and after Hurricane Katrina in August 2005, energy reinsurance rates hardened.

Classes not directly affected may also see some level of rates hardening because the supply and demand ratio changes, but other factors may limit the impact. If rates are softening in any case, a major event may slow the trend, but not entirely reverse it.

Underwriting profit or loss for a non-life or reinsurance company is measured through the combined ratio. It is calculated by taking losses and expenses as a percentage of premiums received, and it excludes investment income. If the combined ratio is 99 per cent, the insurance company will have made a 1 per cent underwriting profit. But if it is higher than 100 per cent, non-life insurance policies may still be profitable after allocated investment income has been taken into account.

Regulatory developments

Contract certainty

In the past, insurance deals have been struck but the paperwork has sometimes not been sorted out for some months, which led to contract uncertainty. The problem became apparent in the insurance demands arising from the 11 September 2001 attacks on the United States.

In December 2004, John Tiner, then chief executive of the FSA, said that he was concerned about the 'deal now, detail later' culture of the London insurance market. The FSA gave the London market two years to find a solution.

By November 2006, Lloyd's managing agents were reporting 91 per cent of contracts as certain at inception and some insurance companies were reporting even higher levels. The FSA took the risk of attesting that the industry had succeeded, but said that the process had to be ongoing.

Contingent commissions

Contingent commissions are where insurers pay commissions to brokers in exchange for steering business their way. In April 2004, New York Attorney General Eliot Spitzer launched an investigation into this area and later alleged that certain brokers had taken pay-offs from insurance providers in return for introducing clients, with the result that the clients were denied best prices for policies. Spitzer alleged that bid rigging had taken place, which is where the broker makes sure that a favoured insurer wins the business.

During 2005, a small number of brokers agreed to pay substantial fines to settle charges initiated by Spitzer, including bid rigging, but many neither admitted nor denied the allegations. Spitzer said that there would be further investigations across the industry.

Within weeks of Spitzer's allegations, seven global insurance brokers announced that they would stop contingent commissions and, by early 2005, they were presenting revised business models. But others continued the practice.

There is some high-level industry sentiment that there is nothing wrong with contingent commissions provided that there is disclosure. The FSA has not yet made automatic disclosure of brokers' commissions mandatory in the UK, which fits with its preference for avoiding prescription, but the issue is under discussion.

ICAS and Solvency II

The FSA has required insurers to match capital closely to the risk of business written. Individual Capital Adequacy Standards (ICAS) is the framework under which firms measure their own risks to calculate the capital needed and the regulator reviews the results.

The regulator gives firms Individual Capital Guidance, specifying the capital it thinks they should have. By 2007, in about a quarter of cases across life and general insurance, the Guidance had been equal to the figure specified by the firm, and the FSA expects future divergence to diminish.

The ICAS is a move in the direction of the EU Directive, Solvency II, in which firms will have much greater freedom to calculate their own capital requirements for regulatory purposes, and the responsibility that accompanies it. The Directive will make more demands on the insurance industry than ICAS, Paul Sharma, head of financial risk review and modelling at the FSA, told delegates at a March 2007 conference.

The Solvency II framework requires insurers, as under ICAS, to establish technical provisions to cover expected future claims from policyholders. In addition, insurers must have resources to cover both a minimum capital requirement (MCR) and a solvency capital requirement (SCR).

The SCR covers all risks faced by the insurer – insurance, market, credit and operational – and will take account of the insurer's risk mitigation techniques, for example reinsurance and securitisation. Insurers can opt for a standardised approach to calculate the SCR or an advanced approach using an internal model validated by the supervisory authorities.

If an insurer's available resources fall below the SCR, its liabilities will be transferred to another insurer, its licence will be withdrawn, or the insurer will be closed to new business and its in-force business will be liquidated. The level of the SCR ensures that, as in ICAS, the insurer has no more than a 1 in 200 likelihood of being ruined in the year. In practice, it is much lower because, once the SCR is breached, supervision must intervene.

The introduction of new qualitative requirements, including risk management, should make insurance failures less likely. In the new regime, the focus will be on risk management. Insurers can invest in any asset they wish, provided they can show they understand the risks involved and can manage them.

Group supervision will be modernised and simplified. A parent may sometimes use SCR to meet part of the SCR of its subsidiaries. Groups will have a dedicated group supervisor.

The Commission is committed to having the new requirements in place in 2010, at least 18 months before insurers will need to start applying the new rules. A stepping stone towards Solvency II is the Reinsurance Directive (see Chapter 29).

Market reform

The Market Reform Group, including representatives from both Lloyd's and company markets, acts as a focal point for setting the direction of the current market reform programme, which focuses on, among other things, contract certainty.

A system has been introduced that provides managing agents, who hire the underwriters, with electronic assistance in checking that underwriting slips meet the need for contract certainty. Other initiatives include an electronic filing cabinet that enables claims, premium and policy documents to be handled electronically, and an electronic wordings repository to enhance clarity and efficiency throughout the market.

The future

As an insurance centre, London has significant underwriting expertise, diversity of business and a reputation for innovation. It has access to backup specialists such as lawyers, consultants and claims adjusters, and provides the best expertise in interpreting contractual clauses for settling claims.

For such reasons, London constantly attracts new capital. But its share of the global commercial insurance market has declined since the 1990s and, in some sectors, even earlier. Since the turn of the millennium, the insurance market in Bermuda has grown at a rate almost seven times that of London. Market sources attribute London's relatively slow performance partly to the greater cost of doing business in the capital, but also to the lack of efficiency and clarity in its processes.

Bermuda is more tax efficient and its regulatory regime works faster and less formally. In Bermuda, it is possible to set up an insurance company in a week, but in London it takes four weeks as a bare minimum.

28

Insurance: Lloyd's of London

Introduction

In this chapter, we will focus on Lloyd's, which is part of the London insurance market. We will examine the history of Lloyd's, how the market works, and the chain of security that underpins it, as well as the centralised underwriting controls.

Overview

Lloyd's represents just over half of the London insurance market, including reinsurance, which is how an insurance entity insures its own position (see Chapter 29). Lloyd's is a specialist insurance market, and business comes into it from more than 200 countries and territories worldwide. It started as Edward Lloyd's Coffee House, a 17th-century coffee house where timely shipping news was made available and marine insurance could be obtained.

Shipping and insurance were closely connected, and ship owners would meet in the coffee shop with wealthy individuals who took the risk of insuring ships and cargo. These were the early underwriters, and they had unlimited liability, which meant that they had to meet claims even if it bankrupted them.

They were called Names because they put their name on a slip of paper, the forerunner of today's underwriting slip, indicating what percentage of risk they would bear in return for a *pro rata* cut of the premium.

In 1769, the shipping insurance community moved to another coffee house, separating itself from other business, and kept the Lloyd's name. In

1811, Lloyd's gained a constitution, regulating admission more strictly, and in 1871, the market was incorporated by an Act of Parliament.

In 1887, Lloyd's issued its first non-marine policies and, 17 years later in 1904, a first motor policy, followed in 1911 by a first aviation policy. In 1958, Lloyd's moved to Lime Street.

The Lloyd's market is uniquely structured, has a high reputation abroad, and is known for innovative underwriting. Lloyd's has had its challenges, not least in the 1980s and 1990s when many insurance claims came from US company employees who had diseases from asbestos exposure. In the early 1990s, this brought the market close to collapse.

But Lloyd's has reinvented itself, focusing on disciplined underwriting, retaining its powerful brand, and recovering its strength, as demonstrated recently by its success in handling two consecutive record-breaking hurricane seasons in the United States in 2004 and 2005. It is in the nature of the insurance cycle that there will be more large losses, but it is hard to say when and where. Lloyd's points out that it has demonstrated resilience throughout its 300 years of history.

How Lloyd's works

Lloyd's consists of over 70 syndicates, each of which is no more than a collection of individuals and companies that have agreed to join together to underwrite insurance risks at Lloyd's. A syndicate may trade under the same name and number for years, but it is a series of annual ventures. The members of Lloyd's include companies, which may underwrite through only one syndicate, and individuals, known as Names, who typically underwrite through several syndicates.

Lloyd's members are not responsible for each other's losses. Nonetheless, a member may end up paying for another member's losses through its annual contribution to the Central Fund, part of the Lloyd's chain of security, which we will look at briefly in this chapter.

The syndicates cover specialist classes of business such as marine, aviation, catastrophe, professional indemnity and product liability. Reinsurance makes up more than half of Lloyd's income. There has been consolidation in the Lloyd's market; over 400 syndicates in 1980 had been reduced to 72 by mid-2007. Notably, British insurer Catlin Group agreed in October 2007 to buy its smaller rival Wellington Underwriting for £591 million to create the largest underwriter at Lloyd's, with synergies by 2008 particularly from moving Wellington's earnings to Catlin's low-tax base in Bermuda. Moody's Investors

Service (Moody's), the source for credit ratings, research and risk analysis, considers that potential for further consolidation remains but is unlikely to any significant extent given the independent nature of the operating units and the different cultures.

A closing syndicate year passes its portfolio of policies and reserves covering claims forward to future years in a procedure known as reinsurance to close. This way, each annual venture is brought to an end, normally after three years, crystallising the liabilities of participating underwriting members.

As a result, a closing syndicate will often have liabilities not only from policies written in the year it has accepted business, but also from policies acquired in reinsuring to close the previous year of account. Participants on the same syndicate in the next year may be different or, in some cases, the same, but with different participations, which means they are effectively reinsuring themselves. Members have the right, but not the obligation, to participate in syndicates for the following year and most of them do so.

The syndicates compete for business, and cover all or part of the risk, depending on their capacity, their specialisations and their view of the risk. They are staffed by underwriters, on whose judgment the market depends.

The lead underwriters make the decisions about the terms on which they will accept the business, if at all, setting the premium payable to the syndicate for underwriting the risk. Other underwriters follow suit, taking a slice of the risk, as presented by the broker, who will then move on to the next syndicate. Brokers need to be registered with Lloyd's to do business in the market, and Lloyd's streamlined the process in 2007 to make it faster and more efficient.

The managing agent employs underwriting staff and manages one or more syndicates on members' behalf. There are 47 managing agents, most of which are now owned by listed companies or backed by insurance-related capital. The only function allowed to a managing agent is syndicate management. Each managing agent employs underwriting staff, provides computer systems, and decides on the syndicates' underwriting policy in conjunction with the underwriters. Moody's believes there is a wide range in the quality and extent of the management within the managing agents.

The members' agent manages the affairs of Names, those individual capital providers who have given way to an influx of corporate capital in recent years and, to a lesser extent, the supply of corporate capital. As part of managing their affairs at Lloyd's, the members' agents will advise the Names on which syndicates they should participate. As at 2007, there were only two members' agents at Lloyd's, reflecting a decline in numbers of individual members. There are now only a very few traditional Names with unlimited liability at Lloyd's.

The Corporation of Lloyd's has the task of running the market. If the Corporation does not consider that a syndicate is acting in a prudent manner, it can ultimately terminate the right of the syndicate and the managing agent to trade at Lloyd's.

Capital backing

In 1994, companies were allowed to underwrite at Lloyd's for the first time. Before this date, it was entirely individuals who underwrote at Lloyd's. Between 1997 and 2007, private capital has reduced from 50 to 16 per cent of market capacity, including through incorporated vehicles, and now the underwriting is 84 per cent from corporate members. There are just over 1,100 Names with unlimited liability, down from 32,000 in 1988, and Lloyd's is taking in no new applications.

Individuals can underwrite at Lloyd's through Namecos, Scottish Limited Partnerships, or Limited Liability Partnerships, where they participate on a limited liability basis. Namecos are registered companies set up on a bespoke basis for Lloyd's Names and other individuals and are advised by members' agents. They usually underwrite on a range of syndicates to spread risk, while corporate capital typically invests in syndicates aligned to the corporate group. Scottish Limited Partnerships and Limited Liability Partnerships each have their own legal status but operate in a similar way to each other.

Another option for Names is to underwrite at Lloyd's through Members' Agent Pooling Arrangements (MAPA), which have participations across a spread of syndicates. At the other end of the spectrum are the integrated Lloyd's vehicles, where the sole corporate member of the syndicate is within the same corporate group as the managing agent of that syndicate. The parent company of the group is often listed on a recognised stock exchange.

The special purpose syndicate is a recent development that enables unaligned capital to participate on aligned syndicates via quota share reinsurance (a proportional treaty where the same proportion is ceded on all cessions; see also Chapter 29).

Syndicate capacity

The capital support from members, known as syndicate capacity, is the maximum amount of insurance premium, net of brokerage, which a syndicate can write in a year while keeping within Lloyd's capital requirements. In 2007, Lloyd's overall capacity provision was £16.1 billion, which has risen from £8.9 billion in 1993.

The average capacity for a syndicate, based on capital provided by members, is £244 million.

Lloyd's security has been threatened in the past and its underwriting standards have not always been under control. To see how it can happen, let us take a flashback.

Boom to bust

Between the 1970s and the early 1990s, Lloyd's experienced a boom-to-bust period. Names flocked to join Lloyd's in the 1980s. Some saw Lloyd's membership as being part of an exclusive club.

Some Names who signed up underestimated what this would mean when the losses later hit. Some alleged that they had been lured into dud syndicates but they never proved their case. Individuals who had become Names with as little as £100,000 in liquid assets were, in a number of cases, ruined.

A main problem lay in the type of business written. The most dangerous was asbestos liability, which had been written on a long-tail basis, meaning that the policy allowed claims to be made many years later. US employees affected by asbestosis sued their former employing companies that they held responsible, often many years after they had first been exposed to asbestos.

The companies claimed on insurance and were awarded huge damages in the courts. Lloyd's ultimately had to pay out much of the costs, and syndicates claimed from their Names.

Catastrophe claims were a major issue. London Market Excess of Loss (LMX) was used to reinsure catastrophe risks, and it led to what became known as the LMX spiral (for more about excess of loss reinsurance, see Chapter 29). Syndicates and insurance companies would pay a first slice of a loss, and would pass the next slice onto a reinsurer. A third slice would be passed to another reinsurer, and the spiral would continue through the market, sometimes winding back to the original insurer or reinsurer, which might take another slice, effectively reinsuring itself.

A series of major catastrophes happened. In 1988, the Piper Alpha oil platform caught fire and fell into the North Sea. In 1989, Hurricane Hugo struck Puerto Rico, St Croix, South Carolina and North Carolina and, in the same year, oil tanker Exxon Valdez ran aground off the Alaskan coast. In 1990, there were severe storms across Europe.

Lloyd's Names ended up paying many of the claims. Some loss-making Names alleged that certain members' agents had known of pending legal actions affecting the syndicates that they advised them to join. The claim was never proven.

In 1988–92, losses at Lloyd's were £8 billion and commentators had started querying whether the market could survive. In 1991, several thousand

Names resigned from Lloyd's, and others reduced or stopped their underwriting commitments. Many refused to pay cash calls. Some took legal action against members' and managing agents for negligent advice, negligent underwriting or closure of years of account, and against auditors.

David Coleridge, then chairman of Lloyd's, appointed a task force under David Rowland, chief executive of broker Sedgwick, which in January 1992 recommended many changes to the Lloyd's market, including new governance arrangements. Among the changes made arising from the Rowland report, smaller Names could pool their limits into the MAPA, which spread their resources across many syndicates and so reduced their risk. Corporate members with limited liability, but also higher deposit requirements to support underwriting activity, were introduced.

Rowland created a Hardship Committee to help Names pay their debts. It was headed by Lloyd's council member Dr Mary Archer, wife of best-selling novelist Jeffrey, and enabled Names in proven financial hardship to pay up in stages or by a deferred arrangement.

In 1993, David Rowland became Lloyd's first full-time paid chairman. In 1996, he completed a market-wide Reconstruction and Renewal settlement plan. The main part was to form Equitas Reinsurance Ltd, which was authorised by the Department of Trade and Industry (DTI) in March 1996, subject to certain requirements, including an agreed level of surplus assets over liabilities.

Lloyd's made a £3.2 billion settlement offer to Names. The amount consisted of £1.1 billion of litigation settlement funds mainly from errors and omissions (E&O) insurers, who insured underwriting (managing and members') agents and auditors against liability for their professional negligence to the Names for whom they acted, and of £2.1 billion of debt credits made up of contributions to the settlement by Lloyd's, members of Lloyd's, underwriting agents and brokers. These debt credits were available only to Names who accepted the settlement offer, reducing their outstanding liabilities and Equitas premium (the role of Equitas as reinsurer is discussed shortly below). By contrast, a non-settling Name was entitled to an allocation from the litigation settlement fund if the action in which that Name was involved settled.

To help Names pay their share of the remaining shortfall, special arrangements were made that allowed for the early release of anticipated surpluses from the 1993, 1994 and 1995 years of account.

Lloyd's sent out its settlement offer to all 34,000 Names at the end of July 1996 and by the first closing date, 28 August 1996, acceptances were sufficiently high for the Council of Lloyd's to declare the offer unconditional. Ultimately about 95% of Names accepted the settlement offer.

Equitas closed all the 1992 and prior years of account of Lloyd's syndicates, writing non-life business by way of reinsurance of those syndicates.

It proceeded with the run-off of the business, giving Names, at this stage, 'affordable finality'. However, there was a residual risk for Names if Equitas should fail to pay liabilities to policyholders in full.

Lloyd's Central Fund has a contingent exposure to Equitas through the two Joint Asset Trust Funds in the United States, which 1992 and prior policyholders may tap if claims are not met. Maintenance of those US funds is a condition of members being permitted by US state insurance regulations to underwrite certain classes of US business.

The exposure to Equitas arises also because Lloyd's has a subsidiary called Lioncover, reinsured into Equitas. It set up Lioncover to reinsure the liabilities of private members on syndicates formerly managed by, among others, PCW Underwriting Agencies Ltd. In 1987, the Council of Lloyd's and others had agreed a settlement with PCW Names, acknowledging that they had been victims of fraud on the part of certain directors and employees of the managing agent. Lloyd's is liable to fund any deficiency of assets in Lioncover.

However, a recent deal struck between Equitas and Berkshire Hathaway is expected to help Lloyd's draw a line under the past completely. This is covered later in this chapter.

More about Lloyd's today

Even through its troubled times, Lloyd's has retained its track record of paying valid claims, which now dates back over 300 years. Let us look at Lloyd's financial strength going forward, as in its chain of security. We will examine the Lloyd's solvency ratio and the benefits of the recent Equitas deal with Berkshire Hathaway. Lloyd's financial strength accompanies its recent more stringent underwriting controls, implemented through the Franchise Performance Directorate, which we will discuss below.

Chain of security

Lloyd's chain of security has three links: premium trust funds, members' funds at Lloyd's and central assets at Lloyd's. The earlier the link, the sooner is the financial claim on it. Let us look at how they work.

First link: premium trust funds

The first link consists of insurance premiums received by a syndicate and held in a premium trust fund as the initial resource from which to pay policyholder claims. Contributions are made to the premium trust funds at syndicate level for a given year of underwriting. On 31 December 2006, these funds were £28 billion.

Premium trust funds can be used only to pay claims, and permitted expenses and outgoings such as reinsurance premiums and underwriting expenses. The funds must be liquid and are mostly invested in bonds.

Second link: Members' funds

The second link, known as members' funds, is capital provided by each member at individual syndicate level to support its underwriting at Lloyd's.

The link between the premium trust funds (above) and members' funds is best shown by a simplified example. If a syndicate receives £100 in premium, it will put this amount in the premium trust fund, and will then calculate what its claims will be, based on actuarial estimates. If it concludes that they will be £90, it will keep this amount in the premium trust funds and transfer the remaining £10 to the members' funds.

On 31 December 2006, members' funds were £11.3 billion. The capital provided by a member in these members' funds provides cover beyond the first link if claims should turn out to be more than expected, as well as future losses generally, for that member only. Funds at Lloyd's support all of the open underwriting years for that member.

Members' funds are intended to satisfy the Individual Capital Assessment (ICA) that the Financial Services Authority (FSA) requires each syndicate to provide to cover underlying business risks, with a worst outcome of a 1-in-200 risk covered, so satisfying a 99.5 per cent confidence level. When each syndicate's ICA is agreed with the Corporation of Lloyd's, it is uplifted (by 35 per cent in 2007) to ensure extra capital is in place to support Lloyd's ratings with insurance rating agencies. For more on the ICA, see Chapter 27.

Third link: central assets at Lloyd's

In both the first and second link in the Lloyd's chain of security, as described above, members have put up their capital on a 'several' basis. For example, Brit Insurance puts up capital and so does Amlin, but Brit money cannot be used to pay Amlin claims, and the reverse is also true. However, the central assets, the third link, are held mutually and can be used to pay any member's unpaid losses at the Council of Lloyd's discretion.

If hypothetically there were 11 members, and each put up £1 billion, and the central assets have £2 billion, there is £3 billion (£1 billion plus £2 billion) to be used to pay any single member's claims if necessary.

The central assets at Lloyd's, based on 31 December 2006 figures, include the Central Fund at £629 million, corporation assets at £114 million, subordinated debt at £497 million, syndicate loans at £214 million (since repaid), and a callable layer (up to and including 3 per cent of capacity) of a maximum £484 million.

The Central Fund is funded by members' annual contributions, which are set at 1 per cent of underwriting capacity for 2007. Each year, Lloyd's collects 1 per cent of capacity from each syndicate for the Central Fund, which in 2007 added up to £160 million, based on £16 billion of total capacity. Over the years, these collections have been the main way in which Lloyd's has built up the Central Fund.

In 2002 and 2003, there was a premium levy of 2 per cent on members, which no longer exists but was another way of building up the central assets. Lloyd's continued the levy, originally introduced after Reconstruction and Renewal to repay a £285m loan, and it increased the rate from 1.1 per cent to 2 per cent in the knowledge that extra claims were pending as a result of the 11 September 2001 attacks on the United States.

Let us now look at other parts of the central assets. The corporation assets include, but are not confined to, cash and investments.

The subordinated debt consists of £500 million that Lloyd's borrowed in 2004 in the capital markets, and a further £500 million in June 2007; it will have to repay this debt, as well as pay interest on it. It can be used to pay claims first, taking priority over repaying debt holders or paying them interest.

Rounding off the figures for illustrative purposes, Lloyd's pays £70 million a year in interest on the subordinated debt. The flip side is that it has invested this borrowed money as well as, in the past, money borrowed through syndicate loans. The investment interest on borrowed money, again rounded for demonstration purposes, is £55 million, which is less than the £70 million paid out on the subordinated debt because it is invested mainly in debt instruments that pay less interest as a result of offering higher security. The £15 million gap is easily met from the £160 million levied from members into the Central Fund. Lloyd's plans to reduce the levies from 1 per cent to 0.5 per cent in 2008, but the gap will still be covered.

The syndicate loans are loans made from syndicate premium trust funds to Lloyd's, and the interest payable was based on a Merrill Lynch 1–3 year UK government total return index (or equivalent US index for dollar loans), which was around 3 per cent on sterling loans for 2006. In 2007, Lloyd's repaid the syndicate loans, using the financing that the second issue of subordinated debt had provided. If the central assets were needed to pay claims, surplus assets could have been used and this use would have taken priority over repaying the syndicate. Because the central assets are mutual, one syndicate loan could have been used to pay another syndicate's claim.

Lloyd's has been criticised for having subordinated debt as part of the central assets that are part of the final link in its chain of security. Lloyd's borrowed from the capital markets because this is essentially cheaper than borrowing from members, although it could have taken this step. Businesses look for a return of capital of more than 10 per cent, but Lloyd's could borrow in the capital markets and pay around 7 per cent in interest, which it found more efficient.

The callable layer is an option to move up to 3 per cent of capacity from each business's premium trust fund into the central assets. If Lloyd's should ever make a first call on the layer, it recognises that this would not take the levy from any syndicates, where it would effectively leave them with less money than they needed in their premium trust fund.

Solvency ratio

The solvency ratio is important because if it fell below 100 per cent, Lloyd's would fail the regulatory solvency test. The solvency ratio may be defined as central assets in relation to outstanding claims in respect of insolvent members (solvency deficiencies). A member is insolvent when it does not have enough assets to meet its underwriting liabilities and solvency margin. In the insurance companies' market, the FSA's focus on a company is increased if its solvency ratio falls below 200 per cent. The Lloyd's solvency ratio at end 2006 was 812 per cent, up from 384 per cent a year earlier, based on assets of £2,054 million, in relation to solvency deficiencies of £253 million. Lloyd's solvency position is regularly calculated.

Equitas developments

In October 2006, Equitas announced a deal with National Indemnity, a subsidiary of Berkshire Hathaway, which credit rating agency Standard & Poor's has assigned an AAA rating, its highest financial strength rating. Lloyd's has said the deal, when fully implemented, would end the contingent exposure of Lloyd's central assets.

Phase 1 of the deal gave cover of US$5.7 billion in excess of Equitas' reserves of US$8.7 billion held as at 31 March 2006. Lloyd's made a £72 million contribution and has committed itself to pay a further £18 million as Phase II occurs.

'Equitas would have to have existing reserves wrong by 66 per cent for this entire cover to get used up and we don't believe that it's likely to happen,' says Robert Smith, vice-president and senior analyst at financial institutions group, Moody's Investors Service.

The American Names Association told its members in November 2006 that the agreement was a momentous achievement, but added that the first phase of the transaction did not in itself remove the original and outgoing legal liability of Names in relation to US policyholders and ceding companies that purchased coverage from Lloyd's syndicates before 1993.

The second phase of the deal is a statutory transfer of Names' liabilities under Part VII of the Financial Services & Markets Act 2000 (FSMA). In terms of fundamentals, it is already certain that Berkshire Hathaway will pay claims, but the Part VII transfer is for legal substance, enabling liabilities to be transferred to Berkshire Hathaway out of Lioncover and Names.

Before Phase II can happen, amendments are required to the FSMA, and the transfer will require the approval of the court and the Financial Services Authority (FSA). If Phase II takes place before 31 December 2009, Equitas has the option to buy up to a further £1.3 billion in reinsurance cover from National Indemnity for up to £40 million.

Taking account of the Berkshire Hathaway deal in advance of Phase II, two credit rating agencies, Standard & Poor's and Fitch Ratings, upgraded Lloyd's from A to A+, which means that they consider it in a stronger position to pay any creditors in the future.

Franchise Board

Lloyd's Franchise Performance Directorate, (FPD) was implemented in 2003 because of some poor underwriting in the past. It aims to ensure that disciplined underwriting for profit prevails in the market. By this move, Lloyd's shifted its focus from that of regulator of the market to its commercial manager.

It is through the FPD that the Corporation reviews the business plans of syndicates. The FPD can reject a managing agent's plan or require explanations about it. All managing agents must submit quarterly monitoring reports to the directorate.

Since the late 1990s, Lloyd's has run a Realistic Disaster Scenario (RDS) framework that assesses the syndicate and market response to a range of natural events, including hurricanes in the United States, a typhoon in Japan and two planes colliding above a major city, which are imaginary events, although with some basis in real experience.

Lloyd's expects that, where catastrophe models are used, there should be more than one, and that modelling is done by skilled and experienced staff, Paul Nunn, head of exposure management at Lloyd's, told delegates attending a June 2007 industry conference. For more on modelling, see Chapters 21 and 23.

If a syndicate's operation poses an unacceptable risk, the board can take action and, at the extreme, terminate the right of a managing agent and its syndicate to trade in the market. It took such action against Goshawk Syndicate Management and, subsequently, in October 2005, the FSA fined Goshawk £220,000 for systems and control failures that were initially the subject of warnings from Lloyd's.

One-year accounting

On 1 January 2005, Lloyd's financial reporting regime moved from three-year fund accounting to annual accounting under UK Generally Accepted Accounting Principles (GAAP), which facilitated comparison with insurance company results using, for instance, the combined ratio (losses and expenses as a percentage of premium received).

The accounting difference can be considerable. Under annual accounting, the Lloyd's loss from the 11 September 2001 terrorist attacks on the United States was accounted for in the 2001 financial year, when the loss occurred, but under three-year accounting, it was split between 1999 (a very small proportion), 2000 and 2001, the years in which the relevant insurance policies incepted.

The 12 months of underwriting that make up an accounting year are held open for three years as claims can come in over this full period, following which the risk is passed on through the reinsurance-to-close process referred to early in this chapter.

The three-year account is still maintained in order to keep equity between members and for distribution purposes. Each member takes its proportional share of the syndicate's profit or loss for a particular year of account, based on the proportion in which it agreed to participate before the start of the year of account.

Accounts are issued at the end of three years from syndicates that are supported by third-party capital.

Regulation

Historically, Lloyd's has been a self-regulating body. Under FSMA, the regulation of Lloyd's was transferred to the FSA, reflecting a shift in Lloyd's role from that of regulator to that of a more commercial entity. At the same time, Lloyd's retains a significant regulatory role, particularly in the supervision of the market. Managing agents at Lloyd's are also now regulated by the FSA, although the underwriting members operating under Lloyd's supervision are excluded from much of the same regulatory framework, subject to certain requirements. The FSA, however, retains certain powers to take over the regulation of underwriting members.

In June 2007, Ed Balls, economic secretary to the Treasury, announced that there would be a legislative reform order to amend Lloyd's Act 1982, with the aim of updating the governance arrangements at Lloyd's to reduce costs and unnecessary bureaucracy. The initiative is part of a broad cooperation between the government and the City to help keep the City globally competitive. The government plans to publish its proposals for consultation in 2008.

International progress

On the international front, Lloyd's has a large global licence network and Lloyd's underwriters write business in 200 territories and countries. This has not always been easy because of how others react to the unique Lloyd's structure. Lloyd's has licences in over 70 countries, the latest being an offshore reinsurance licence in China, and it has a representative office in India.

Lloyd's does the highest proportion of its business in the United States, accounting for 39 per cent of the total, which compares with 24 per cent in the UK and 15 per cent elsewhere in Europe. It is licensed for writing only surplus lines business in the United States except in two states. On Lloyd's and other European insurers' objections to the 100 per cent reinsurance collateral required of overseas reinsurers dealing with US ceding companies, see Chapter 29.

The future

Lloyd's expense levels in relation to net premiums look relatively high, according to credit analysts. The expenses are partly due to the type of business Lloyd's writes, which involves a long distribution chain, compared with, for instance, the more direct business writing model in Bermuda.

To address the expenses issue, Lloyd's is focusing on efficient processing as a top priority. Lloyd's has helped to lead London insurance market electronic processing initiatives in recent years. These have been successful, although there have been pockets of market resistance (see Chapter 27). The initiatives have involved some trial and error. In January 2006, Lloyd's withdrew funding for its electronic trading platform Kinnect after spending £70 million on it over five years. The technology seemed inadequate and many said that the project lacked practical benefits.

Lloyds has a rolling three-year plan that outlines how it aims to achieve its vision of being the marketplace of choice. Work is under way to build on the five key benefits that Lloyd's sees as applicable to working in its market. These are: a performance management framework that supports the achievement of superior operating returns; capital advantages in which the benefits of mutuality outweigh the costs; security and strong market ratings capable of attracting specialist insurance business; access to major markets supported by a global brand and licence network; and operations and processes supporting the cost-effective, efficient transaction of business.

While this plan is underway, the insurance cycle is heading, as from late 2007 onwards, for a downturn with pressure on most classes of business, particularly aviation. Lloyd's is benefiting from improved risk management at syndicate level and underwriting controls imposed by the FPD. This has not yet been tested in a downturn although, according to Smith at Moody's, Lloyd's FPD is likely to curtail the extent of losses seen in previous downturns.

Structurally, Lloyd's unique diversity of capital is under threat given the shift from individuals underwriting with unlimited liability. But this shift helps to protect Lloyd's from the risk to reputation arising when Names cannot or will not pay liabilities, and undertake high-profile court action or settlement negotiations as they allege unacceptable practice and fraud.

If Lloyd's position is to be maintained, new ways must be found for unaligned capital providers to access syndicates in a way attractive to both managing agents and the capital providers, according to the Annual Venture Review carried out by Lloyd's in 2006.

29

Reinsurance

Introduction

In this chapter, we will see how reinsurance works. We will take a quick look at times when it has come into the hands of fraudsters. We will touch on financial reinsurance, and check out some of the latest capital markets solutions. Reinsurance is part of the insurance industry. Read this along with Chapters 27 and 28.

Overview

Reinsurance is a product for insurance industry professionals. It enables them to lay off their own risk onto a reinsurance company but it does not change the total risk exposure.

The process of reinsurance works as follows. The insurer wants cover for the risk it has taken onto its books, so seeks to reinsure it by passing on the liability to a reinsurance company. As the ceding office, it pays a premium to the reinsurer, which is the company that accepts the cession and assumes responsibility for claims. Any of the business that the insurer keeps, rather than passing onto the reinsurer, is known as retention.

In this way, reinsurance helps insurance in its main aim, which is to spread risk. Reinsurance enables insurers to limit loss exposure and so to offer higher coverage limits or to cover a greater number of risks. It increases the capacity of insurers to take on more business that it is safe for them to write, and helps them to stabilise earnings when major events arise. The reinsurer provides support services such as technical training and accounting.

A reinsurance placement is typically shared among more than one reinsurer. A 'lead' reinsurer will set the terms and 'following' reinsurers will subscribe to the agreed contract. Reinsurance can be written through brokers, who can represent a number of participating reinsurers, each assuming part of the risk, or it can be written directly from ceding companies.

In reinsurance, loss data is often less available than in insurance, which makes the underwriter's job more critical. Reinsurance is an international business and through reinsurance contracts, the London market links with the United States, Bermuda, continental Europe and elsewhere.

Proportional reinsurance

In proportional reinsurance, the reinsurer takes a percentage share of the policy, receiving a fixed percentage of premium income from the original policyholder and paying the same percentage of claims payments. Under this arrangement, if the reinsured pays the reinsurer 40 per cent of the premiums, it will recover 40 per cent of the losses.

The reinsurer also pays a ceding commission to the insurer to cover the costs of writing business and administration, which may include a profit element for providing the business.

One form of proportional reinsurance is quota share business, where premiums and losses are shared *pro rata*. Another form is surplus treaty, where the ceding company retains a defined amount as a line, keeping all the premiums and losses, beyond which there is a proportional split.

Property insurers prefer proportional reinsurance because the sum insured is usually known, making proportional divisions practical.

Non-proportional reinsurance

Non-proportional reinsurance is paid only if the loss is beyond the retention of the insurer, which is the amount of the loss it will accept. It is commonly excess-of-loss reinsurance, where the ceding office pays the initial layer of every valid claim. The reinsurers pay the balance of losses up to a set figure, and this is known as 'working layer' or 'lower layer' excess-of-loss reinsurance, beyond which further excess-of-loss cover may apply.

Losses in the lower layer are more predictable than in the higher layers because of greater historical frequency, and this enables underwriters to price the risk more accurately.

Reinsurance contracts

The two basic types of contract are treaty and facultative. Both may be written on a proportional or non-proportional basis, or as a mixture of both.

Treaty reinsurance

Treaty reinsurance is an agreement covering a class or classes of business, and it automatically covers risks written by the insured without evaluation of individual exposures.

The treaty reinsurer will review the ceding company's underwriting practices, risk management and claims settlement processes, and its evaluation will affect the pricing of the treaty. The reinsurer is ultimately dependent on the underwriting decisions of the primary policymaker.

Reinsurance treaties can be written on a term basis, with an expiry date, or be continuous, but with a notice period built in. The most usual buyer is a senior insurance company executive.

Facultative reinsurance

Facultative reinsurance provides an insurer with coverage for specific risks, typically large or unusual, which are not covered in its reinsurance treaties. Each facultative reinsurance contract is agreed individually, which requires significant resources to implement but enables the underwriter to price the contract more accurately. Unlike in treaty reinsurance, the most usual buyer is the insurance underwriter who underwrote the original policy.

Retrocession

Retrocession is where a reinsurer reinsures its own business under a retrocession agreement with another reinsurer, the retrocessionaire, to cover risk exposure or obtain extra underwriting capacity.

The reinsurance of reinsurance process may continue until the original receiver receives back some of its own business, which is known as a spiral, as in the LMX spiral (see Chapter 28). In the past, retrocessionaires involved in spirals have sometimes refused to pay.

The reinsurer and the reinsured

To understand the relationship between the reinsurer and the reinsured, let us focus on two doctrines: utmost good faith, and follow the fortunes.

Utmost good faith

Parties to a reinsurance contract should be honest with each other. The reinsured should disclose all material facts, and should enter appropriately into any settlement with the original policyholder.

The reinsured should give adequate notice of any claim to the reinsurer, giving it time if it should wish to participate in defending the claim, as well as to find funds.

Follow the fortunes

The reinsurer must follow, and act in accordance with, payments to the original policyholder by the reinsured, so following its fortunes. The doctrine is not infallible, as court findings have shown.

Financial reinsurance

Let us now look at financial reinsurance, which has given rise to some controversy; it started in the United States. Financial reinsurance can take various forms, but it has in common that it is arranged for financial or strategic reasons and there is little or no risk transfer from the insurer to the reinsurer. Unlike in traditional reinsurance, the level of claims makes no difference to the level of premium the insurer pays and the profit the reinsurer makes.

One aim of financial reinsurance is to smooth the insurer's profits. The insurer transfers money to the reinsurer in good years that can be used to offset losses in bad years. Another aim is to provide increased reinsurance protection as a way to strengthen the balance sheet, giving the impression that the company is stronger than it really is.

Financial reinsurance should be disclosed and accounted for properly, failing which it can be construed as concealing the financial position of a company, according to the Financial Services Authority (FSA). The regulator's position is that if reinsurance genuinely transfers risk, it should be risk-accounted and recognised as such in the company's accounts, while a contract that does not meet the risk-transfer criteria should be deposit-accounted, and treated as a loan in the balance sheet.

In July 2006, the FSA, in conjunction with the Australian Prudential Regulation Authority (APRA), issued a final notice against John Byrne, former chief executive of the alternative solutions business unit of the General Re group, prohibiting him from performing a controlled function in the UK for five years. The regulators concluded that Byrne was involved in arranging and structuring financial reinsurance transactions that he knew lacked sufficient risk transfer.

In this way, the FSA showed not only that it understood the complicated concept of financial reinsurance, but also that it had the teeth to take effective action against its misuse.

Reinsurance reassessed

The 11 September 2001 attacks on the United States served as a trigger for insurers to make a closer inspection of their reinsurance arrangements, including the quality of their reinsurers. In recent years, insurers have become less inclined to use reinsurance as a substitute for their own good underwriting. They are giving brokers less discretion in choice of reinsurer, particularly for long-tail business, where the liability may be discovered and claims made many years after the loss was caused. Some £200–£300 million insurance payouts to parties who claimed on long-tail asbestos-related diseases have served as a warning, and insurance contracts may allow for a review of liabilities later.

Reinsurers tend to set aside loss reserves for incurred but not reported (IBNR) claims, which are necessarily only an estimate of future loss. There is an increasing use of downgrade clauses by which, if a reinsurer's rating falls below a trigger level, the primary insurer may be permitted to void the contract or require collateral to be posted.

In keeping with the caution of reinsurers, credit rating agencies have lowered the financial strength ratings of some reinsurers, although they rate the sector outlook as stable. Many reinsurers feel that the rating agencies have too much power, and use outdated methodologies.

Capital markets convergence

To meet demands for capacity, traditional reinsurance has converged with the wider capital markets, which Lloyd's chairman Lord Levene has described as bringing a 'new creativity' to the market.

Cat (catastrophe) bonds, the oldest of the structured insurance products, have existed since 1997 as a form of reinsurance cover sold as debt. Insurance risk is converted into a bond, which a special purpose reinsurance company, established in an offshore location, sells to investors. The bond sale proceeds are placed in a collateral trust and are invested in highly liquid paper and are used to pay losses by the reinsured.

The cat bond is an excess-of-loss arrangement, and investors will lose money only if the excess is triggered. The detachment point can vary. In the late 1990s, overcapitalised reinsurance companies assumed catastrophe risk more cheaply than investors in cat bonds, which slowed the product's development.

After the 2004 and 2005 hurricane seasons and scares such as bird flu, some shortage of retrocession capacity in catastrophe cover arose. Cat bonds as well as newer structured insurance products such as sidecars flourished as a means of transferring risk. Another use of structured insurance products is to achieve capital relief in line with regulatory requirements. Solvency II, the EU Directive planned for implementation in 2012 (see Chapter 27), is encouraging this.

The sidecar is an alternative to a cat bond. It is riskier because it takes on a proportion of the reinsurer's risk but, to reflect this, it pays investors a higher return. The sidecar is a form of captive – an insurer owned by the reinsurance company for which it provides cover – and is registered typically in Bermuda or, less often, in the Cayman Islands.

The sidecar provides catastrophe coverage to its sponsor reinsurance company for a period of perhaps two years. In this way, it takes risk off the parent's book, so enabling it to write more business. It is designed to capitalise on market conditions that may be temporary, and it can be dismantled quickly.

Short-term securities are issued to institutional investors to fund the sidecar. The premiums from the reinsureds and equity capital from investors are typically paid into a trust account, which can collateralise each policy written by the sidecar on a probable maximum loss basis or up to the policy limits.

Another form of insurance securitisation is the embedded value securitisation, which is the monetisation of the future profits of a portfolio of life contracts. The monetisation aims to decrease the capital that life insurance companies must hold, and to get cash up front from investors, repaying them by the profits from the life insurance contracts.

So far, the deals have generally been structured in a way that transfers only a low level of risk to note holders, said Moody's, the rating agency, in a 2007 report, *Life Insurance-Linked Securities: Impact on Sponsor Ratings*. Moody's foresaw a rapid increase in the transfer of more extreme risk to capital markets as solvency regimes round the world become more sophisticated.

The money invested in structured products is still small compared to conventional reinsurance, and much of it is from hedge funds and private equity, particularly in the United States where there is greater willingness to take a risk for the high returns.

For investors, what matter most are the returns. In 2006, the average sidecar had better returns than most stocks, but by mid-2007 stocks were showing much better returns than the previous year. The risk of investing is priced into the product. Investors may have a problem getting money out of sidecars after a loss event, given that reinsured parties, otherwise known as cedants, may hold money back to cover unknown losses.

When implementing the Reinsurance Directive, the FSA exercised its option to allow credit for reinsurance transactions, using insurance special purpose vehicles (ISPVs). By August 2007, no ISPV had been set up in the UK, largely due to current unfavourable tax treatment, but the FSA was considering a first ISPV application.

The Reinsurance Directive

The Reinsurance Directive is a component of the European Commission's Financial Services Action Plan and should be implemented across member states from December 2007. The UK had implemented many of the Directive's provisions before the deadline but some EU member states will almost certainly fall behind it.

The Directive is an interim solution for reinsurers, pending finalisation of the broader Solvency II, and it aims to create a single regulated market for pure reinsurance business, creating a level playing field across the EU. For many member states, it introduces regulation of the reinsurance industry for the first time.

Reinsurers have tended to do business through subsidiaries across Europe with separate solvency and reporting requirements, but the Directive enables them to write business through a single entity across the EU, based on one licence and supervised by a home regulator. On this basis, reinsurers will be able to hold their capital in a single entity and manage it better and to save on costs. Life and non-life reinsurance may be written from the same entity.

The Directive encourages consolidation and provides an incentive for reinsurance groups to select a home state in the most favourable regulatory and tax environment. In March 2007, Zurich-based Swiss Re, the world's largest reinsurer, said that it would optimise its legal entity structure in the EU by forming three legal entities, based in Luxembourg, which will serve as risk carriers for most of its European reinsurance and insurance business, operating via branches in the rest of the EU. Swiss Re aims to have the new structure in place by mid-2009.

In London, the Reinsurance Directive has brought about a significant increase in compliance and reporting obligations. The Directive eliminates reinsurance-related collateral requirements across Europe. The hope has been that it will encourage the United States to eliminate collateral requirements on foreign reinsurers; the London market and European insurers have pushed for this, although entire elimination now seems over-optimistic.

Offshore reinsurance collateral requirements in the United States

Overseas reinsurers in the United States must post collateral equal to 100 per cent of all reinsurance obligations assumed, which is not required of domestic reinsurers. Much business is affected. In 2006, US insurers and reinsurers ceded more than US $22.2 billion worth of premium to unaffiliated companies in 95 foreign jurisdictions. European reinsurers, including Lloyd's, have campaigned against the requirement for offshore reinsurers in the United States to post collateral. Part of their case is that US licensed reinsurers operating in the UK and in some other main reinsurance jurisdictions do not have to post collateral.

In September 2007, the US National Association of Insurance Commissioners (NAIC) published a proposal that reinsurers should be able to passport their business across the United States after being credit-rated by a single US state to determine their collateral requirements. The proposals ditched an earlier idea that the NAIC should establish its own entity, the Reinsurance Evaluation Office (REO), to conduct the ratings. Instead, a new organisation, the Reinsurance Supervision Review Department (RSRD), would be created and have only one job, which is to review the quality of regulation in other countries and identify those that offer regulatory equivalence to the United States.

The RSRD, which reports to the NAIC's E-committee, would circulate a list of approved jurisdictions. Reinsurers from appropriate countries would be able to go to a US state of their choice to obtain a rating, which determines the collateral required for conducting business in the United States. This would make sense because state regulators are more accountable for their ratings than the originally proposed REO would be, according to lawyers. For example, an EU-based reinsurer could go to New York and say 'rate me', and New York could give it a rating and would be its port-of-entry state and sole regulator.

The collateral required, as determined by the rating, would be unattractively high for overseas reinsurers both in absolute terms and relative to those for US reinsurers. The strongest overseas reinsurers, given an AAA credit rating by rating agency Standard & Poor's (S&P), would have to put up collateral worth 60 per cent of reinsurance obligations assumed to conduct business in the United States, and strong overseas reinsurers (A+ from S&P) would have to put up 80 per cent collateral. For US reinsurers, there would be a zero per cent collateral requirement for every class, except Class 5, which means a US reinsurer with a BBB S&P rating would not need collateral.

Domiciliary states of the ceding company (placing business with the reinsurer) have to agree to a state regulator's rating of the reinsurer if it is to conduct business, or could change the collateral.

The failure of the new proposals fully to create a level playing field with US reinsurers over collateral requirements reflects some of the political pressure points that have been brought to bear on the issues, as well as regulatory inertia, lawyers say. The NAIC has, nonetheless, said many times in writing that there is a need for a new system that is not parochial, is internationally agnostic, and judges reinsurers on their financial strength. This is a move in that direction. The proposals were to be debated at an NAIC meeting at the end of September 2007 and, by the time this book is in your hands, there may have been significant progress.

Dispute resolution

When disputes arise between insurers and their reinsurers, the most usual way to resolve them is through arbitration. The arbitration process is acknowledged as slow, expensive, adversarial and risky, and although every case is supposed to be confidential, parties involved sometimes leak details. In May 2007, new guidelines from the Chartered Institute of Arbitrators restricted parties to an arbitration from liaising inappropriately with prospective arbitrators before deciding whether to appoint them.

Litigation applies in only a small percentage of cases, but it is seen as more efficient than arbitration. The court system is streamlined, and both barristers and judges are reinsurance savvy.

There is a growing interest in mediation as an alternative to arbitration. The process tries to preserve relationships, which are an important part of the London market. It remains, as one underwriter put it, 'as rare as hen's teeth', partly because parties to the dispute feel that they have already exhausted avenues for agreement. On a positive note, mediation resolves some disputes, offering genuine confidentiality. There is no obligation to settle and, if it fails to work out in the allotted time period, it may have provided insights.

30

Retail insurance, savings and domestic property

Introduction

In this chapter, we will look at retail mortgage, insurance and savings products. The link with the City is that sometimes these products are sold within the Square Mile, and the premiums and deposits arising are invested by asset managers who may be based there. We will focus on some regulatory developments, including the Insurance Mediation Directive, and on complaints and compensation procedures. Read this with Chapter 31, which covers pensions and annuities.

Overview

In March 2006, the Financial Services Authority (FSA) published a survey in which it found that many people were failing to plan ahead adequately for retirement or for an unexpected expense or drop in income.

The FSA is leading the National Strategy for Financial Capability, which is bringing together the financial services industry, consumer and voluntary organisations, Government and media to find ways to improve the UK's financial capability.

Let us now take a look at some of the main financial services products on offer, how they are sold, and changes underway.

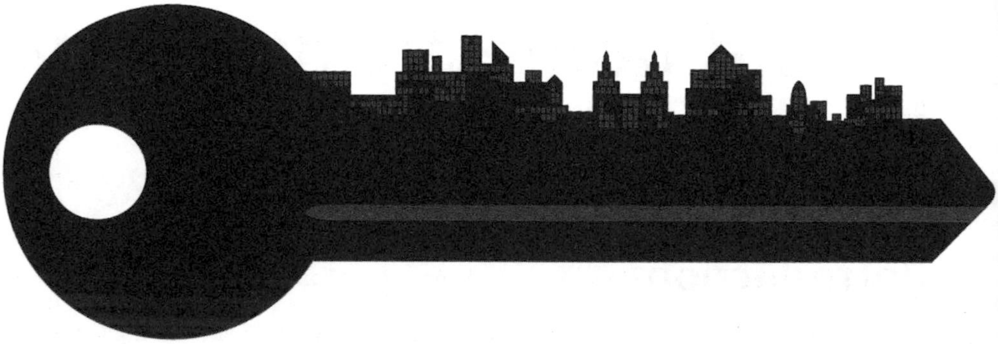

Products

Property and mortgages

The biggest personal investment most people make is their home. There is now no tax relief on mortgages for the purchase of a home. Stamp duty is payable on properties priced above £125,000, on a rising scale according to the cost of the property.

If you use your property as security on a purchase loan, you will take out a mortgage. This is the most usual way to acquire your home. In 2006, a record £346 billion was lent on UK mortgages, up 20 per cent on the previous year, according to the Council of Mortgage Lenders (CML).

First-time buyers now struggle to enter the housing market and are sometimes receiving parental help in putting down a deposit on a property. In March 2007, first-time buyers spent an average 18.3 per cent of their income on mortgage payments, up from 16 per cent the previous year, reflecting interest rate rises, according to the CML.

A mortgage may be repayment, interest only, or a combination. The repayment mortgage requires you to pay your lender a monthly sum that combines repayment of capital borrowed with interest on the loan. If you make all your payments, the loan will be repaid at the end of the mortgage term.

If you have an interest-only loan, you will pay only interest to the lender every month and, at the end of the term, you will pay back the original debt in a lump sum. You will need a savings vehicle, perhaps a pension, or an ISA to build up enough money over the years to pay it off, although you can also pay as you go throughout the life of the loan.

In the past, endowments were taken out for this purpose. Unfortunately, many endowments were mis-sold in the late 1980s and early 1990s on the basis that they would pay off the mortgage. Declining stock markets and overall returns meant that there was often a shortfall. Companies have been paying some compensation and there is no longer any real market for new endowments.

Some mortgage providers offer lower rates for a certain period, which provides reassurance for those concerned about interest rate volatility. This may be provided through a fixed-rate mortgage, which guarantees the level of monthly payments. In 2006, two-thirds of those buying or remortgaging chose the certainty of a fixed-rate deal, compared with just over half in 2005, according to the CML.

Other forms of lower-rate mortgage offers include a discount mortgage, where the rate is set at a margin lower than the lender's standard variable rate for an initial specified period, and a capped rate mortgage, which sets an upper limit. A tracker mortgage is where the interest is set at a margin above or below the Bank of England's base rate.

An offset mortgage is one where the credit that you hold with the lender is offset against what you owe on your mortgage. The main advantage is that it is tax-efficient because your savings can be used to pay off parts of the mortgage rather than earning interest at a taxed rate. Another advantage is flexibility, meaning that you can make such repayments when you have the cash to do so, but withdraw from your mortgage when you need the cash for something else.

In 2006, 170,000 offset mortgages were taken out, worth £29.3 billion, which was equivalent to 7 per cent of all lending, according to the CML. Between April 2006 and March 2007, the growth of offset mortgage lending was 49 per cent by value, compared with 15 per cent for non-offset lending.

Among more seasoned property buyers, buy to let is popular. In 2006, there were 330,000 buy-to-let mortgages, representing 11 per cent of all new lending, according to the CML. It was a 48 per cent increase in volume and a 57 per cent increase in value over 2005.

If you are unable to make the agreed repayments on a mortgage, the lender can sell the property to repay your debt. There were 17,000 possessions in 2006, up 65 per cent on 2005, but broadly similar to the 2001 level, according to the CML.

In mid-2007, the FSA raised concerns about the UK sub-prime mortgage market, which provides home loans to consumers with less-than-pristine credit records and, on industry estimates, accounts for about 5–6 per cent of total industry gross advances. The equivalent US market had already suffered defaults that cast a ripple round world markets (see Chapter 12).

At this point, the FSA had started enforcement action against five unnamed firms, known to be intermediaries, after it found weaknesses in responsible lending practices and in the firms' assessments of consumers' ability to afford a mortgage.

Life policies

The two key non-investment life products available are whole-of-life and term insurance.

Whole-of-life policies will pay out when you die. You will pay regular premiums to build up a pot of money, which is invested, and the cover is not limited to a set period. Gains on a qualifying policy are free of any further tax charge. The product is useful for inheritance tax purposes. If you have children who will be beneficiaries of your estate but are subject to an inheritance tax liability, you can take out a whole-of-life policy and write it in trust for your children, with the result that it will provide a lump sum to pay on that liability.

This is an area where specialist advice is needed.

Term insurance is cheaper than a whole-of-life product. It pays out a tax-free lump sum, or a family income benefit, only if you die within a specified period, failing which the cover ends. Many have term insurance in conjunction with a mortgage.

Pension term insurance (PTA) gave policyholders tax relief on the premiums paid at their marginal rate, as for a pension product. The product was scrapped by the government only eight months after it was introduced in April 2006.

Protection products

The key protection products are private medical insurance, income protection insurance, critical illness insurance, long-term care insurance and payment protection insurance. Let us consider each.

Private medical insurance covers the cost of private medical treatment of acute conditions, defined as illness or injury, where treatment will lead to recovery. Premiums increase with age.

Income protection insurance pays a tax-free monthly income for an agreed period if you are unfit to work because of sickness or accident, resulting in a loss of earnings.

Critical illness insurance pays a tax-free lump sum if you suffer from any illness or condition, or have any surgical procedure, covered by the policy. The product tends to pay salespeople a higher commission than income protection. There is a high level of rejected claims. As the FSA has found, customers have not realised that prior medical conditions are material and have to be disclosed.

Long-term care insurance covers the cost of long-term care in your home, or in a residential or nursing home. It includes a wide range of care services.

Payment protection insurance (PPI) policies are designed to help you repay your borrowings such as mortgages or credit cards should you become unable to work due to an accident, illness or because you unexpectedly lose your job. The FSA has recently cracked down on poor selling practices and a lack of proper compliance controls among firms promoting PPI. The product is usually sold in conjunction with something such as a car. Exclusions have not always been made clear and consumers typically do not shop around before they buy.

Investments with life insurance

In this section, we will refer to products that are primarily investment, not protection, but include an element of life insurance. These are either endowments or investment bonds.

For practical purposes, the endowment (see above in this chapter) is a regular savings version of the investment bond, but is more tax efficient (see above, under 'Property and mortgages'). Investment-type insurance is based around endowments.

The investment bond is a savings vehicle. The key benefit is that it enables you to defer, or possibly to avoid, any additional higher-rate tax on gains and income generated by the bond. The product is useful for those who pay higher rate tax but, in the future, will no longer be paying it. Financial advisers can receive a high commission to sell this product, and so have often been known to recommend it above cheaper and more tax-efficient alternatives.

Other savings products

Bank and building society accounts

In the past, a savings account with your bank or building society was either instant access, which paid a little interest, or a notice account, which paid more. In today's more competitive environment, some accounts have high rates, and may not have much of a notice requirement, if any, but there may be catches. The rate may fall away after six months or an even shorter time or, if you make more than a certain number of withdrawals within a set period.

ISAs

An Individual Savings Account (ISA) is a wrapper that protects investments held in it from income and capital gains tax. Your ISA can be pre-wrapped as a cash account or fund, or it may be free-standing, where you select the investments to hold in it.

Every year the public has invested about £28 billion in ISAs, with increasingly more in cash and less in shares. On 1 February 2007, HM Treasury announced the government reforms to make the ISA regime simpler and more flexible for users from 6 April 2008, a year earlier than originally planned. From this point, the upper limit for a stocks and shares ISA will be £7,200, and for a cash ISA will be £3,600.

National Savings and Investments

National Savings and Investments, the UK's second largest savings institution, started life in 1861 as the Post Office Savings Bank, and it manages around £73 billion in government funding, about 8 per cent of the UK retail savings investments market. It promotes secure, sometimes tax-free, government-backed savings products, but the returns tend to be uncompetitive. Interest rates payable may be fixed, variable or index-linked.

Will

A will is a formal arrangement to distribute your assets after your death. To be valid, it must be in writing, signed by the testator, and witnessed. If you do not make a will, your estate will be distributed under the laws of intestacy.

Should your estate be worth more than £300,000 (tax year 2007–2008) or £312,000 (2008–2009), it will be subject to rules on inheritance tax.

How the products are sold

If you are willing to buy without advice, you will have access to a wide range of financial services products at a discount from, for example, an internet supermarket or, in some cases, an online broker. Most of the discounted products are collective investments (see Chapter 19).

The traditional way to buy personal finance products is from a financial adviser, who assesses your needs and recommends what is, or should be, suitable. A series of mis-selling scandals have damaged public trust in advisers.

You can choose between an appointed representative, who works for one financial services company and only offers its products, an independent financial adviser (IFA), who theoretically advises across the marketplace, or, following depolarisation in December 2004, a multi-tied agent, often a bank, that sells products from a select number of companies.

Some customers use multi-tied agents without fully understanding that they are receiving a more restricted service than provided by an IFA, although it is no cheaper. Some firms are a combination of IFA and multi-tied. Some banks are multi-tied in investment products but not in insurance products, and they sell their own brand of insurance only, which can be expensive.

The IFA must offer customers a choice of paying either a commission on products bought or a fee for time spent. In the past, many IFAs offered fee-based services, but many worked only on commission. In practice, most consumers prefer to go down the commission-paying route.

Customers must receive clear information about the service that the adviser is offering, including an upfront indication of the cost. Until mid-2007, IFAs were required to provide information through initial disclosure documents and a Menu document that explains the cost of the firm's services and the different payment methods. In May 2007, the FSA proposed to scrap the requirement for these formats, which are not required by the Markets in Financial Instruments Directive. An FSA-commissioned study found no consistent evidence that the Menu had put downward pressure on commission levels, or increased the level of fee-paid advice for consumers, and found limited evidence that it had reduced provider bias in sales.

In its Retail Distribution Review, unveiled in June 2007, the FSA proposed a new two-tier system for financial advisers. At the high end would be professional financial planners, whose remuneration was agreed by the customer and who, being free from bias in advising on products, could be called independent. At the low end would be general financial advisers, who could be paid on commission and, because this would give rise to conflicts of interest, could not be called independent.

To reduce distribution costs and so make advice on financial services affordable to consumers on a middle-to-low income, there could be a new type of regulated advice service, primary advice, which might point the consumer towards a limited range of products.

The industry showed an initial mixed reaction to the proposals that, as the second edition of this book went to press, were under consultation. There were concerns about the distinction between the two types of adviser and whether the 'independent' label would truly mean there was no bias. Some felt that the idea of primary products had been tried before and did not work, and could lead to mis-selling because some products like index funds were simple to explain but not low risk.

Meanwhile, a review is underway to research and prepare a national approach to 'generic' financial advice, led by Otto Thoreson, chief executive at insurer Aegon UK. A generic adviser should take a holistic view of the consumer's finances and recommend that the customer move to the stage of buying products only when it suited his or her circumstances.

The generic adviser would not be regulated to sell products but might refer the client to a financial adviser. The government and industry could share the cost of any new service, which could be called guidance, or otherwise information, education or coaching.

Insurance Mediation Directive

The Insurance Mediation Directive (IMD) was implemented in the UK and three other EU countries on time by 15 January 2005, but in other countries later. It introduced minimum professional requirements for insurance intermediaries across Europe, and required that consumers should receive specific information before they concluded a contract. Insurance intermediaries must be registered with a competent authority in the home member state, enabling them to offer cross-border services on a single passport. Complaints procedures must be available.

EU countries have taken different approaches to the IMD, and there has been significant gold plating of the Directive's minimum requirements (that is, regulation on a home state basis has gone beyond the rules laid down at EU level). In the UK, the Directive has been expensive to put into practice, and there have been fears that the costs and regulatory burden might drive some small operations out of the market. At a March 2007 conference, John Tiner, chief executive of the FSA, described the IMD as the worst directive he had ever seen, with no cost-benefit analysis behind it and no sense of whom it was trying to protect.

The FSA's regulation of insurance intermediaries has meant that not just the IMD but also other rules in the regulator's *Handbook* have applied to them. In the UK, unlike in France and Germany, the IMD has been applied not just to intermediaries but, beyond the Directive's scope, to the direct selling of insurance products.

Significant changes are underway. In the second half of 2007, the FSA was consulting on a proposed rewrite of its Insurance Conduct of Business Rules (ICOB). The proposal was that NEWICOB, as the revised version would be known, would separate insurance protection products, which require heavier regulation (controversially inclusive of term insurance), from 'other' products, which are all the rest. The FSA accepted that other products were over-regulated and proposed to remove ICOB requirements beyond minimum IMD rules. It would transfer the more detailed rules such as unfair inducements into guidance.

Brokers have criticised the NEWICOB proposals. The British Insurance Brokers' Association (BIBA) supports the idea of heavier regulation for insurance protection products but disagrees with proposals to remove ICOB requirements in relation to other products. It has noted that the proposals would leave insurers less burdened with regulation than brokers. The complaint of brokers is that this creates still less of a level playing field than before. For example, in non-advised sales, insurers would not be required to send out suitability letters and demands and needs statements to customers but brokers would. BIBA has given the FSA evidence that customers are confused about the different status of insurers and intermediaries and it believes that all disclosure should be the same.

Complaints and compensation

The Financial Ombudsman Service

If a financial services firm, including a stockbroker, has operated incompetently or dishonestly, private investors should first complain to the firm. If this does not get a satisfactory result within eight weeks, there is in most cases access to the Financial Ombudsman Service (FOS), which is an independent organisation with statutory powers to settle individual disputes between consumers and financial services companies.

Every year, the FOS deals with half a million enquiries and settles 100,000 disputes, and the service is free to consumers. Most cases are resolved within six to nine months. Consumers do not have to accept any decision by the FOS and can go to court instead. But if they do accept an ombudsman's decision, it is binding on both them and the business.

Financial Services Compensation Scheme

The Financial Services Compensation Scheme (FSCS) is a statutory fund of last resort. It pays compensation for financial loss if an authorised firm is in a state of default and so cannot meet the costs of compensation claims.

The scheme will pay a maximum of £31,700 per person for a claim on a deposit when a bank, building society or credit union cannot repay its depositors (first £2,000 guaranteed, plus 90 per cent of the next £33,000), and up to £48,000 on a loss from bad investment advice or poor investment management, or for a loss for mortgage advice and arranging. For most kinds of insurance, the Scheme will pay 100 per cent of the first £2,000 on a claim plus 90 per cent of the rest, and for compulsory insurance such as motor insurance it will pay 100 per cent of claims. The FSCS has recently committed much of its resources to paying money owed to people who bought mortgage endowment policies.

Funding from the scheme is from levies on authorised firms. In March 2007, the FSA set out proposals to reform the funding of the FSCS, with the idea of creating a more robust funding system than at present, with the cost of compensation apportioned between regulated firms as fairly as possible.

The future

The financial services professionals accept that their industry is not perfect but see it as worrying if people prefer to take investment advice from their mate down the pub rather than from themselves. Financial journalism offers a source of information and guidance, although it is not always as independent or well informed as it may appear.

A possible long-term solution is to provide personal finance education to a younger generation that has not been exposed to the mis-selling in the industry. There has long been an interest in putting financial services on the school curriculum and, by mid-2007, government plans were underway to introduce lessons in economic well-being and financial capability. This educational initiative has won expected support from the financial services industry, but some are cautious.

In a letter published in *The Times* of 11 July 2007, Professor Richard Verrall and Professor Julie Logan of Cass Business School applauded the initiative but said there was no quick fix. They said that their own teaching about the City in schools had shown the subject was popular, but the key to success, they said, was to make it relevant. Teachers had often not had direct exposure to business and were uncomfortable teaching it, they said, and the initiative should not boil down to just another target for already pressurised teachers.

31

Pensions in flux

Introduction

In this chapter we will see how pensions and annuities work from a retail perspective. We will focus on pension scandals, and legislative developments, including new government proposals.

Overview

The pensions industry has been dogged by scandal, and financial advisers see this as a major factor in having created public mistrust. Although it was as long ago as 1991, the Maxwell fraud did a lot to undermine confidence in pension management. Robert Maxwell, owner of the Mirror Group Newspapers, had illegally borrowed more than £400 million from the *Daily Mirror*'s pension fund, and the Department of Trade and Industry in a subsequent report had been critical not just of the tycoon's business but also of those in the City who had profited from it and who had not made proper checks.

Mis-selling has been another problem in the pensions industry, including for personal pensions between 1988 and 1994. In its own mis-selling scandal, Equitable Life wrote pension funds with generous guaranteed annuities that, after interest rates declined, it was unable to pay. Equitable responded by asking some policyholders to take a cut in bonuses, but, in 2001, it was required to pay out, leaving a £1.5 billion asset shortfall in its balance sheet.

Financial advisers see such scandals as a major reason why, on the government's own estimates, around seven million people in the UK are not saving enough for investment. The government established the Pensions Commission, headed by Adair Turner, to focus on the pension problem and, in 2005, it made its proposals.

Based on the Turner proposals, the government has developed two packages for change. The first is the state pension package, which is to be implemented through the Pensions Act 2007. The second is the proposal for Personal Accounts, a form of occupational scheme, which is not part of the act but is part of the same overall reform. We will be covering both in this chapter. Let us start by looking at the basic state pension.

The basic state pension

Pension arrangements in this country start with the basic state pension. It is payable in full to those of the requisite age, which is 65 for men, and between 60 and 65 for women, depending on when they were born (to become 65 from 2010) who have paid enough national insurance contributions over the years.

The state second pension was introduced in April 2002, and provides an additional state pension. It replaced the state earnings-related pension scheme (SERPS), which was an earnings-related part of the basic state pension.

As an employee, you are included in the state second pension, unless you contract out, which is to give up the entitlement and build up a sum instead in your own pension fund. HM Revenue and Customs rebate part of your National Insurance contributions into your personal pension. You are free to contract back in.

State pension package

The Pensions Act 2007, which received Royal Assent in July 2007, is mainly about state pension reform. It has three strands.

People will receive the state pension later than before. This will be on a phased basis. In 2024–26, they will start taking the pension at the age of 65–66, and in 2034–36, they will start at the age of 66–67. In 2044–46, they will take it at the age of 67–68 years.

The basic state pension rises every year with the Retail Prices Index. From 2012 or slightly later, it will rise instead by earnings, which should make the pension more generous.

To receive the full state pension, men must have made national insurance contributions (NI) for 44 years and women for 39 years but, from 6 April 2010, only 30 qualifying years are required in either case. Anybody who has paid NI contributions for fewer years than required can make a proportionate claim.

The state pension provision does not pay individuals enough to live on comfortably after retirement. The government encourages people to take out their own pension as well. This may be an occupational pension, provided by the workplace, or a personal pension. Let us look and compare.

Occupational and personal pensions

The government encourages you to make your own pension provision by providing tax breaks. In general, your personal or occupational pension (you can have both) is a tax-efficient savings vehicle designed to provide you with a tax-free sum on retirement of up to 25 per cent of your accumulated pension funds, should you wish to draw on this, followed by a taxable income for the rest of your life. Your pension is a wrapper into which any funds may be put, and you get tax relief on contributions. Tax is paid on dividends but no additional personal taxation is payable.

Whether you have an occupational or personal pension, or both, your pension money is invested in funds. You may choose the funds in which you invest, and in which combination, depending on your risk appetite and circumstances. For those who want to avoid making decisions, a managed fund is available, which is balanced and not high-risk, but for others there is a wide choice, including more exotic funds such as Far East equities.

Poor performing funds significantly outweigh the good and, as financial advisers confirm, investors tend not to switch out of the duds. Older pensions can have penalties for switching funds or for stopping and restarting contributions.

In the past, an individual has been able to invest only a limited amount annually in a private or occupational pension but, under rules introduced from 6 April 2006, known as A Day, there is much more flexibility. Anybody may contribute up to 100 per cent of their earnings to any pension scheme, subject to an annual allowance of £225,000 in 2007/08 or £235,000 in 2008/09.

The maximum allowable pension of two-thirds of final income was replaced by a lifetime allowance, which for 2007–08 is £1.60 million and for 2008–09 will be £1.65 million. Any pension fund above this level is taxed.

Another benefit introduced from A Day is that it has been easier to mix personal and occupational schemes. Employees may take pension benefits while they remain at work and, if they wish, accrue a further pension. From 6 April 2010, the earliest age at which you can withdraw a pension will rise from 50 to 55.

Let us now see how occupational and personal pensions work.

Occupational pension

A company does not have to operate an occupational pension although, as we shall see later in this chapter, the rules will change in 2012, with the introduction of Personal Accounts. At present, companies with five employees or more must at least offer a stakeholder pension (see below), and do not have to contribute to it, although they often do.

The occupational pension is a workplace pension. The employer sponsors it, and usually makes contributions, and a board of trustees runs it. As an employee, you may contribute to the pension, and may top up these payments with Additional Voluntary Contributions (AVCs). In many public sector schemes, the employer makes all the contributions.

An occupational scheme often has other benefits, such as life insurance and a pension if you retire early because of poor health. Many employers pay for the scheme's administration, rather than taking the cost out of the fund. Most occupational schemes are contracted out, which affects members' entitlement to a second state pension (see above).

An occupational pension may be final salary, which comes into the category of defined benefit, where the pension provision is a proportion of your salary when you retire. It may otherwise be money purchase, also known as defined contribution, where the value of the pension is defined by the value of the funds built up.

Final salary (defined benefit) schemes

From the employee's perspective, the final salary scheme is seen as the best type of occupational pension because there is some predictability about how much the pension will be, and the pension income will usually rise annually. The final salary pension that you receive is calculated according to how many years you have been a scheme member, your final salary before retirement, and an accrual rate, which is the fraction of final salary earnings allowed for each year of membership. People who receive a pension after 40 years of membership on a 1/80th accrual rate could expect it to be half their final salary.

'The world of defined benefit [including final salary] pensions is sick,' Stephen Haddrill, director general of the Association of British Insurers (ABI), said at the Punter Southall Summer Conference in June 2007. For the first time, the amount of money flowing into defined benefit pension schemes is less than the amount flowing into defined contribution [money purchase] schemes, he noted.

In keeping with this trend, the Association of Consulting Actuaries found, through a survey published in July 2007, that four out of five of defined benefit (including final salary) schemes run by companies responding to the survey were closed to new entrants. Major factors in the decline of the final salary scheme are weaker stock market returns, rising longevity and more payment guarantees. Another influence, it is felt, may have been the July 1997 move by Gordon Brown, then Chancellor of the Exchequer, to scrap tax relief on dividends paid into pension schemes.

When final salary schemes are inadequate or the scheme becomes insolvent, two compensation schemes are available. The first is the Financial Assistance Scheme (FAS), a government body established under provision of the Pensions Act 2004. It helps individuals who lost pension rights because they were members of qualifying under-funded final salary pension schemes that started winding up between 1 January 1997 and 5 April 2005.

Under the earliest version of the FAS, not many received benefits because the Treasury decided that only those within three years of retirement when their final salary scheme collapsed were eligible. The criteria have since been modified and most recently, in his budget statement of March 2007, the chancellor said that the FAS would have significantly more public funding. A key development is that all members of qualifying pension schemes will have their pensions topped up to a level broadly equivalent to 80 per cent of core pension rights accrued in their scheme.

The second compensation scheme available is the Pension Protection Fund, which is an independent body answerable to the government, which provides compensation in relation to final salary schemes that started winding up from 6 April 2005.

The Pensions Regulator was created under the Pensions Act 2004, and has the role of regulating work-based pension schemes, with a key objective of reducing the risk of claims on the Pensions Protection Fund.

Money purchase (defined contribution) schemes

In a money purchase (defined contribution) scheme, cash is invested in a retirement fund to create for the employee, on retirement, a pot of money. The employee may take out a tax-free sum of up to 25 per cent of the fund, and the remaining money is used to buy an annuity, unless alternative arrangements are made (see below). The size of the pension depends significantly on how well the retirement fund performed.

Group personal pensions are not trust based, like occupational pensions, but are contract based. The contract is between the pension provider, such as Norwich Union, and the individual. The employer usually pays into the scheme, but does not have to, and may be able to negotiate favourable group terms from the pension provider. See also below under 'Personal pension'.

Personal Accounts

The National Pension Savings Scheme (NPSS), based on part of the Turner proposals referred to earlier in this chapter, is the government's plan for changing the savings culture in the UK so retirement saving becomes the norm. The scheme is to be introduced in 2012 and will mean employees for the first time will have the right to a workplace pension with matching contributions from the employer.

Under the NPSS, employees are to be automatically enrolled in their company pension scheme if one exists. If it does not, they will be automatically enrolled into Personal Accounts, which are a large form of occupational pension.

Employers will contribute 3 per cent of an employee's salary, and employees will pay in a further 4 per cent, with 1 per cent tax relief from the government.

The pensions industry supports the concept of Personal Accounts but has expressed fears that employers could see them as a cheaper alternative than their current provision, and could put new recruits or employees not currently in their scheme into personal accounts at a lower contribution level than at present.

The government has said that Personal Accounts are designed to complement and not to compete with the existing company pension provisions. Personal Accounts are aimed at low to moderate earners (£5,000 to £33,000 per annum), who are not now in occupational pensions.

Personal pension

The personal pension is usually a money purchase scheme (see above). You can buy it independently of the workplace and it has no employer contributions, but is portable and flexible. A personal pension may be suitable if you are self-employed or do not have a workplace pension.

You may buy your personal pension directly from a provider or through an independent adviser, who will help you to select from the wide range available. As you pay in your contributions, the personal pension provider will claim tax at the basic rate, adding it to your fund. If you are a higher rate tax provider, you can claim the additional tax rebate through your tax return.

On retirement, you may take up to 25 per cent of your pension fund as a tax-free lump sum and with the rest of the fund can purchase an annuity or take an alternative route (see below).

Stakeholder pension

The stakeholder pension, introduced on 6 April 2001, is a cheap and flexible form of personal pension, which must meet specified government criteria. The government designed the product to encourage savings through pensions and to make them more accessible and affordable to middle income consumers.

You can pay as little as £20 a month into your stakeholder pension, in some cases less. Unlike with some personal pensions, there can be no penalties if you miss payments or move your fund to another scheme.

Like any personal pension, the stakeholder pension provides the option of taking a tax-free sum of up to 25 per cent on retirement and buying an annuity with the rest of the pension pot. The stakeholder element is about the fairness of the wrapping and not about fund performance.

The cap on stakeholder charges was raised in April 2005 from 1 per cent to 1.5 per cent (falling to 1 per cent after 10 years). The rise boosted sales because it gave advisers a greater financial incentive to recommend the product, but the charges are still low.

A possible disadvantage in the stakeholder pension is that it tends to offer conservatively run in-house funds, without the wider choice available through other forms of personal pension.

Self-invested personal pension

The active investor may opt for a self-invested personal pension (SIPP), which enables him or her to choose where to invest from a wide universe, including investment funds, shares and commercial property, and to switch investments. It is possible to employ an investment manager to make these decisions.

Charges on a SIPP are levied on the underlying instrument. There are also charges on the wrapper although these have reduced from earlier levels.

Since April 2007, the FSA has begun to regulate the operation of SIPPs and the sales advisory process. It has warned financial advisers not to be influenced by the high sales commissions into advising customers inappropriately to buy a SIPP, a problem on which the press had been focusing some attention.

Annuities and unsecured pensions

Annuities

When you retire, the bulk of your pension fund may be used to purchase an annuity. This is a contract from an insurance company that converts your pension fund into regular income that you will receive for the rest of your life. Since 6 April 2006, an annuity purchase has been optional.

If you are buying an annuity, you may first take out a tax-free sum from your pension pot. As we have seen, this may be up to 25 per cent of the fund. You will then use the rest of your capital to buy the annuity. Your capital will become the property of the annuity provider, an insurance company or similar specialist company, which will then pay you an income until you die.

The level of income you receive has declined over the years. It depends on the annuity rate at the time of conversion, which is derived from average life expectancy, and the long-term interest rates on government bonds. The annuity can vary significantly between providers, and you should shop around to find the best deal.

There is more than one type of annuity. The level annuity pays you the same income annually. The escalating annuity pays you a lower starting income but this rises every year, either by a fixed amount or in line with inflation. A single life annuity will not pay to anyone after your death, but a joint life annuity will pay income, after you die, to your partner for his or her life.

Anybody with a medical condition that could reduce life expectancy such as cancer, or who has smoked at least 10 cigarettes a day for 10 years, could qualify, subject to medical underwriting, for an impaired life annuity, where the rates are higher.

Phased retirement is where you convert your pension fund into annuities at different stages. Some personal pension funds are a single plan, but others are a cluster of plans called segments, which you may use to buy a lifetime annuity at different times. When you convert a segment to an annuity, you can take part of it as tax-free cash.

Unsecured pension

An unsecured pension involves short-term annuities or income withdrawal, and you can combine the two.

You may use some of your pension fund to buy a short-term annuity, leaving the rest of your fund invested, with the volatility that arises from its exposure to equities. At the end of the annuity's term, you may buy another short-term annuity.

With income withdrawal, you will draw a taxable income from your pension fund, which is up to 120 per cent of the income that you would receive from an equivalent level single-life lifetime annuity. The rest of your fund stays invested, again with the risky exposure to equities. The amount that you take from your fund must be reviewed every five years to ensure it is within HM Revenue and Customs limits. At any time you can stop income withdrawal and use the rest of the fund to buy an annuity.

If you have an unsecured pension by the age of 75, you must secure an income from your pension funds – usually a lifetime annuity, but it may be an alternatively secured pension (ASP). The ASP is similar to an unsecured pension but with different rules, and has been available only since 6 April 2006.

From 6 April 2007, the government has stopped ASP funds passing tax-effectively to non-dependent family members as a pension scheme. Any such payment would now be unauthorised, and could be subject to a tax charge of more than 80 per cent.

A word to investors

Final word

The book is over, but this could be a new beginning. The City is always developing and I hope what you have gained from this reading will help you to keep up with it. The books recommended in Appendix 2 and the websites listed in Appendix 1 will deepen your understanding.

Keep up also with ongoing developments. Read the business pages of *The Times* and, for intra-day developments, *Times Online* (www.timesonline.co.uk). You will soon gain a breadth of knowledge that you can put to practical use. Good luck!

Appendix 1: Useful websites

Here is a list of some financial websites that have proved useful to me. Use it as a starting point for your own requirements.

Accounting and corporate governance

Accounting Standards Board, www.asb.co.uk
Financial Reporting Council, www.frc.org.uk
International Accounting Standards Board, www.iasb.co.uk
PricewaterhouseCoopers, www.pwc.com

Banking and building societies

British Bankers' Association, www.bba.org.uk
The Building Societies Association, www.bsa.org.uk
European Central Bank (English site), www.ecb.int
London Investment Banking Association, www.liba.org.uk

Bonds

Debt Management Office (gilts), www.dmo.gov.uk
International Capital Market Association, www.icma-group.org

Collective investments and similar

Alternative Investment Management Association, www.aima.org
The Association of Investment Companies, www.theaic.co.uk
Investment Management Association, www.investmentuk.org

Morningstar.co.uk, www.morningstar.co.uk
Standard & Poor's – funds website, www.funds-sp.com
Trustnet – a particularly good funds website, www.trustnet.com

Complaints and compensation

Department of Trade and Industry, www.dti.gov.uk
Financial Ombudsman Service, www.financial-ombudsman.co.uk
Financial Services Authority – financial services regulator, www.fsa.gov.uk
Financial Services Compensation Scheme, www.fscs.org.uk
Office of Fair Trading, www.oft.gov.uk
Press Complaints Commission, www.pcc.org.uk

Corporate governance and social responsibility

Financial Reporting Council, www.frc.org.com
Ethical Investment Association, www.ethicalinvestment.org.uk

Derivatives and commodities

Baltic Exchange, www.balticexchange.com
The Futures and Options Association, www.foa.co.uk
Ice Futures, www.theice.com
London Metal Exchange, www.lme.co.uk
Numa Financial Systems, www.numa.com
NYSE Euronext, www.nyse.com
World Gold Council, www.gold.org

Economy

Bank of England, www.bankofengland.co.uk
HM Treasury, www.hm-treasury.gov.uk
National Statistics, www.statistics.gov.uk
Organisation for Economic Co-operation and Development, www.oecd.org
Samuel Brittan – economic commentator for *The Financial Times*, www.samuelbrittan.co.uk
David Smith, economics editor of the *Sunday Times*, www.economicsuk.com

Factoring and leasing

Factors and Discounters Association, www.factors.org.uk
Finance and Leasing Association, www.fla.org.uk

Foreign exchange

ICAP, www.icap.com (register with the ICAP Knowledge Centre for courses)

Insurance

Association of British Insurers, www.abi.org.uk
British Insurance Brokers' Association, www.biba.org.uk
Chartered Insurance Institute, www.cii.co.uk
International Underwriting Association of London, www.iua.co.uk
Lloyd's, www.lloyds.com

Investor relations

Buchanan Communications, www.buchanan.uk.com
Investor Relations Society, www.ir-soc.org.uk
IR On the Net, www.ironthenet.com

Law enforcement and similar

Assets Recovery Agency, www.assetsrecovery.gov.uk
City of London Police, www.cityoflondon.police.uk
Serious Fraud Office, www.sfo.gov.uk
Serious Organised Crime Agency, www.soca.gov.uk

Money laundering and fraud

The Egmont Group, www.egmontgroup.org
Financial Action Task Force, www.fatf-gafi.org
Insurance Fraud Investigators Group, www.ifig.org
International Association of Insurance Fraud Agencies, www.iaifa.org
Service provided by the British Bankers Association for the Joint Money Laundering steering Group, www.jmlsg.org.uk
Nick Kochan – a journalist's site with some interesting articles, www.nickkochan.com
Proximal Consulting – run by Peter Lilley, www.proximalconsulting.com

Money markets

Wholesale Market Brokers' Association, www.wmba.org.uk

News, data and research

Advfn, www.advfn.com

AFX News, www.afxpress.com
AWD Moneyextra, www.moneyextra.com
Bloomberg News, www.bloomberg.co.uk
Breakingviews, www.breakingviews.com
Citi Smith Barney, www.smithbarney.com
Citywire, www.citywire.co.uk
Corporation of London, www.cityoflondon.gov.uk
Digital Look, www.digitallook.com
The Economist, www.economist.com
FT.com, www.ft.com
Hemscott, www.hemscott.com
Interactive Investor, www.iii.co.uk
Investors Chronicle, www.investorschronicle.co.uk
Mergermarket, www.mergermarket.com
MoneyAM, www.moneyam.com
The Motley Fool UK, www.fool.co.uk
Reuters, www.reuters.co.uk
Securities & Investment Institute, www.securities-institute.org.uk
ShareCast.com, www.sharecast.com
Times Online, www.timesonline.co.uk

Pensions

Association of Consulting Actuaries, www.aca.org.uk
Financial Assistance Scheme, www.dwp.gov.uk/fas
Financial Services Authority pension website, www.moneymadeclear.fsa.gov.uk/pensions
National Association of Pension Funds, www.napf.co.uk
Pension Protection Fund, www.pensionprotectionfund.co.uk
Pension Sorter, www.pensionsorter.co.uk

Post-trade services

Euroclear UK & Ireland, www.euroclear.co.uk
LCH.Clearnet Limited, www.lchclearnet.com
SIS x-clear – the central counterparty service, www.ccp.sisclear.com

Private investors

Association of Private Client Investment Managers and Stockbrokers, www.apcims.co.uk
UKSA – UK Shareholders' Association, www.uksa.org.uk

Regulation in UK and Europe

Committee of European Securities Regulators, www.cesr-eu.org
Competition Commission, www.mmc.gov.uk
Complinet.com, www.complinet.com
European Union, www.europa.eu.int
Federation of European Securities Exchanges, www.fese.be
Financial Services Authority, www.fsa.gov.uk
International Association of Insurance Supervisors, www.iaisweb.org
International Organization of Securities Commissions, www.iosco.org

Stock exchanges, capital raising and equity trading

British Venture Capital Association, www.bvca.co.uk
Chi-X, www.chi-x.com
Deutsche Börse, www.deutsche-boerse.de
Equiduct, www.easdaq.be
London Stock Exchange, www.londonstockexchange.com
NASDAQ, www.nasdaq.com
NYSE Euronext, www.nyse.com
Plus Markets Group, www.plusmarketsgroup.com
Pink Sheets, www.pinksheets.com
virt-x, www.virt-x.com

Technical analysis

Barclays Stockbrokers (download free short course, Technical analysis explained, from the education centre online), www.stockbrokers.barclays.co.uk
Building wealth through shares. (The website of Colin Nicholson, technical analyst and teacher), www.bwts.com.au
Society of Technical Analysts, www.sta-uk.org

Appendix 2: Further reading

Invest your time

The cost of buying books is negligible when weighed against the information they can provide and the ideas they can spark. The real investment is your time.

For the second edition of this book, I have decided to cut down my book recommendations to those that, in my view, could really make a difference. My recommended list is idiosyncratic – I would not insult you with anything less – and it does not purport to be complete.

I have mainly included books that provide an overview rather than specialist detail. If you have related to this book, you will certainly appreciate some of the books below, and find them useful. Reading good investment books is also hugely enjoyable.

You can buy books online or by telephone, often at an excellent discount, through Global-investor.com (www.global-investor.com), which is my favourite bookshop because it has a high level of personal service, delivers reliably, and has some interesting features on its site. Otherwise, try Amazon (www.amazon.co.uk), which publishes useful book reviews and offers some seriously reduced prices, particularly through resellers.

General guides to the City

The sequel to *How the City Really Works*, although written before it, is *How to Understand the Financial Pages* by Alexander Davidson, Kogan Page, 2005. It is another title backed by *The Times*, and it has a practical bent.

If you want to focus on the *Financial Times*, and on the press generally, an authoritative guide is *The Financial Times Guide to Using the Financial Pages* by Romesh Vaitilingam, Financial Times/Prentice Hall, 5th edition, 2005. It can be a bit dull in places, but is comprehensive and helpful.

For a book explaining how the City works in easy language, I recommend *All you Need to know About the City: Who Does Why and What in London's Financial Markets* by Christopher Stoakes, Longtail Publishing, 2nd edition, 2007. This book is presented in bite-size chunks and in an easy-to-read style.

If you are ready for a slightly more advanced, but still accessible, approach, setting the City in the European context, read the classic *An Introduction to Global Financial Markets* by Stephen Valdez, Palgrave, 5th edition, 2006. This will give you a good overview, and it is used in some investment banks to inform younger recruits.

Stock market

The Complete Guide to Online Stock Market Investing: The Definitive 20-day Guide by Alexander Davidson, Kogan Page, 2006, is worth reading if you want to become a successful stock market investor. It is a substantially updated version of my earlier bestseller, and it tells you all that you need to know about investing online.

The Naked Trader by Robbie Burns, Harriman House, 2nd edition, 2007, is a tongue-in-cheek beginner's guide to trading written from experience and is largely based around the ADVFN website. This is a cheeky, irreverent young person's book, and it contains home truths, with the author's own new rules alongside the old. Read it if you want to have a crack at gaining financial independence – through investing or anything else.

The UK Trader's Bible by Dominic Connolly, Harriman House, 2005, is a lucid guide to the mechanics of how share trading works in London. It fills you in with a lot of detail not always known by private investors, including how electronic trading at the London Stock Exchange works.

Taming the Lion: 100 Secret Strategies for Investing by Richard Farleigh, Harriman House, 2005, explains the author's own highly successful investing approach. The semi-autobiographical approach helps to bring the text to life.

The Disciplined Trader by Mark Douglas, New York Institute of Finance, 1990, shows you how the territory represented by stock markets is, unlike the world we know, uncaring, unforgiving and ruthless. This classic book changed the way I looked at the stock market more than any other, and it is a must read, the appropriately dark content and original perspectives more than compensating for a wordy writing style.

An accessible book from a successful investor is *The Next Big Investment Boom: Learn the Secrets of Investing from a Master and How to Profit from Commodities* by Mark Shipman, Kogan Page, 2006. The author explains his own proven methods.

The Only Three Questions That Count: Investing by Knowing What Others Don't by Ken Fisher with Jennifer Chou and Lara Hoffmans, John Wiley, 2006, makes interesting reading. In this book, market pundit, columnist and author Ken Fisher provides an intellectual framework through which to make investment decisions. He stresses that asset allocation matters more than stock selection.

Derivatives

Derivatives require a specialist focus. One of the clearest books on the subject has recently gone into a second edition. This is *The Investors Toolbox; 2nd edition: How to Use Spread Betting, CFDs, Options, Warrants and Trackers to Boost Returns and Reduce Risk* by Peter Temple, Harriman House, 2nd edition, 2007. The author is a former equities analyst and is a prolific investment writer. If you are a beginner to derivatives trading, you are in safe hands.

To understand how derivatives can go wrong, read *Rogue Trader* by Nick Leeson, Time Warner Paperbacks, 1997. It is the autobiography of the trader who brought down Barings Bank. The event helped to spur regulatory changes in the City. The events described are historical, but the author offers universal insights into how derivatives traders work.

If you want to learn about commodities derivatives, I recommend *Hot Commodities* by Jim Rogers, John Wiley, 2007. This is an easy-to-read text from a master investor and it is unashamedly bullish about commodity markets. Rogers has strong opinions on which commodities will do well, and provides a reasoned case. The author is a renowned globetrotter and the book is international in its scope.

Fundamental and technical analysis

The Little Book that Beats the Market by Joel Greenblatt, John Wiley, 2005, is a particularly accessible introduction to value investing, which is based on buying cheap on fundamentals.

Fundamental investing is based on the numbers. The problem about most books on accounting in relation to quoted companies is that they are pre-International Financial Reporting Standards (IFRS), and so out of date. Forget these. To get to grips with modern accounting, read *Interpreting and Forecasting Accounts Using International Financial Reporting Standards* by

Nick Antill and Kenneth Lee, Harriman House, 2005. The book is written for practitioners, by practitioners, but remains accessible.

Technical analysis has a controversial status in the City but enough of a following in some markets to influence price movements. To find out more, read *Technical Analysis of the Financial Markets: A Comprehensive Guide to Treading Methods and Applications* by John Murphy, New York Institute of Finance, 2nd edition, 1999. This is probably the best overall book on technical analysis, and is the core text of the professional courses run by the Society of Technical Analysts.

For a lighter approach, try *Investor's Chronicle Guide to Charting: An analysis for the intelligent investor* by Alistair Blair, Financial Times/Prentice Hall, 2002. This is a cynic's introduction, and is entertaining as well as providing a good overview.

Forecasting Financial Markets: The psychology of successful investing by Tony Plummer, 4th edition, Kogan Page, 2003, explains the mass psychology behind stock market rises and falls from a technical perspective. It is a fascinating book.

You will find IFRS accounting and technical analysis basics in my book *How to Understand the Financial Pages* (see under *General Guides to the City* above). It can be your starting point.

Economics

My favourite book on economics for beginners is *The Investor's Guide to Economic Fundamentals* by John Calverley, John Wiley, 2003. This is a clear overview from a chief economist and strategist at American Express Bank. Some of the case studies are now a little old but the book captures the spirit of how bankers see and make use of economics.

For details on how economic indicators work, try *First Steps in Economic Indicators* by Peter Temple, FT Prentice Hall, 2003. It is rare to find such clear explanations.

Last but not least, read *Free Lunch* by David Smith, Profile Books, 2003. It is a lightweight but thought-provoking introduction to economics, penned by the economics editor of the *Sunday Times*.

Corporate finance

The Greed Merchants: How the Investment Banks Played the Free Market Game by Philip Augar, Penguin, 2005, is a critical and sometimes entertaining look at investment banking from a one-time insider. The author's case is that the investment banking model is fundamentally flawed because it is riddled with conflicts of interest, and recent regulatory initiatives have not properly addressed this. The book has insights, particularly for those not in the loop.

The Penguin Guide to Finance by Hugo Dixon, Penguin Books, 2000, is a journalistic primer on corporate finance. It is no textbook, but it provides a good overview and some back-of-the-envelope calculation methods and, almost unheard of, makes the subject entertaining.

The Real Cost of Capital by Tim Ogier, John Rugman and Lucinda Spicer, Financial Times/Prentice Hall, 2004, is a useful introduction to measuring cost of capital. The authors, a team of three at PricewaterhouseCoopers, explain the Capital Asset Pricing Model (CAPM), but warn of its deficiencies. The guidance on estimating the international weighted average cost of capital – using mainly versions of CAPM – breaks new ground, and there is an assault on DCF forecasts, for which cost of capital is used as a key interest rate. The book explores real options valuation as an alternative.

Risk management

Dealing with Financial Risk: A Guide to Financial Risk Management by David Shirreff, Economist Books, 2004, is a journalistic trot through the basics of financial risk management. It is a cynical, sometimes entertaining book and provides a valuable introduction.

Money laundering

Dirty Dealing: The Untold Truth about Global Money Laundering, International Crime and Terrorism by Peter Lilley, Kogan Page, 3rd edition, 2006, offers a lucid and lively introduction to how money laundering works, and how regulators and legislators are trying to combat it.

The Washing Machine by Nick Kochan, Gerald Duckworth, 2006, is an entertaining guide to how money laundering works today. The book is in some respects more cynical than Lilley's. The author, an investigative journalist, gets under the skin of the anti-money-laundering bravado, demonstrating how ineffectual much of it is.

Index

Index of Advertisers